"Cycon's analysis and experience, as well as his humorous and engaging style . . . bring stories to the light of day that would not and could not be told, simply because no one else has his range of experience."

—**Winona LaDuke**, indigenous rights activist, author of *All Our Relations*

"*Javatrekker* is a great read because it is, first and foremost, entertaining in the swashbuckling style of Anthony Bourdain or Jack Kerouac. But Dean's stories possess a depth of spirit and a love for his subjects that many adventure writers lack. And his core subject—coffee—is so universally familiar (and yet little understood) that I believe his potential audience is enormous."

—**Stephen Braun**, author of *Buzz: The Science and Lore of Alcohol and Caffeine*

"Dean is truly a singular character in the world of coffee roasters. While most roasters and importers brag about their 'third world' experiences, Dean travels to the 'fourth world,' getting down and dirty with the indigenous groups growing the coffees, beyond where most folks will go."

—**John Cossette**, Royal Coffee, Inc.

"In spite of all the movements on behalf of Fair Trade, organic, birds, shade, eco this and that, it's still rare to find someone who is truly working for the farmers' interests and not their own."

—**Bill Fishbein**, co-founder, Coffee Kids

JAVATREKKER
DISPATCHES FROM THE WORLD
OF FAIR TRADE COFFEE

DEAN CYCON

CHELSEA GREEN PUBLISHING
WHITE RIVER JUNCTION, VERMONT

Javatrekker® is a trademark of Dean Cycon

Developmental Editor: Benjamin Watson
Project Manager: Emily Foote
Copy Editor: Collette Leonard
Proofreader: Nancy Ringer
Designer: Peter Holm, Sterling Hill Productions

Printed in the United States of America
First printing September 2007
10 9 8 7 6 5 4 3   16 17 18 19

Library of Congress Cataloging-in-Publication Data
Cycon, Dean, 1953–
  Javatrekker : dispatches from the world of fair trade coffee / Dean Cycon.
    p. cm.
  ISBN 978-1-933392-70-7
  1. Coffee industry. 2. Coffee growers. 3. Coffee. 4. Cycon, Dean,
1953– Travel. 5. International trade. I. Title.

  HD9199.A2C93 2007
  338.4'766393—dc22

2007028222

Our Commitment to Green Publishing
Chelsea Green sees publishing as a tool for cultural change and ecological stewardship. We strive to align our book manufacturing practices with our editorial mission and to reduce the impact of our business enterprise on the environment. We print our books and catalogs on chlorine-free recycled paper, using soy-based inks whenever possible. This book may cost slightly more because we use recycled paper, and we hope you'll agree that it's worth it. Chelsea Green is a member of the Green Press Initiative (www.greenpressinitiative.org), a nonprofit coalition of publishers, manufacturers, and authors working to protect the world's endangered forests and conserve natural resources.

  Javatrekker: Dispatches from the World of Fair Trade Coffee was printed on Natures Natural, a 30-percent postconsumer-waste recycled, old-growth-forest-free paper supplied by Thomson-Shore.

Chelsea Green Publishing
85 North Main Street, Suite 120
White River Junction, Vermont 05001
(802) 295-6300
www.chelseagreen.com

DEDICATION

To the next generation of coffee farmers and drinkers—
may this book help them know each other better to make
the world a better place.

ACKNOWLEDGMENTS

An ancient Ethiopian blessing before each coffee ceremony, the *beraka* (whose name has the same roots as *bracha*, the Hebrew word for "blessing"), recalls that all that is set before us has been touched by many hands that have contributed to its nurture, fruition, and delivery. So it is with this book.

I give humble appreciation to Ingrid, Winona, and Rigoberta, who brought me into the international struggle for indigenous rights as early as 1979. To David Abedon and Billy Fishbein, my cofounders at Coffee Kids, who introduced me to the world of coffee, affording me a vehicle for my life's work and outrageous adventures. To Bill Harris, Bongo Bob, Matt, Chris, Jody, Monika, and the rest of the gang at Cooperative Coffees, my fellow Javatrekkers in bringing progressive change to a very mainstream industry. To Sue Mecklenburg at Starbucks and Rick Peyser at Green Mountain Coffee, for listening to my ranting over the years and for receiving my sometimes pointed judgments with an open mind and a good heart.

To my wife, Annette, and my girls, Sarah and Aliya, who have always supported my hectic travel and welcomed many visitors, third-world stuff, tattoos, and diseases into our home with grace and good humor. To John Cossette, my coconspirator in coffee travel and adventure, who continues to help me unscramble the Da Vinci code of coffee availability and finance. To the hearty crew at Dean's Beans, who let me come and go so erratically and hide away in my office to write this book while they kept cranking out tons of great coffee.

And, of course, thanks to Tadesse, Esperanza, Kekas, Iggy, Hiderico, Rigo, Merling, Lucia, and the hundreds of farmers who opened their homes, their hearts, and their books of accounts to this short, frenzied Javatrekker who so often appeared to drop in on them from another planet.

I raise my cup to you all.

CONTENTS

Acknowledgments • **vi**

Prologue: The Inner Worlds of Coffee • **ix**

I—AFRICA

1. Miriam's Well, the Emperor's Bed, and Kaldi's Goats (*Ethiopia, 2002*) • **3**
2. Fermenting Change, but Don't Cross the Big Man (*Kenya, 2005*) • **33**

II—SOUTH AMERICA

3. Bridging the Gap (*Peru, 2003*) • **67**
4. Global Warning: Climate Change, Conflict, and Culture (*Colombia, 2007*) • **86**

III—CENTRAL AMERICA

5. The Flickering Candle of Freedom (*Guatemala, 1993*) • **111**
6. Tracking the Death Train (*Mexico/El Salvador, 2005*) • **137**
7. Coffee, Land Mines, and Hope (*Nicaragua, 2001*) • **165**

IV—ASIA

8. Good Friends, Cold Beer . . . and a Water Buffalo (*Sumatra, 2003*) • **185**
9. The Three-Hundred-Man March (*Papua New Guinea, 2004*) • **207**

Epilogue • **237**

The Inner Worlds of Coffee

When you sit back with a good cup of coffee you are engulfed in the aroma, the taste, the acidity, and body of the brew. You take in all the dimensions of the cup—yet this is only the surface. Swirling beneath are worlds within worlds of culture, custom, ecology, and politics. All of the major issues of the twenty-first century—globalization, immigration, women's rights, pollution, indigenous rights, and self-determination—are being played out through this cup of coffee in villages and remote areas around the world. The coffee trade is immense, second only to that of oil in its value. It is also complex, with several levels of middlemen removing the 28 million growers in fifty distant countries far from the ultimate consumers, far from your cup.

There are as many different cultures growing coffee as there are coffee-growing regions in the world. In some countries, coffee is intricately intertwined within the culture, expressed through ritual and custom in daily life. In Ethiopia, farmers like Tasew Gebru start each day with three small cups of coffee, the beans roasted over a charcoal brazier—a tacit acknowledgment of the centrality of coffee to their way of life. In other countries coffee is just a crop, and a poverty crop at that. For instance, it's hard to find a decent cup of coffee in much of Central America. The only coffee available in most restaurants is the ubiquitous "Nes," as instant Nescafé is called.

Not all coffee growers look like Juan Valdez, a Latin male with a big moustache and a smile, dressed in clean white linen. Coffee farmers come in all shapes and sizes, colors, and genders. There are coffee growers from all Christian persuasions and from an abundance of indigenous religions, as well as Muslims, Hindus, and Buddhists. There is even a coffee-growing community of Black Jews in Uganda. Underlying the various coffee cultures are profoundly different understandings of the dance of good and evil, of communal responsibility and personal freedom—and of the very nature of the gods themselves. Yet what they all share are the common dreams of good health, love, food on the table, an education for the kids, and a great sense of humor.

Most of the coffee farmers I have worked with around the world don't speak the dominant or national language. Rather, they speak a local dialect or distinct tribal language. In Latin America, for example, many farmers do not speak Spanish. In Guatemala they might speak Tzutujil, Quiche, Cakchiquel, or other ancient Mayan tongue. In Peru, many speak Ashaninkas in the south or Kechua in the north. Thus, you can enter coffee villages throughout the Americas, speak fluent Spanish, and not be understood at all. In Kenya, the national languages are Swahili and English, yet many farmers I met in the Embu region of the Central Plateau spoke neither well. They spoke Akamba. In Ethiopia the national language is Amharic, which shares its ancient roots with Hebrew. Yet our farmers speak Oromifa. Imagine my surprise when I delivered my well-rehearsed opening speech to the farmers in Amharic on my first visit to Ethiopia, only to be met with blank stares and embarrassed smiles!

Similarly, dress style can differ dramatically, even within the same community. In some places, communities hold firmly to their culture and traditions, and clothing (or lack of it) plays an important role. Many farm families in countries as far from each other as Indonesia and Guatemala weave their own fabric on backstrap looms tied to trees. The patterns may be centuries old and specific to the local ethnicity. Or they may be old patterns with a new twist, evidence of the strength and flexibility of the culture. Yet in the next house, farmers may be wearing T-shirts with Nike or Boston Red Sox logos that seem absurdly out of place until you realize that much of the clothing we wear is produced in sweatshops in the world's coffeelands. In the mountain villages of the Eastern Highlands of Papua New Guinea, farmers may be naked or wear nothing more than a penis gourd carved from a water buffalo horn and decorated with beads or strips of old blue jeans. Indigenous growers in Peru wear a bark-dyed shroud and face paint, while their neighbors dress like small-town Iowans. Muslim coffee growers in Sumatra and Ethiopia wear clothing ranging from modern Western styles to traditional white woven shawls, with head or face coverings for the women.

Coffee grows in a rich belt of lands from the Tropic of Cancer to the Tropic of Capricorn, straddling the equator by thirty degrees north and south. The ecology of these coffeelands ranges from tropical rain forest to deserts. Since the 1950s the trend has been toward large, monocultural coffee plantations or "estates." Although many of these large holdings are well tended, many more suffer from the soil erosion and water pollution that are often the by-product of this kind of agriculture. Highly toxic pesticides are often used by workers who can't read the warning labels in Spanish, English, and German, or who have had insufficient training in pesticide application. However, the vast majority of coffee is still grown on small farms of a few acres. In many countries the farmers are keenly aware of the importance of interplanting and maintaining biodiversity for the health of the land and of their families. "Shade-grown" and "Bird-friendly" were concepts well known to small farmers long before international environmental groups took an interest in the coffeelands. These beautiful and varied landscapes can also be subject to nature's immense fury, as earthquakes, mud slides, hurricanes, and tsunamis destroy crops, roads, warehouses, and lives.

The economic situation of coffee communities is varied, as well. The price paid to coffee farmers has little to do with the cost of growing and processing the crop. Nor does the price include a reasonable profit for the farmers to maintain or improve their lives. Rather, coffee prices are dictated largely by the forecasts of financial speculators, banks, and multinational corporations in New York and London. One month a farmer may receive a reasonable reward for his or her labors, and the very next month the price can plummet. Nothing has changed at the farm level, so the farmer shakes his head and carries on. During the first five years of the new millennium coffee prices were often lower than the cost of production, driving hundreds of thousands of coffee families off their lands and into crowded cities or across borders. Sometimes this forced exodus ended in death, with desperate migrant farmers falling off trains in Mexico or abandoned in locked vans in the Texas heat.

Well-intended private initiatives and international efforts to provide an ethical alternative to the current pricing system (Fair Trade, for example) have kept thousands of farmers on their lands but, while growing, represent only the smallest fraction of world coffee commerce. Even during the best of times, farm communities have rarely been able to make meaningful improvements in the basics of water supply, education, health care, and housing. Not only does the coffee crop not generate enough money, but the World Bank, the IMF, and the international lending community have greatly inhibited the ability of national governments to assist farming communities by forcing them to slash rural health care and environmental and educational budgets under "structural adjustment" policies. As a result, many coffee communities have turned to grassroots, self-help efforts as the only viable means to improve their people's lives. The resulting development projects, wells, and health clinics, among others, may be small in scale, but they can immediately and directly improve the lives of coffee farmers and their families.

The coffeelands are often zones of conflict, where war and its aftermath can deeply affect the economics and cultural cohesion of the coffee communities. Almost every coffee country I have worked in is currently or has recently been engaged in an autonomy or independence struggle from a colonizing society or suffers under the yoke of a corrupt or dictatorial regime. Sometimes the coffee farmers are actively engaged in these struggles, as in Chiapas. More often, in places like Colombia and Sumatra, they are innocent bystanders with no place to go when the tides of conflict wash through their lands. Armed conflict can even prevent farmers from harvesting their crop. Truckloads of coffee representing a year's hard work get hijacked, leaving farmers with nothing. Roads get closed and "tolls" must be paid to one side or another. A farmer's wife disappears in Timor, an entire village is massacred in Guatemala. Even decades-old conflicts like the one in Nicaragua can reach out of the past to inflict death and despair. Old American or Czech land mines litter abandoned coffee fields or rise up to the surface after storms. They maim farmers at work or children walking to school. Nobody remembers which side planted them or where they are. Yet zones of conflict may in time become zones of hope. Longstanding conflicts end, new opportunities for political participation can be created.

Culture and custom, ecology and economics, conflict and creativity swirl beneath the surface of your cup. Ultimately, the differences among coffee communities and between "us and them" are more than the sum of these parts. All of it draws me in. Each trip I make to the coffeelands is a return to the crucible. Each expedition offers a challenge to some deeply held or unexamined belief and an opportunity to participate in meaningful change in people's lives on a very personal level. Each visit gives me the chance to put my skills and heart at the service of the people who grow the beans that provide for my family and result in such great coffee for our customers. That is why I became a Javatrekker.

The Evolution of a Javatrekker

The truth is, 99 percent of the people involved in coffee commerce, from roasters to baristas, have never been to a coffee village. They get their information about the lives of coffee farmers from the advertising and imagery put out by major coffee companies. Ergo Juan Valdez. Even among the handful of coffee company execs and employees who do get out to the coffee countries for a short visit, very few of them spend more than a few hours in the field, and none that I know of sleep in the homes of the farmers. Once, when I was arguing with a well-known environmentalist–coffee retailer about the existence of malnutrition in southern Mexican coffee villages, she snapped, "Don't you think I know that? I've flown over those villages!" Yet today coffee represents more than a mere commodity to a small band of intrepid, engaged coffee people. Their businesses are the means by which they immerse themselves in the deeper worlds of coffee. These are the Javatrekkers, and since 1987 Javatrekking has been my life.

Although I have been a coffee roaster for over a dozen years, I came to the world of coffee via a circuitous route. I was a lawyer and an activist, with one foot in the mainstream legal world and the other in indigenous rights and environmental issues at home and abroad. I thought the law would be a great vehicle for social change. It can be, but I did not have the constitution for it. I couldn't stand the paperwork, the legal maneuvering, and, frankly, the stacked deck of corporate power and money within the justice system. At one point I was working on the Fort Belknap Indian Reservation in Montana, trying to get the U.S. and state governments to require an environmental impact statement for the world's largest cyanide heap-leach gold mine (never happened!). During one really rough patch, Charlie, a longtime Indian activist, asked me how long the reservation could survive if there were no jobs for the young people. But if the only jobs were dangerous, low-paying, and disruptive to the local culture, were they any better than no jobs at all? We both came to realize that until businesses changed their fundamental operating principles, our efforts would only amount to putting out brush fires started by corporate greed and lack of awareness.

I took a fellowship at Woods Hole Oceanographic Institution in 1985, researching and lecturing about the impacts of development on indigenous communities. I continued to provide free legal work to indigenous peoples in the areas of environmental protection and human rights. Word-of-mouth among those communities brought me meaningful opportunities for service and adventure in several countries. In 1987 I gave a lecture at the University of Rhode Island on the many causes of rain-forest destruction. Afterward I was approached by Professor David Abedon. He asked me if I could talk to a friend of his who had a coffee shop and who wanted to create an organization to help coffee farmers. Since the vast majority of coffee growers are indigenous peoples, doing focused development work in the coffeelands seemed like a good combination of my skills and interests. We met, and the three of us immediately founded Coffee Kids, the first development organization dedicated to coffee communities. Bill Fishbein, the coffee shop owner, would raise money from the coffee industry to support our efforts. I would go into the villages, meet with the farmers and their families, assess needs, and evolve programs and strategies to address the problems identified by the farmers. I was deliriously happy. I had the perfect job (even though Bill, David, and I weren't getting paid for it). We set up microcredit banks for women in Guatemala and Mexico, a water project in Sumatra, and several other initiatives. It was solid, grassroots development.

Then one day something shifted. I was thinking about a well project in Guatemala. A charity-minded coffee company would give us five thousand dollars to build the well. The company would take pictures, tell the story, and trumpet their good works to the consumer. But the company would continue to pay very low prices to the farmers. Nothing would really change. In fact, the consumer would be getting a false impression that things were fine in the villages, that the industry was "taking care of its farmers," as one corporate executive put it. I wondered what would happen if the company simply paid the farmers real money for their coffee; maybe the farmers could afford to build their own well and would not need the "charity" of the company. What would happen if the company took a level of responsibility for the conditions found in the villages it was buying from and became involved in the lives of its suppliers through direct development work and other forms of support to the community? Could the dynamics of poverty, which seem endemic to coffee growing, be challenged and overcome? Could the company still be profitable? If so, what excuse would other companies have to behave otherwise? In this moment of clarity and reflection Dean's Beans was born.

It was 1993. I started with a little roaster and eight bags of coffee. I was teaching part-time and still doing a little law on the side. I would buy only organic coffee because I was aware of the impact of pesticide use on the third-world environment and farmers' health—many of the common coffee pesticides were banned for use in the United States. I would buy only from small farms and cooperatives that were made up largely of indigenous peoples trying to maintain their cultures and dignity in a hostile world. Development assistance and activism would be an essential part of the relationship. This would be our acknowledgment that the price and structure of the world market reflected a century of unfair dealings that left coffee communities in a state of underdevelopment. And I traveled and continued my lifelong love affair with the lands and peoples of the planet.

The ideals of Dean's Beans and the quality of our coffee soon took hold. We grew slowly, steadily, and conscientiously. Many people said we would be "the Ben and Jerry's of coffee," but that company was transforming rapidly into just another big business owned by a multinational with rich but disgruntled founders. No thanks. I wasn't doing this to become a "grow it and sell it" millionaire. Nor did I want to cash in on my "social responsibility" as the new owners kept the public persona but hollowed out the core principles of the business—a frequent dynamic with "progressive" businesses these days. I was trying to develop and prove a new business model—one based on respect, ethics, and justice—to support my family and employees, and to have a good time doing it. The model had to be flexible as well. We needed to be able to change our approach to development, pricing, and any other aspect of our relationship with the farmers that might need adjustment as time and experience revealed. This approach drove my mainstream business buddies crazy, as flexibility and being more dedicated to the process than to the ultimate size of the bottom line clashed with their world of plans, projections, and growth targets.

I began to meet other people in the coffee trade with whom I felt a kinship. In 1998 seven of us got together in Atlanta to form Cooperative Coffees, the world's first roasters' cooperative. We joined forces for two reasons: First, to enable us as a group to buy coffee directly from the farmers under Fair Trade terms and to work to improve that system. Second, we found that we were fellow travelers on a path combining business and social justice in an industry where such a combination was rare. I had discovered fellow Javatrekkers.

As Javatrekkers we became deeply involved in the struggles of our farmer partners. Each of us has our own level of involvement, and we manifest our beliefs in justice and engagement in our own ways. There are other Javatrekkers out there as well. There are progressive and caring brokers, importers, and roasters scattered amongst the many for whom coffee is business as usual and for whom farmers are just a means to a very profitable end. Over the past decade it seems that the industry as a whole has been evolving. The Javatrekkers' impact is being felt. But that's another story.

Now I invite you to get a second cup of coffee (the first must be long gone or cold by now). Are you ready to enter the worlds within worlds inside your cup? Come with me to coffee communities around the world. Experience their customs, their cultures, their struggles, and their hopes. Learn how a Javatrekker participates in the lives of the farmers and their communities. The tales you are about to read are sometimes uplifting, sometimes sad. Some are humorous, some sobering. And all of them are whopping good travel yarns.

Drink deep. Your coffee will never taste the same.

PART ONE

AFRICA

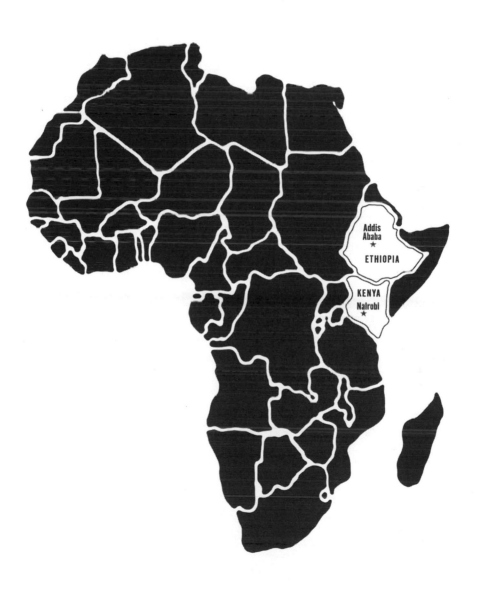

1

Miriam's Well, the Emperor's Bed,and Kaldi's Goats

ETHIOPIA, 2002

There are four well-paved main roads in Ethiopia, emanating in the cardinal directions out of the capital, Addis Ababa. Each road was built by a different European aid organization, and each ends where the money or the interest ran out. It is February 2002 and we are headed due south on the road built by the Germans. We are traveling down the Great Rift, a massive valley that slices Ethiopia from stem to stern, evidencing the powerful birth pangs of a young Mother Earth. This is the "Cradle of Civilization," where "Lucy," our diminutive, apelike ancestor, and her millenniums-old relatives have popped up now and then. The Great Rift created the endless dry plain through which we travel. It continues on for a thousand miles, through Ethiopia and neighboring Kenya. It is a ten-hour straight shot to Yirgacheffe, one of the world's premier coffee regions. Adele, our ever-smiling driver, plays pirated hip-hop CDs. He sings along in phonetic English, blissfully unaware that the words to "Take Me to the Candy Shop" would shock his Evangelical

Christian soul if he understood them. Tadesse, the general manager of Oromia Coffee Farmers Cooperative Union, rides shotgun and seems oblivious to the pounding music and groaning, bump-and-grind singers. He is the founder of the cooperative and holds the future of eighty thousand farmers and their families in his heart, his head, and his thick black notebook.

Cooperatives have a long and checkered history in Ethiopia. The concept was originally introduced as a proper socialist-organizing tool by the Marxist Derg (Committee) that ruled the country after imprisoning and murdering Emperor Haile Selassie in the 1970s. As the regime tightened its control over thought as well as action, co-ops transfigured into instruments of taxation, recruitment for the army, and information mining. When the Derg was driven from power in 1987, cooperatives fell into disfavor and were largely ignored by farmers. It was remarkable, therefore, that when a young agricultural extension worker named Tadesse returned from a fellowship in Japan in 1994, on fire with the potential of well-organized cooperatives, he was given a hearing at all. Tadesse went from office to office trying to get someone to watch his twenty-minute videotape about co-ops in the USA, Europe, and Japan. Finally, someone caved. Tadesse was told he could try his newly acquired skills with the coffee farmers of Oromia, Tadesse's ethnic group (and the largest in Ethiopia, if not the most politically empowered). If he succeeded it would be a great coup for the Ministry of Agriculture. If he failed he could go back to farming the small plot owned by his father and nine uncles.

For ten years Tadesse traveled the enormous distances between Yirgacheffe, Sidamo, Jimma, and Harar to organize, educate, and advocate. He brought in foreign soil scientists and agronomic experts, drawing upon any resource he could to bring assistance to the farmers of the far-flung Oromia Coffee Farmers Cooperative Union. He cajoled financing out of tight-fisted Dutch importers and traveled to Europe and Japan to introduce his coffees to the world. Tadesse listens to every idea that comes down the road, and he reads everything he can about new technologies, modes of organization, and, of course, coffee. He has overseen the building of warehouses and coffee pulping and washing stations, all ready to prepare the beans for their best presentation to the coffee-buying world.

Tadesse is a big man, with a big belly and a big smile. He has a booming laugh, like an Oromo Santa Claus. And he is loved, very loved.

During the drive, Tadesse spends most of his time on his cell phone, accepting offers from European importers, approving loans to individual farmers, checking in with his kids. He breaks his manic multitasking only to answer important questions from his passenger.

Looking out the window, I notice hundreds of people streaming northward on my left, while another human horde streams southward on my right. Women, swathed in multiple layers of brightly colored cloth, bow under impossibly heavy loads of firewood. Pip-squeak donkeys clump down the road with mountains of reed grasses for roofing on their backs or 800 pounds of water in plastic jerry cans. These sad little creatures are tormented by five-year-old boys and girls who snap at their rumps with branches. The back of each donkey shows brown coarse hair in the pattern of the Cross. The locals say this is a blessing on the donkeys for carrying the Virgin Mary on their backs, but it looks more like a symbol of their current suffering in service to mankind. The people form an endless line in both directions.

"Tadesse, where are all those people going headed north?"

"They are going to the market."

"And where are all those people going in the other direction?"

"They are also going to the market."

"So why don't they all just go in one direction to the same market?"

Tadesse looks at me curiously, then erupts with his huge belly laugh.

"Ha ha ha! You are a very funny man!"

"I take you to the candy shop. I'll let ya lick the lollipop," sings Adele cheerfully.

I never did find out why they all just didn't go to the same market. But Tadesse did turn the tables on me when I took him to Vermont on his first trip to the United States. As we drove up Interstate 89, through the pristine woodlands of Vermont, Tadesse looked out the window.

"Dean, where are all the people?"

"There are no people here, and if there were, they'd be driving to market, not walking."

Tadesse had trouble believing that America was sparsely populated anywhere. He looked at me like I was pulling his leg. He nodded and grinned.

"Ha ha ha! You are a very funny man!"

Lords of the Ring

As each mile unfolded past this unchanging pattern of Ethiopian rural life, the price of coffee on the world market was plummeting. Half an earth away in New York City, a room full of overcaffeinated young men (who'd probably never heard of Yirgacheffe) were shouting themselves hoarse bidding down the lifeblood of rural Ethiopia. In the middle of this room was the circular trading floor of the New York Board of Trade (NYBOT), known to its denizens as "The Ring." Here, investment houses, banks, financial speculators, and large coffee companies bid on the future price of coffee. For the companies, the goal is to ensure a future supply at a known price—a necessary planning tool for a business based on an agricultural commodity. But for the rest of the frenzied traders the point is to make a profit on the "float" between what they pay for coffee futures and what they hope to sell them for later. For two centuries, coffee had been a dull commodity, traded on a somnambulant market. Yet somewhere in the last decade, it had morphed from a morning brew into a raging speculative commodity on the trading floor.

In this wired world, these Lords of the Ring are supplied with up-to-the-minute financial, political, meteorological, and other data from an army of consultants. An early frost in Brazil? The flowers necessary for the budding coffee fruit to develop could wither and die, shrinking the coming harvest. Supply down, price up; bid two cents more for March deliveries. A rumored peace deal in Colombia? Easier deliveries in three months; hold off and let the price drop. The rumors and intelligence are translated into buy and sell orders, little slips of paper carried across the floor by the Runners, the traders-in-training. Their street clothes covered in tunics carrying the colors of their houses, the Runners grab the slips from the phone and computer banks owned by the Lords and race them down to their warriors in the Ring, who scream out their offers to buy for a penny more or sell for a penny less. These players make the prices rise and fall in an incestuous system unrelated to the true cost of growing and processing the crop, and with no consideration at all for the needs of the growers to feed their families and keep their kids in school. As one trader told me: "Traders are not guys with moral fiber when it comes to the conditions of the farmers' lives. We're seeing money and we're making money."

While we flew down that road to Yirgacheffe, the market price dropped below sixty cents per pound—the price it costs a farmer to grow and harvest the coffee. From that day forward, each pound produced would drive the farmer who grew it deeper into debt and bewildered despair. For the next half decade, farm families would suffer malnutrition and infant mortality would soar. At the same time, corporate profits would rise to historic heights, as the Lords of the Ring made their killing.

Yirgacheffe—The Richest Coffee from the Poorest People

As we leave the plains of Ethiopia, the elevation increases slowly. Dry scrub turns to light then heavy forest cover, not unlike New England's. The concrete, boxy sprawl of Addis gives way to small towns made up of squat mud-brick houses. The dusty road through each town takes us past goats, horse-cart taxis called *garis*, and a surprising number of foosball tables in the streets, each with a gaggle of teenaged boys rooting for their side. In later years, the foosball tables will compete with Ping-Pong tables, as China becomes a player in the constant global struggle to wrest what few minerals or strategic resources exist in the parched Horn of Africa.

Eventually, the villages disappear, replaced by family enclaves and small settlements of beehive huts. We have crossed the boundary from obeisance to the New World Order into the historic patterns and rhythms of an ancient land. The walls of the twenty-foot-diameter huts are made of stout poles, buried in the earth and lashed together with reeds. The roofs are long thatched grasses. The huts have a half-wall partition in the middle; the family sleeps on one side and the animals are brought in at night on the other side to capture their body heat against the crisp night air. The fire pit in the center sends smoke upward to cleanse the thatched roof of any insects or other pests. The smoke seeps out of the entire roof, making it look like the house is on fire. Small subsistence gardens of pumpkin, squash, and *tef* (an Ethiopian grain) surround the huts. *Tef* is used to make *injira*, the flat, gray national bread that serves as edible plate, silverware, and napkin at every meal.

Further up the road the forest thickens, and a sharp eye can spot the willowy coffee plants interspersed under the forest canopy. The trees do not grow in neatly tended rows here. Rather, they appear here and there, some grouped, some flying solo, as if sprouted in a random yet fully natural pattern. And in this part of Ethiopia, that's exactly how these coffee forests grow. These are the typical coffees of Africa—tall, spindly, untamed, and fully reflective of their wild ancestry. These Yirgacheffes are set apart from other coffees with their earthiness, lemony undertones, and full body. As I stand in this healthy coffee forest next to Tasew Gebrew, a sinewy six-foot-four man who heads Negele Gorbitu, one of the Oromia Yirgacheffe cooperatives, I can't help wondering about the relationship between tree and farmer. Just as different types of pets seem to look like their owners, coffee trees seem to mirror the physicality of the farmers who tend them. Here, the trees and farmers stand tall, strong, and skinny. In Latin America, the trees are short and stocky, the beans pulling downward on the muscular, resistant branches just as the largely indigenous Mayan, Aztec, and Incan farmers seem squat and immovable in their eternal struggle with ecology and centuries of political and economic colonization.

I stand before the assembled farmers. They mostly sit on the ground, although some of the older members are on chairs brought out from the office to the bean-drying area where we are meeting. I had spent hours with an Ethiopian family in Amherst, Massachusetts, learning a great opening speech in Amharic, the national language. I've really got it down, even the clever inflections. After Tadesse introduces me formally, I launch into my passionate speech, praising the farmers and their land, offering the respect of America, sharing our vision for the future. I am soaked with perspiration from the emotion I bring to the speech. Then it is over. Silence. Tadesse leans over to me and whispers, "That was a truly great speech. But none of these people speak Amharic. They only speak Oromifa. They didn't understand a word you said." Big belly laugh. Tadesse gets up and stretches. He gives his version of my speech. It doesn't seem to take as long as mine did, but the farmers' faces shine and they give me loud applause.

The members of Negele Gorbitu have a lot of questions. Why are we being offered only sixty cents when last year we got a dollar? Our coffee is the same and the quality is very high. Why wouldn't the banks give us loans this year to harvest the beans? Half our crop rotted on the plant because we didn't have the money to pick it and ship it to the processors.

How do I explain the Lords of the Ring? How do I tell them that even though some of us care about their families, the people who determine the price simply don't? I am the first Fair Trade purchaser and the first American coffee buyer ever to come here, and I don't relish the role of bringing bad news. The truth is, even the Fair Trade purchases will be only a drop in the bucket here. I can feel great about how I treat these farmers, but all around Negele are farm families that don't sell to Fair Traders. The kids who run by with swollen bellies and streaks of reddish hair are all the evidence I need to know that a diet of false banana, the only starchy staple readily available, leads to malnutrition.

The coffee forests of Yirgacheffe are in bloom. The air hums with wild African bees getting drunk on coffee nectar, occasionally bouncing off our heads in a stupefied revelry. Black colobus monkeys with white tails and faces follow us overhead, among the treetops, now and then scolding us or pelting us with some hard nut from their natural arsenal. A baboon troop crosses the path ahead, their bright red butts bringing us to a halt as if they were car taillights. These are not the manicured, pesticide-doused fields of many large plantations. The farmers carry long poles with hooks on the ends to bow down the ancient trees that have grown so far beyond their reach. They stop to inspect the bright red beans from the random tree. The low murmur in Oromifa is totally unintelligible to me, but I can tell that the farmers are satisfied with their inspection.

Back at the co-op's office, a ten-by-ten cement room festooned with charts of payments to farmers, we go through the co-op's books with a thoroughness that would make Enron shudder. The co-op keeps exact records of all advances, loans, payments—all financial transactions with the members—in handwritten ledgers organized by the harvest. I note that last year's payments are not recorded. Tasew takes a deep breath.

"That is because there were no final payments last harvest. We had no money. Much of the harvest rotted but we still had to pay off old loans to the banks and help our members with doctor money and money to buy food for themselves."

"Tasew, why wouldn't the banks loan you money? They do every year, don't they?"

Tasew gives me a wry smile. "Yes, but the prices for the coffee keep going down, so the banks worry that we won't make enough money to pay them back."

"There is something else," adds Tadesse. "Many of the *sabsabi*, the coffee collectors, the middlemen who buy coffee directly from the farmers, are big guys at the banks. They influence the bank's decision. They want to weaken the cooperatives because we don't need coffee collectors anymore. So if they hold off on the loan and our coffee starts to rot, the collector can come in here and make a high-interest loan or buy the coffee cheap."

We all meet in a circle outside the office after I have finished reviewing the books. I feel compelled to be optimistic for the future, but I don't know how long coffee prices will stay low, or whether the prices will rebound in time to prevent a public health disaster here. As part of the first American group to buy Fair Trade coffee here, I can't even offer a guess as to how many other companies will follow suit—that will take a lot of marketing on Tadesse's part. But there is another way to help here. We can help design and pay for something that will be immediately useful in the life of the community. In my mind, this is not charity. Rather, it is a leveling of the unfair trade terms that these people have experienced in the marketplace. In a sense, it is simply a different form of payment for the coffee.

We talk about the most pressing needs of the community. What is holding you back from having the life you want? What are your highest priorities? The farmers take the exercise seriously. They have no trouble identifying their greatest need: *bishan kunkulu*—clean water.

A farmer explains, "Everything depends on water here. Water brings nourishment to the coffee plants and keeps the land from eroding away in this ancient place. Water is essential for our bodies. We cannot cook without water."

"We cannot even pray properly without clean water," laments one of the women.

Coincidentally, at the other end of the continent, another group is talking about the importance of water. In Johannesburg, South Africa, the United Nations is sponsoring the World Summit on Sustainable Development (WSSD). As we are walking through the coffee forest, down to the clogged stream that is the main water source for Negele, multinational corporations such as Monsanto and Nike are scrambling to be the first to ink their commitment to the newly identified Millennium Development Goals. There is a festive, self-congratulatory air in the swank convention center where the WSSD is being held. Outside, cordons of riot police hold back demonstrators and keep away grassroots groups trying to be heard. The thick, bulletproof glass in the center muffles the noise, allowing the clinking of champagne glasses to ring through the assemblage. The WSSD identified lack of access to clean water as one of the highest development priorities. It committed the world community to providing such access to the billion or so people around the world who need it over the next two decades. It simply forgot to say how.

The stream water comes down from the hills into this gully. Along the way, cattle and wild animals have access, their spittle and defecation introducing giardia and other waterborne intestinal diseases to the humans downstream. I have had giardia, amoebic dysentery, and other nasties over the years, but I also have had metronidozole, a good HMO plan, ample clean water, chicken soup, and the luxury of bed rest to combat the most severe symptoms and to foster recovery. The farmers and their families in Negele have no such comforts. The nearest health clinic is about fifteen miles away. Coming into the village, we had passed a group of men headed for that clinic, carrying a woman on a homemade stretcher. The clinics don't have full medical staffs or many supplies. The government is responsible for building wells in all communities, but the resources and political will in Addis Ababa don't extend far beyond the capital, and the paper proclamations from the WSSD can't be used to filter out giardia.

Closer to the town, a small wellhead dribbles water out of a one-inch pipe. Children cluster around the pipe, taking hours to fill their jugs and go home. This isn't seen as wasted time in Negele, as there are no nearby schools for the kids to attend anyway.

Down at the stream, the farmers describe what a water supply system for Negele might look like. A holding tank would capture the water as it comes out of the ground, before it could be contaminated. A piping system would run from the tank to the village center, or maybe near the coffee processing sheds. From there, villagers could collect water for daily use. Maybe in the future, branch pipes could take the water into homes. I have been involved with similar projects in Indonesia and Guatemala; I know their plan is a good one. They have thought about this for a long time.

Tasew Gebrew stands up and stretches his lanky frame. "If only we had the money."

Later, at home, I began to research well building. I contacted a host of nonprofits that had done work in Africa. They were all interested. Generally, they said it would take about forty thousand dollars to do what we wanted. Forty thousand dollars to dig a hole and make a cement tank and run some pipe? Well, they all had overhead of about 25 percent, they needed to hire outside consultants to come in at two-hundred-dollar per diems and thousand-dollar-per-day professional fees. I went back and forth with these groups and finally stopped asking. I began e-mailing Tadesse to ask him to consider what it might look like if the farmers built their own water supply system, with a little help from their friends. It took Tadesse almost a year to organize water committees in the majority of the member co-ops, to analyze costs, and to develop a protocol for deciding who might get the first well. Tadesse calculated that with local labor from the farmers, a water supply system should cost between eight and ten thousand dollars. The farmers of Yirgacheffe agreed that the farmers of the Jimma region needed water help more than they did. Maybe even the farmers of parched Harar, to the east near Somalia and Djibouti, but no one from Yirgacheffe had ever been there.

The Emperor's Bed

Tadesse was a happy man when we left Yirgacheffe. His first Fair Trade visit had not disappointed the farmers. He had a new project to sink his teeth into. He was ready to party. He decided to treat me to a night in splendor; we would stay at Wondo Genet, the summer resort of Haile Selassie. We drove off the main road and up into the mountains.

Wondo Genet is a bit of a shock after Yirgacheffe. New cars line the parking lot. Waterfalls and hot springs surround the 1950s-style bungalows. Well-dressed Ethiopian couples stroll about, looking lovingly into each other's eyes. At the desk, Tadesse requests the Emperor's Bungalow for his distinguished guest. The receptionist sizes me up slowly, shrugs in apparent approval, and hands me the key. Tadesse parades me to the bungalow, which stands slightly apart and on a small rise away from the other bungalows. Tadesse stops at the door, looking reverent.

"It is an honor to sleep in the Emperor's Bed," he intones. "It is not for everybody."

I am deeply touched and mumble some self-conscious thanks. We enter the anteroom. The rushing water outside and these red velvet walls make me feel like I'm in the Emperor's Ventricle. Tadesse opens the door to the bedroom in a sweeping gesture. There before me is the Emperor's Bed, a massive wooden structure with carved lions at the headboard, a velvet duvet offering a regal welcome. My reverie is broken when I realize that the bed is only about five feet long. The Emperor was very short, even shorter than I am at five-foot-four (and a quarter!). Tadesse is smiling. I don't know if he is pleased with his gift to me or laughing at an Ethiopian inside joke. In any event, I get a great night's sleep. (Note to self: never buy a king-sized bed in Ethiopia.)

In the morning, we take a more leisurely drive back to Addis before turning west toward Jimma, the Oromia outpost near the Chad border. We drive through a town that is full of white and black Rastafarians, Bob Marley music—and the unmistakable odor of ganja. This is Shashamane, the town set aside by the Emperor for his returning flock from Jamaica and beyond. Here, many people believe that the Emperor, His Imperial Majesty Haile Selassie I—Conquering Lion of the Tribe of Judah, King of Kings, and Elect of God—is still alive. That his alleged death in 1974 was a stunt designed to discredit him, and that the bones unearthed from the shallow grave where he was suffocated do not belong to him. The current government is tolerant of the faithful but tries to limit the illegal ganja smoking by staging occasional raids and mass contraband burnings. I decide not to share my account of sleeping in the Emperor's Bed with the locals when we stop (as we do every hour or so) for an espresso. My reticence was proven wise a year later when I told a Rastafarian named King David on the Caribbean isle of Bequia about my experience. He followed me for three days and kept hounding me to repeat the story. He said I was sent to Bequia so that he could be close to the presense of Ras Tafari, the soul of the Emperor.

We continue on, past several large lakes that are major bird habitats for both indigenous and migratory European species. Huge flocks of yellow-billed storks come in for a landing. Pelicans belly-flop into the lake for a quick snack. Hornbills and guinea fowls amble down the road or line the trees. High above, unique bearded vultures circle, watching and waiting. Tadesse stares at the lakes.

"I was thinking that Oromia could operate a fleet of eco-tourist boats on the lake for the Europeans who like to watch the birds."

It sounds like a good idea until he tells me about the massive freshwater crocodiles that attack small boats frequently. Locals disappear frequently.

"Maybe bigger boats," he ponders.

Jimma

Ethiopians are proud to say that their country is the only one in Africa that has never been colonized. While this is technically true, the Italians did try in a colonialist version of keeping up with the Joneses. After all, the British, French, Germans, Dutch, and even Portuguese had African colonies; why shouldn't they? The Italians used the new tactic of aerial bombardment with the banned mustard gas to burn villages to the ground and strafed fleeing civilians, but the best they could do in the heat and dust of the African Horn was to grab Eritrea to the north and hold Ethiopia through the early years of World War II. But the Italians left an indelible legacy in Ethiopia. All over Jimma, the manhole covers read "Pisa Foundry," spaghetti is on every menu, Ethiopians say *ciao*, and—most significant of all—the Italians introduced the espresso machine. America should hang its lattéd head in shame at the number of espresso machines that are found throughout the Ethiopian countryside. Every hamlet, with or without electricity, has at least one. Famous Italian names like Cimbali and Faema adorn these ancient marvels. Hand pumps pressurize many rural units, manned by kids in tattered T-shirts who can pull a shot like Dr. Illy himself. The milk comes in fresh every day, carried by nomadic cowgirls in hollow gourds decorated with leather straps and beads. The milk tastes curiously smoky; the girls invert the gourds over a charcoal fire each night to kill any germs from the day's carriage.

Jimma is also a region where the old religion and social systems still survive, albeit *sub silentio*. Here, among the mosques and churches that pepper the landscape, people still practice Quallu, the animist worldview of an older Oromo society. One night in Jimma we pass an Irreessa, an outdoor prayer ceremony held before the harvest. During this ritual, a farmer will become *ayyaana*, inhabited by the Quallu spirit. The spirit will take the prayers and work on them in otherworldly realms, speaking through the mouth of the possessed farmer.

The Oromo in Jimma and beyond still abide by an ancient system of governance, the Gada, that exists as a parallel universe in the countryside. This tribal hierarchy has its own local and regional councils and a congress that acts as national representative of the Oromo people. Like traditional systems elsewhere, it is tolerated by the "modern" government, embraced when it is useful and ignored when it is not. Yet the Gada plays an important role in the daily lives of the Oromo, regardless of how it plays in Addis. The Gada regulates land use, blesses marriages, settles disputes, rewards achievement, and punishes transgression against the social order. It is an age-based hierarchy, with people gaining greater respect and responsibility as they mature.

Whenever I visit a rural coffee area in Oromo lands, we usually have an introductory meeting with the Gada elders before doing business. We sit under a tree. At my first meeting I stood to give my introduction speech. Some of the elders were miffed because I was standing while they were sitting. I begged them to understand that in America it was a necessary sign of respect to stand when speaking to elders, and that I thought I was being polite. They forgave my inadvertent insult. I also make contributions for the regional Gada gatherings during my visits. A hundred bucks feeds a lot of elders during those gatherings, but more significantly it demonstrates my respect for the traditional order of the Oromo. I have never met anyone in the coffee industry who has even heard of the Gada.

Probably more than anywhere else in Ethiopia, the people of this region have coffee in their cultural blood. Every day in most households begins with a coffee ceremony. Tadesse takes me to the small house of sixty-year-old Hadjj Hussein, a co-op member, to experience the ritual.

Hadjj Hussein lives far out of town. As is the case for many Ethiopian farmers, his coffee is "sun dried," meaning the coffee is processed by laying the coffee fruit out in the sun to dry like raisins. These are then picked up by the co-op and taken to Addis for further processing. Farmers sun-dry coffee when they are far from a coffee washing station that would allow the beans to be soaked and fermented in water immediately after harvest, and where they live in dry regions like Jimma or Harar. Sun-dried coffee sells for less than half the price of wet-processed coffee, so the farmers are that much poorer. Hadjj Hussein has fifteen children and twice as many grandchildren. I can't tell which are which. Supersized families are not uncommon among rural Ethiopians. Back in Yirgacheffe, Tasew Gebru at seventy is about to have his tenth child, who will be named Toduru, meaning "What Will the Neighbors Say?" When he is born he will be Uncle Toduru to seven nieces and nephews in their early teens.

One of Hadjj Hussein's younger daughters, twelve-year-old Rehima Hussein, comes out of the house swathed in brown-checkered fabric, her head wrapped in a proper Muslim white head scarf. She is the same age as my oldest daughter and carries that same shy smile. Her sisters spread sweetgrass on the ground and burn frankincense to purify the air around us. Fourteen-year-old Minah stokes a small charcoal brazier. Three-year-old Nejat sits dangerously close to the glowing coals. Rehima puts an old blackened skillet on the brazier and places several handfuls of green coffee beans on the skillet. She stirs the beans with a wooden spoon until they are smoking and cracking like popcorn—the first sign the coffee is nearly ready. Rehima skillfully stirs the beans until they are almost black.

"The coffee is ready when it is the color of a chicken's eye," says Hadjj Hussein approvingly. Yes, I did spend several minutes trying to look into the eyes of the few scrawny chickens in his yard, but to no avail. They were too fast for me.

Rehima pours the beans into a wooden mortar and crushes them with the rhythmic movement of a pestle, humming the whole time. She empties the ground coffee into a clay coffee pot, a *jabana*, the symbol of Ethiopian coffee. There are giant mock *jabanas* at the entrance to many coffee towns in Ethiopia. Rehima pours boiling water into the *jabana* and swishes it around for a minute. Her sister brings out a tray of porcelain teacups, like the ones in a Chinese restaurant.

"We bought them in Jimma market," says Hadjj Hussein proudly. "They are made far away in China."

Rehima pours each cup. She begins about six inches from the cup and pulls the *jabana* up to three feet away as she fills it. Each filling is a little ballet of black liquid. We each receive a cup. This is *abol*, the first round. We drink it quickly and say, "*Buna gari*" (Good coffee). There is a second round, the *tonah*, and then the third, the *beraka* or "blessing" round. *Beraka* is an Amharic word. It shares ancient roots with Hebrew and is thought to have been introduced to Ethiopia by the Queen of Sheba and the early Semitic migrations. The Oromo, though, are not a Semitic people. They are Black African pastoralists who migrated throughout this region over the centuries and have been "internally colonized" by the Amharic peoples for a long time. But at least here, during the coffee ceremony, such things are not discussed. *Buna gari*. The ceremony has ended and the day's work can begin.

I take a photo of Rehima, proudly holding out the tray of small cups full of her family's bounty. This photo would become iconic in the Fair Trade movement. Later, I would pay for her high school education in return for the use of the photo. Even later, Tadesse would tell me that Rehima had graduated from high school and was being sent to Saudi Arabia as a "domestic servant," as her family had no money to keep her in school and there were few jobs in the small towns around Jimma. I visited with Hadjj Hussein and offered to pay for her college tuition and upkeep; after all, I was still using the photo. He had aged immensely in the past four or five years but still held himself with immense grace and dignity. I gave him a framed copy of the photo, his young daughter's beautiful face shining out of the past. The old man nearly cried, but he accepted my offer to pay for her schooling and in a brief ceremony made me Rehima's "Second Father." Rehima would not go to Saudi Arabia. We then visited the now seventeen-year-old Rehima, who was living with a sister at that time. When Masgabu, our translator, told her outside her sister's house that her father had accepted my offer and she could stay in Ethiopia, she seemed only mildly interested. But when her sister invited us inside her one-room house, Rehima threw her arms around me and hugged me tightly.

"I accept you as my Second Father. I love you, I love you," she whispered forcefully. She held my hand as we sat down on the floor and had coffee. I realized that outside, with a gathering crowd of about a hundred Muslim men, women, and children, she had felt uncomfortable expressing emotion to a *ferangi* (a foreigner). She needed to study English, as all university courses in Ethiopia are taught in English, and she wanted to study computer technology. Two months later I received my first letter in English from my new daughter. It began "Dear Dad," and ended with, "I thank you for your innocent gift. Your daughter, Rehima."

Kaldi's Goats Bring Coffee to the World (Maybe)

Ethiopia is the only country in the world so heavily steeped in coffee ritual. And little wonder, as it is generally considered to be the birthplace of coffee (except by certain Yemenis, who say they had it first)—right here, in fact, in the forests outside Jimma over fifteen hundred years ago. Tadesse took me on a pilgrimage to this holy site. As the story goes, it was here that the goatherd Kaldi saw his goats shucking and jiving like crazy. Upon investigation, he found that the goats had been munching red berries from a certain plant. He took the berries (but not the goats) to a local monastery, monks being the rational scientists of the era. Did the monk eat the berries? Did he boil them and drink the brew? Did he strip off the red berry, dry the beans inside, and roast them to a lovely velvet until the oils started to emerge? This is where the story gets murky, but in the end the nameless monk figured out that the beans got you—and your goats—wired (alas, only Kaldi gets the credit).

Another version of the story, apocryphally told by Coptics and Evangelicals alike, has the angel Gabriel appearing as the beatific Bearer of the Buzz at the same spot as Kaldi. Intriguing, although what Gabriel was doing hanging around with a bunch of goats in an isolated patch of Ethiopian forest has more the makings of a Greek comedy than a religious revelation.

At the edge of the forest we met Ayene, an Oromo elder charged with guarding the sacred site. As we trudged through the ancient coffee forest and climbed toward the site I expected to come upon KaldiLand, an amusement park full of rides and attractions, or at least Birthplace of Coffee National Park, with rangers keeping the snotty-nosed little kids from pulling all the red berries off the venerated plants. All of the theme-parked history a kid raised on Disneyland and Six Flags, on Plymouth Plantation and donkey rides into the Grand Canyon, was sure to see. But all that awaited us at the top was, well, a clearing on a hillside. No angels, no prancing goats, no Small, Small World puppets. Nothing. I asked Ayene to tell me the story of Kaldi. I gently shared with him that some people (those Yemenis!) said that the Kaldi story had been made up by American coffee companies in the 1950s, along with Juan Valdez and Dr. Marcus Welby. Ayene looked puzzled and hurt. He scratched his grizzled chin.

"I do not know this doctor. I know the story of Kaldi from my grandfather when I was a boy. He told me that he had heard it from his grandfather."

Ethiopia one, Yemen nothing.

But fairness demands the Yemenis be given a hearing. After all, these two countries have a rivalry over who first brought coffee to the world as fierce as that between the Yankees and the Red Sox, as old and bitter as the coffee at an all-night truck stop in Ohio.

There is a snow-capped mountain of academic literature to back up the claim of each side. As Javatrekkers, however, it is incumbent upon us to go to the source. I confess that I have never been to Yemen (and never met anyone who has), but I do have a primary source. His name is "the Arab." He is a dealer in rare coins, maps, antiques of dubious origin, and Allah-only knows-what-else in Mombasa, Kenya. After a visit to the farmers in Embu, Kenya, I took a little side trip to Mombasa, as I have this insatiable desire to visit ancient trade ports and search for treasures. After fending off street urchins *qua* guides for an hour ("Would you like to see the hiding place of Osama Bin Laden when he lived in Mombasa?" "I can take you into the dungeon beneath the old Portuguese fort; you can buy one of the cannons.") I finally reached the ancient Arab Quarter of the city. It was aptly named, as the narrow, labyrinthine streets, veiled women, and muezzins calling the faithful to prayer could have been Cairo or Damascus. As I entered the Arab's house, I noticed the massive wooden front-door frame—a carved series of chains surrounded the door.

"My ancestors were slave dealers" came a deep, smooth voice in impeccable Etonian English. "It was a point of pride in those days, so the doors of the dealers' houses carried the mark of a slaver—the chains." The Arab was tall and thin, swaddled in white robes and wearing the *khaffiya* headdress—and he was from Yemen. Jackpot! After perusing his old coin collection, drawing deep on a hookah containing whatever, and downing the omnipresent Coke. I asked the big question.

"So why do you think coffee originated in Yemen and not Ethiopia?"

"My country had the first recorded coffee port, at Mocha," he said with obvious pride. "If the Ethiopians were the first, where did they sell their coffee? Why does no one know this, eh?"

Score one for Yemen. The Arab was right. Why wasn't coffee pouring out of a Djibouti port, or any of the other sandy, shallow ports along the coast on the Ethiopian side of the Gulf of Aden? Although the coast is now controlled by Somalia and Djibouti, leaving Ethiopia landlocked, back in the Kaldian era the whole area was part of the Abyssinian empire, so there should be some historical record to support the coffee claim.

"Ahh, but I have something that will prove what I say." This guy was a born salesman. He called a young, veiled Rubenesque woman over and gave her sharp, curt directions. She returned with a cardboard portfolio. The Arab opened it and my eyes nearly popped.

"This is a manuscript chart of the coffee port of Mocha. It was drawn in the early 1700s by the sea captain Jan Zacherias Nauwman of the Dutch East India Company—the VOC. If you look in the hills surrounding the port, you will see that the captain drew little coffee trees."

Sure enough, the good Dutch captain had drawn the soundings in the harbor, the anchorages, minarets in the town, and the coffee in the surrounding hills. VOC captains were required to make charts to update the company's Secret Atlas, which contained the greatest collection of sea charts known at that time. Manuscript charts are incredibly rare—and valuable. More hookah, please. A quick trip on the back of the Arab's scooter to the only working ATM in the Arab Quarter and the manuscript chart was mine, along with some coins from the long-lived VOC and the short-lived British Imperial East Africa Company. People are often shocked at the notion that most currency from the sixteenth through eighteenth centuries was minted by private companies. But to me, these coins are merely the hallowed precursor to the credit card—a publicly used currency printed and backed by private enterprise instead of governments.

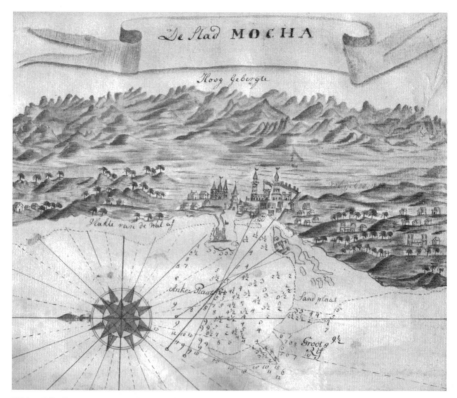

This 18th Century manuscript sea chart of the port of Mocha shows coffee trees surrounding the town.

Even though I now own this cool chart, I can't be bought off that easily. I just can't get behind Yemen as the Birthplace of Coffee. Look, in the streets of the smallest town in Ethiopia, beggars come up to you and plead, "Can you spare a *birrh* for a cup of coffee?" Yet Anthony Wild supports the Yemenis in his book *Dark History*. Wild says that if the Ethiopians invented coffee, why was it not mentioned in the Bible when the Ethiopian Queen of Sheba was giving welcome gifts to visiting kings? This claim made Tadesse apoplectic.

"You must put this in your book," he urged. "It was not the Ethiopians but the Oromo who discovered coffee. That's why it is not in the Bible. The Queen of Sheba was Amharic, not Oromo. Oromo people used coffee for centuries before the Ethiopian or Abyssinian nation was created. We fried the beans in butter and put them in our cheeks to stay alert for long treks with our cattle. We could go all day on these *buna kalla* without food and water. We used the leaves for tea and put the grounds on cuts. You must correct this Wild man."

Lately, radical revisionists have even defiled the sacred grove of Kaldi. Some claim that India was the true birthplace of coffee, based on carbonized beans found in ancient archaeological sites. But the Kaldi story is so much a part of coffee lore that pitching India as the real place of origin has as much punch as trying to convince Italian-Americans that the Basques, Vikings, or Chinese got to America before Columbus. Honestly, is nothing sacred?

Like Water for Coffee

The water management committees of Oromia had chosen Haro Cooperative in Jimma as the location for the first water supply system. We had created a program of revolving loans to build the wells. It was a unique project and one that the farmers had trouble accepting. The idea was that we would grant Oromia eight thousand dollars to start the fund. Oromia would lend the money to a member co-op for construction of the water system. The co-op would build and manage the system and pay the loan back to Oromia, without interest, at the rate of a penny per pound of coffee harvested. When the fund was replenished, it would revolve to the next member co-op, and so on. We named the project Miriam's Well, in honor of the biblical prophetess who found water in the desert wherever she went. As many Ethiopians are big-time Old Testament Christians, the name was solid, evocative marketing. Even the Muslim members could get behind a project named for their ancient cousin.

In November 2006, I returned to Haro Cooperative to celebrate the opening of the water system. I carried the elder's cane, the *dula*, that was given to me on my first visit. The *dula* is a beautiful cane made of different colored sections of buffalo horn, separated by silver discs. At the time, I was only forty-eight, so I wondered why I was considered an elder. Then I found out that according to the United Nations, the average life expectancy of an Ethiopian male was forty-six. Since my bad knee had gotten worse over the years, I actually used the *dula*. But since it was too long, I had to cut off six inches from the end and put a rubber cap on it. When the

Oromia members saw my shortened cane, they asked why I had cut off the tip of my *dula*.

"It's an old Jewish tradition," I said with a smile.

It took a few seconds for the cross-cultural joke to sink in, but soon all the farmers were howling. I was thereafter introduced as "The Dula Man."

Unfortunately, we could not hold the celebration when originally planned. A week before my arrival, Christian youths shot up a truckload of Muslim worshippers in the small town where Rehima lived, killing several. A mosque was burned, and all of Jimma was tense over the first serious signs of interfaith conflict in this region. The Christian president sent police and troops to the area, which was seen by many Muslims as a show of Christian power and did nothing to lower the flame. Five days into my visit, Tadesse said it was safe to go in.

The design of the water project was just as the Yirgacheffe farmers had described. We walked downhill for more than a mile via winding trails through ancient coffee groves to get to the spring. There, young girls were filling their containers with water to take back to their villages on the other side of the mountain. They were not members of Haro, but the farmers had said that the clean water was a gift for everybody and had invited the three thousand villagers in the surrounding area to tank up here. A large cement tank held about five hundred gallons as it bubbled out of the ground. Two-inch metal piping emerged from the tank, snaking out into the forest and away toward Haro village. The villagers had dug trenches by hand through the coffee forest, in places as deep as nine feet, to keep the pipe relatively level, allowing for a good head of pressure to build. We trekked back up the hill, talking with some Haro women about what it was like to carry those forty-pound jugs of water on their backs uphill for over a mile. The question puzzled them, as they had no alternative and just accepted it as necessary to provide water for their families. A mother of six, Mardiya Gelaye, told me, "Now that we have water in the village I don't have to walk so far to collect it. I have more time now to help my husband with coffee farming, and cooking the meals is much easier."

Her friend added, "Our community is much happier now. We can wash before prayer all seven times each day!"

As we came to the village center, the sweet sound of young girls, voices reached out in welcome. A crowd of several hundred villagers came out to thank us for helping them get *bishan kunkulu*. We went first to the square, where a new cement water station with four spigots sat happily dripping away. Next, we marched to a nearby field, where we were welcomed by more songs from the children. I sat with the local elders under a cloth canopy and we shared the three cups of the coffee ceremony. The old man to my right sat slumped in his chair, his rheumy eyes unfocused on the ceremony. I patted his hand and whispered to him, "*Bism'allah rachman al rachim*" (God is compassionate and merciful), the first words of the Koran. He looked over to me slowly, smiled and nodded, and patted my hand in return. Several of the co-op members and local dignitaries made speeches of welcome and thanks. I was wrapped in a beautiful handwoven shawl of white muslin and blessed by the local *imam*. I gave my speech in English this time, with a few Oromifa words sprinkled in as crowd-pleasers. Tadesse beamed at my new language skills. "You will be speaking Oromifa in six months!"

The festivities devolved into visiting. I had a chance to sit with many of the farmers and their families. I asked what the new water system meant to them, how it had impacted their lives. They talked about immediately noticeable health benefits, such as less diarrhea and stomach pains, as well as less pain in the backs of the women and kids who generally carried the water. Damtew, one of the younger farmers, said that they were looking forward to a good harvest to pay back the loan, so that another co-op could share in this "gift from God."

On the road back to Addis, Tadesse wanted to stop to show me something "very special." We pulled over at a cement bridge crossing a slow-flowing brown river. At one side of the bridge sat a small guardhouse, occupied by Officer Aba Diga, an old man who looked like a weary palace guard in his tattered uniform. Tadesse gave him some *birrh* and the old man walked out onto the bridge. He cupped his hands and bellowed in a clear, strong voice, "Robi! Robi!" He waited a few minutes, staring at the water. "Robi! Robi!"

About twenty yards upstream, a comical fat head with tiny ears popped out of the water. It was a hippopotamus! The old guy called up a hippo! We stood there delighted, giggling like kids while the old man beamed. He said a few words lovingly to the *robi* and it sank slowly under the water. We thanked him and left.

Seven hours later we pulled into the Sheraton Hotel in Addis to check on my return flight for the next week. The lobby and bar were crowded with aid workers and consultants who were staying at the Sheraton at a nightly rate equal to an Ethiopian coffee farmer's annual earnings. It was obvious why those wells would cost forty grand if we worked with one of those groups. We moved on to the Atlas Hotel, eight bucks for the night. The receptionist smiled at me and whispered, "Take me to America. I will be your wife forever."

We stepped over the sleeping prostitutes in the hallways, barricaded our door with our suitcases, and sank into a good night's sleep.

Harar

Ethiopia is a very big country. It takes another ten hours due east from Addis to reach Harar, the ancient and crumbling walled trading center of the thirteenth century. A typical third-world bazaar of cheap goods and hustle has grown up around the walled city. Along the way we pass nomadic Afar tribespeople swathed in white muslin, a seven-foot spear in one hand and a rifle in the other. I notice that the older nomads carry World War II–era Belgian Fabrique Nacionale rifles or ancient French Zouave muskets. The younger men sport AK-47s. All of them have rough, handmade daggers tucked under their waist sashes. Many Afar live in small huts made of branches and grass. The huts are no more than five feet high and look like the *sukkot* huts of the ancient Israelites. The Afar herd their camels down the road. I stop to take a picture of the camels. A young boy runs out screaming at me.

"He says you cannot take a picture," translates Dessalegn, the finance manager of Oromia, who has joined us for the trip to Harar.

"Okay, should I give him some money for a photo? I just want his camels, not him if it matters." Hey, I'm still a tourist, after all.

Dessalegn talks to the kid, who ultimately throws up his hands and pounds on a camel's rump with his spear, causing my photo op to vanish in the desert.

"He said if you take a picture, it will suck out the blood of the camel and it will get sick and die."

"You mean I will capture its soul in the camera?" That was a fear of many indigenous groups long ago. Dessalegn looks at me curiously.

"No. Not the soul. How could it do that? It would suck out the blood like I told you." Dessalegn obviously thinks I'm a little thick, as I didn't get it the first time, but we have known each other for many years now and he is very forgiving. Fortunately camels are in abundance down the road, and I manage to sneak in some bloodless shots over the next few days.

We also pass many Somali herders. This part of Ethiopia is close to the Somalia border. The Ethiopians claim northern Somalia as part of Greater Abyssinia, while the Somalis claim southeastern Ethiopia as part of Greater Somalia. Doesn't this stuff ever end? We are passed on the road by tractor trailers hauling huge old Russian T-54 tanks toward the border. It is November 2006, and the Ethiopians are part of an international coalition sent to prop up the flagging transitional government of Somalia under the assault of the Somalian Union of Islamic Courts. In a case of really bad marketing, the Ethiopians managed to be the only nation in the coalition to send troops into Somalia, so it looks like a plain old land grab to the Somalis and everybody else around here who is willing to talk about it. War is just around the corner. There is also a new flood of Somali economic and political refugees in this region, and the tension between the Afars, Oromos, and Somalis is palpable. Everyone is armed to the teeth and marketplaces turn violent quickly. We limit our coffee stops going through this region.

We pass a burned-out British light tank, a remnant of the Eritrean war in the early 1990s. I ask Dessalegn to stop so I can plaster a "Make Coffee Not War" bumper sticker on it and take a photo. A group of Somalis and their camels wander over, totally bemused at the sight of someone taking a picture of a burned-out tank. I get in the turret and make some goofy gestures, trying to move the tank forward. The herders laugh, say something to Dessalegn, and move on, shaking their heads and mimicking my gestures. As we drive off, I ask Dessalegn what they said. He smiles.

"They thought it was very brave of you to go into that tank when everyone knows it is the den of many deadly snakes. They use it to avoid the sun."

We are passed by heavily loaded Isuzu trucks on their way to Addis. Behind the wheels are crazed-looking drivers, their drooling, open mouths green with the spittle of chewed *qat*. *Qat* is a shrub that grows wild throughout Ethiopia and Somalia. It is a mild, addictive narcotic. I have heard that Somalis spend as much as 65 percent of their household income on the dry green leaves, literally chewing up any future for themselves and their families. The truck drivers chew all day to make the long runs to and from the capital more bearable, and to finish the job as quickly as possible. The towns around Harar thrive on *qat*. We drive through market after market of nothing but women sitting next to huge bundles of branches and leaves. It is easy to grow and easy to sell. Why work for a living? Many farmers in Ethiopia have abandoned their coffee plots for *qat*, which is not subject to the vagaries of the world commodity markets. Several people told me that there is a booming export trade in *qat* that is dominated by government officials and their wives, who make enormous profits in the drug trade. At the top of the list, apparently, is the wife of a high minister. Her name is Sura, the Qat Queen. Some folks consider Sura a Robin Hood figure, as she gives money to the poor while driving around in one of several Mercedes. It seems as if everyone in Harar has a Sura story to tell, and she gets bigger, fatter, richer, meaner, and more generous with each telling. That night I meet a well-to-do family at the hotel. I ask the pretty teenaged daughter what she wants to be when she grows up. A doctor, an engineer? She waits until her dad is out of earshot before replying.

"I want to export *qat* to Europe and become very rich. Don't tell my father."

Before we go up into the mountains to visit the farmers, I have to search the bazaars of Harar for old coins. The streets of old Harar are an endless labyrinth of winding, narrow, cobblestone paths with high painted mud walls on each side. Looking like a lost tourist draws sympathetic passersby to my aid. I ask if anybody knows where Fatuma lives, as I have heard she has old coins for sale. A khaki-clad official-looking fellow steps forward and tells me the "easy way" to find Fatuma's house.

"At the end of this lane you will find a begging leper woman; go left. Stay left and left past the Muslim Market. She lives near there and many people will help you find her."

Twenty minutes later I am hopelessly lost, surrounded by eight-foot mud walls, not a leper in sight. Some children run after me, shouting and pointing. I want to get away from them, so I duck into the alley ahead. The children fade away. I look down and realize why the kids were trying to keep me from going this way. I have found the alley that serves as the public toilet for all of Harar and most of the visiting camels. One hand on my nose, the other held out for balance, I tiptoe through this minefield of *merde* until I emerge out the other side. Hey, the Muslim Market!

Nobody knows where Fatuma lives, but I do get many offers from Muslim women to buy my gold earring. They have never seen a man with an earring, so I am the star attraction for the day. Finally, Fatuma emerges. She is very large and very dark. I follow her to her home, wishing I had dropped bread crumbs so I can find my way out. Her home doubles as an informal ethnographic museum of nomadic culture, with knives and shields covering the walls, the floors littered with milk gourds, basketry, and sleeping, fleabag puppies. The tray of coins she offers turns out to be the pocket change of every Italian and German traveler who has visited Harar in the last fifty years. No, this isn't what I wanted. I manage to find someone in the ogling crowd that has gathered to explain that I want very old coins from the days of trade. Harar was once a major trading post from the African south and the Arab north, from Yemen to the east and Sudan to the west.

Fatuma produces a small woven sack and empties the contents into a silver tea tray. Jackpot! Silver and bronze coins a half inch in diameter full of strange Arabic and old Hebrew markings fill the tray. I choose six and spend the next half hour eyeball to eyeball with the toughest old bird I have ever met. She would do well as a New Jersey divorce lawyer. She gets most of my assets and I am left with a few coins. But I am delirious. What have these coins traded for? Guns and swords? Did they buy the freedom of a slave or transfer ownership of a camel? How far have they traveled and how many hands have touched them? What karma do I hold in my hands?

Another four-hour ride to get to the farmers. The ecology changes dramatically again as we climb into the mountains surrounding Harar. Even the omnipresent *tef* disappears, as the harsh landscape can only support the tougher sorghum. This plant looks like angry cornstalks, topped with a fiery red crown of seedheads. Even the dryland shrubs give way to a wild variety of cacti and yuccas. Small green weeds and ground cover struggle for survival in what looks to my New England eyes like a Darwinian nightmare. I share these feelings with Dessalegn. To him, it is a celebration of the tenacity of life.

We pass through the town of Aware, which Dessalegn tells me is the largest financial center in the country after Addis. It is a miserable collection of mud huts and curious open-air stalls. The stalls are made of blue tarps that read "UNHCR," salvaged or stolen from the Somali refugee camps set up by the United Nations a little further southeast. Other stalls have metal walls, hammered together from flattened gallon cans reading "USAID Food Aid: Gift of the People of the USA." The town is nothing more than a giant *qat* market. Dessalegn tells me that the coffee farmers in this area have supplemented their earnings with *qat*, even forming a cooperative of *qat* growers in a bizarre twist on the lessons of Fair Trade.

We arrive at the headquarters of Ilili Darartu Cooperative at midday. The two mud-brick, one-room offices are swarming with families picking up the newly delivered zinc roofing sheets for the new school. As poor as these people are, they have made the decision to pool their Fair Trade premiums instead of disbursing them. They have built the first school in the area. After reviewing the books of the co-op and sharing welcoming speeches, we trudge down the road to the school. From a distance we can hear the recitation of the heavily accented English lesson: "I have two eggs today. I will have an egg tomorrow . . ."

The teacher, a twenty-year-old woman named Daria, leads us inside. The small, dark room is jammed with students. This is the third and fourth grades. Children sit on long benches, some crammed three abreast at small wooden desks. The back row is populated by fifteen- and sixteen-year-olds. I ask Daria why they are there.

"We rank the children by what they know, not age. These young boys and girls have never had any education, so they are at the third-grade level." She looks their way and smiles. "This is a great chance for them, and they come here every day."

I ask Daria to show me what the students know about math. She puts examples on the blackboard.

"Savan plus wan equals?"

Twenty hands shoot up eagerly. Daria chooses a young girl who marches up to the blackboard and chalks an irregular "8." Daria asks the class if she is correct. They all respond, "Correct!" Three more exercises occur until one little boy gets one wrong. "Not correct!" the class shouts, maybe a little too gleefully. I feel bad for the kid, as he seems embarrassed before their guest from "the USA." I ask Daria to do one more, and let me answer. She writes and says, "Seex an tree equals?" My hand shoots up and she calls on me. I walk to the board, think about it, and write a big, loopy "8."

"Not correct!" shouts the class happily. Daria asks for someone to correct me. She chooses the little boy who got the last one wrong. He slowly walks up to the blackboard and puts on a screwed-up face of deep concentration. He writes a determined "9," breaking the chalk in the process.

"Correct!" squeals the class, and I lead a round of applause for the clever student. He sits down with restored self-confidence.

Outside, we pass two more buildings under construction.

"These will be five–six and seven–eight," says co-op manager Abere. The co-op members are very excited to have schools for their children. My excitement about this contribution to Fair Trade in Ilili Darartu is tempered by the dozens of children running around us who are not in school. Everywhere we have gone in Ethiopia we have been awash in a sea of children with little or no education. They can't all be farmers. What will they do?

The coffeelands of Harar are radically different from the other areas in Ethiopia. The trees have not been here since the Kaldi era and are not integrated into any natural forests. Instead, they stand apart in fields, under mixed shade or in open sun. The farmers take us through the tight rows of coffee plants, standing around six feet tall and chubby with green leaves and red berries. At the foot of each plant, the farmers carefully place a thick bed of mulch to hold the precious moisture that comes irregularly during the year. I put my hand under the mulch and feel the dampness—a sharp contrast to the dry air that envelops us. The rows are difficult to negotiate, as they are filled with bean vines, pumpkins, and squash. The interplanted vegetables do more than provide for the farmer's table; they retain moisture and fix needed nutrients into the dry soils.

All of these coffee beans will be sun-dried. There is no water to spare for a wet-process harvest. In fact, there is hardly any water to drink here. In the town square a water distribution spigot stands deserted. Abere tells me that this water spigot was built by the government a few years ago, but it is clogged up or broken. No one from the government will come and fix it. Maybe, he ventures cautiously, the water has been diverted closer to the source a few miles away. We walk the three-inch pipeline a quarter mile, talking about water problems. We come across two women, sitting by a leaking pipe joint. Under the excruciatingly slow drip, the women have placed a shallow plastic bucket. Every fifteen minutes or so they empty the bucket into a larger container. I ask the women how long it takes them to get the water they need for their families every day. The women are uncomfortable talking to me. Maybe I am from the government and I think they are stealing the water. Dessalegn explains that I am trying to understand the water problems they face in this region and maybe I can help some day.

"Three hours" is the curt reply.

It is our last night in Harar. We are going to see Yussef, the Hyena Man. Yussef lives in a small house outside the northern wall of Harar. Every night he feeds the wild hyenas that come down from the hills surrounding the city to scavenge through the dark lanes. Curiously, the hyenas eat the local mutts but never bother the cats. The hyena feeding is supposed to be something of a tourist attraction, so I figure we will be jostling for a view among busloads of German and Italian tourists. Actually, the entire time we are in Harar, I don't see another Westerner.

Our taxi driver takes us to Yussef's house just after dark. He leaves his headlights on so that we can see the action. The tourist crowd I feared consists solely of Yussef's three young nephews. The Hyena Man, a dark, scrawny fifty-year-old, sits on the ground next to a bucket of butcher scraps. He taps the side of the bucket and calls names out into the night. Slowly, six hairy, hunchbacked shapes come prowling around the perimeter of the light. Dear God! These things are huge! I thought they would be the measly canines of Disney cartoons, or the size of the coyotes that skulk through New England backyards at night. But these creatures stand as tall and as broad as bull mastiffs. They become more comfortable with the light and inch toward Yussef's outstretched hand, a slab of meat and gristle hanging off a foot-long stick enticing them forward. They lunge for the stick, snatch the meat, and back off. Now and then two will compete for the grab, with the larger one growling or snapping the other away. Yussef shortens the stick until it is only a few inches long. Then he puts it in his mouth, and the hyena's snapping jaws clamp the meat a kiss away from his lips. It is mesmerizing. I have read that the Hararis had a mystical relationship with the hyenas, and something wild is going on here. I find my feet shuffling toward Yussef. He beckons me forward and hands me a stick. I stab a hunk of meat from the bucket and hold it out. The biggest hyena inches forward, keeping her eyes on mine, not on the meat. It is a weird experience, but I am compelled to draw the meat in closer. Closer to my face. My body freezes when the meat dangles two inches from my lips. There is a blur of teeth and fur before me as the hyena lunges in then retreats several feet to watch me as it tears the meat apart. I abruptly come out of my odd reverie, hand Yussef a bunch of *birrh*, and back off to the taxi. The driver slaps me on the back, laughs, and says I am "crazy like a Harari."

By the close of 2006, coffee prices had risen dramatically. Oromia had grown from thirty-five member cooperatives to almost one hundred. Over eighty thousand farmers were now enrolled in the largest and most successful co-op in Ethiopia. They had sold a remarkable ninety containers of Fair Trade coffee in 2006, yet there was considerably more coffee sold at conventional prices. Tadesse was the star of a documentary about the struggle for Fair Trade in Ethiopia called Black Gold, *and he was speaking at showings all over the USA and Europe. New elementary schools had been built by the farmers from Fair Trade premiums in Negele Gorbitu and Ilili Darartu, and a new health clinic was under construction in the former. A new water supply system is being designed for Ilili Darartu under the Miriam's Well program. The farmers have asked me to help design a coffee museum for the birthplace of coffee. Meanwhile, the Millenium Development Goals feature prominently in many glossy reports on corporate social responsibility.*

2

Fermenting Change, But Don't Cross the Big Man

KENYA, 2005

Nuk-nuk-nuk- . . . The stentorian tones of the antique British wall clock in the waiting room of the Ministry of Cooperatives Development were a reminder that we had been sitting there for an hour and a half. The waiting room was well appointed, containing beautiful Kenyan arts and crafts. It was in sharp contrast to the poverty on the street just outside the office building. To my left on the hard wooden bench was Francis Kyoko, a determined, middle-aged Kenyan who lived in America and had cofounded Kenya Fair Traders (KFT) to bring the Fair Trade system to his native land. On my right was Alexia Baldascini, a project administrator with the United Nations Food and Agriculture Organization (FAO) in Rome, with whom I had worked for over a year.

The tall, skinny majordomo with the ill-fitting shirt and tie came out of the Minister's office now and again but never deigned to acknowledge

our presence. He barely hid the smirk behind the indifference behind his
professional demeanor. No sound came from the inner sanctum, except an
occasional throat clearing and turning of newspaper pages. The Minister was
in before we got there. There was no one in the waiting room besides us. We
were experiencing the typical bureaucratic blow-off that establishes "power
over" the supplicants. Back home, time is often seen as an impediment
to efficiency. Here, it is a tool of power to be stretched, massaged, and
manipulated to fit the moment. We got the message. Francis Kyoko looked
uncomfortable. He had expressed strong opinions about what had to be done
here, but now he seemed very meek. Alexia, an experienced U.N. administrator
who had worked in several African countries, took it all in stride.

Minister Peter Ndwiga called us in after another fifteen minutes. He was
impeccably dressed in a dark Savile Row suit and silk tie—a sharp contrast
with my flowered shirt and Alexia's hip European jeans. He welcomed us
to Kenya with handshakes and smiles, then proceeded to read verbatim a
seven-page speech.

> 1.0. Welcome
> 1.1. It is my greatest pleasure to welcome you to Kenya on behalf
> of my Government, my Ministry, the Co-operative Movement,
> and on my own behalf.

A half hour later, he ended his tour de force of the Kenyan coffee industry
and cooperative movement.

> 5.0. Conclusion
> The Government believes that a strong co-operative movement
> will maximize coffee farmers' incomes as it is the avenue for
> channeling credit, distribution of inputs, marketing, and value
> addition processing thereby reducing the endemic poverty
> among our people.
> It is in this regard that my Ministry welcomes any joint
> venture in the coffee subsector, as this will enhance the returns
> to our coffee farmers.
> Thank you.

Okay, so the Minister had treated us to a bureaucratic show of power and a long-winded speech. He was still a member of Parliament from the new National Rainbow Coalition that had swept into power a year earlier, promising to end the reign of corrupt Big Men who had monopolized power in Kenya since independence in 1963. There was an impressive "Corruption Reporting Box" in the lobby of each government building; some of the old rascals were being investigated; the new government had installed longtime (and long-suffering) environmental activist Wangari Maathai as vice minister for the environment and promised a sweeping cleanout of Kenya's notorious kleptocracies. We were here to help them find an alternative way of doing business in the coffee sector.

The project came about in a serendipitous manner. I had been working with Alexia in an FAO group exploring ways to help sustain mountain communities, and Kenya was one of the countries of major concern to the group. At the same time, some members of Cooperative Coffees, our roasters' cooperative, had been speaking to a group of Kenyans, including Francis, who had formed KFT and were interested in developing Fair Trade in their country. KFT had received a ringing endorsement from the Minister for a pilot project to arrange and sell "the first shipment of Fair Trade coffee to the world market" on an exclusive basis.

I had reservations about our ability to do anything in Kenya. After all, there were many good organizations working on organics and Fair Trade, and to date none of them had been able to put anything together in Kenya. There had to be good (or bad) reasons for this. But there was a new government dedicated to change and transparency, and we had been invited by the Minister to undertake this venture, so my caution was swept away in the excitement. My only caveat to Cooperative Coffees was to refrain from actually purchasing anything until after my visit. This way we could understand the flow of coffee from the co-ops in Kenya out through their rather unique, state-controlled system and also trace how the money would flow from us to the farmers to ensure a fair and transparent distribution down the line.

However, a week before I left for Kenya, Cooperative Coffees bought a container of coffee from KFT. It would be on the water by the time I got to Kenya and the funds released by the bank. *Oh well*, I thought, *at least I'll have a real transaction to trace.*

The Minister had made a tight travel schedule for us and put us in the care of Justus Kiago, his very competent (and equally well-dressed) assistant. The Minister then reviewed the itinerary, which was designed to help me examine the efficient functioning of the Kenyan coffee sector. We would visit the processors and the auction and have full access to all documents and financial records relevant to our purchase. Then we would meet with the farmers of Rianjagi and Gakundu Cooperatives, who grew the coffee we had purchased. We would end the visit with a large farmer assembly attended by the Minister himself, where I would have a full opportunity to talk to the farmers about Fair Trade and setting up new relationships.

"You will see for yourself the flow of beans out of the farmers' hands and the flow of money into their pockets," said the Minister grandly.

I had never done work in the coffeelands through a government before and was not thrilled at this arrangement, but Justus seemed truly concerned with the plight of the small farmers, and the schedule promised everything we needed to get the job done. I had originally met Justus at the Specialty Coffee Association conference in Atlanta the year before, where he had participated in the early meetings between Cooperative Coffees and KFT. I then got Justus invited to participate in a planning session organized by Alexia at FAO in Rome, as the creation of Fair Trade and organics in Kenya came before the group as a development option. After one long session, Justus and I had gone out dancing with Joseph, an agricultural extension worker from Uganda, in the very hip Trastavere district. Joseph and I rocked the dance floor, holding hands in proper African male style, while the shy Justus hung back at the bar. At one point, I looked over and saw the tie-and-jacketed Justus giggling nervously, surrounded by a gaggle of admiring men. I didn't know it was a gay bar.

I had thrown a small glitch into the Minister's planning by setting up a separate meeting of nongovernmental environmental and agricultural groups that afternoon to put together an in-country team to carry out the work, but the Minister had accommodated the meeting in the cramped schedule. Already two hours behind, we left the Minister's office and headed to the headquarters of the Kenya Planters Cooperative Union (KPCU) in downtown Nairobi.

Small farmers in Kenya are required by law to be members of cooperatives and to sell their coffee exclusively through their co-op. The farmers bring their red cherries into the co-op's "factory," or primary processing plant, where the fruit is stripped off and the beans soaked for up to three days in water. Most coffee around the world is soaked for twenty-four hours, so the Kenyan coffee has a fermentation time in the tanks three times longer than in other places. This accounts for the highly prized acidity of Kenyan coffee. The dried beans are trucked to the KPCU mills, where they are dehulled from the parchment, graded, and bagged for sale at the state-run auction. When the beans are sold at auction, KPCU receives the money on the farmers' account, subtracts government-mandated fees and milling and processing costs, and credits the remainder to the co-ops' bank accounts. Besides processing the coffee, KPCU is one of the limited number of licensed bidders at the auction. Often, KPCU will buy beans for its own account, keep them in its warehouse, and resell them later. KPCU was legally owned by all of the farmer cooperatives that sent their coffee to the processor, but in reality it acted as an independent entity with little accountability to the farmers. The officers were appointed not by the farmers or their co-ops, but rather by the government as political patronage. KPCU officials had been accused of stealing farmers' money, of overcharging them, of delaying payments, of losing coffee, and of committing most crimes short of murder (although assault and battery were on the list). As we approached Wakulima House, their imposing offices, I imagined a boardroom full of characters out of *Pirates of the Caribbean*.

There were no Pirates, at least according to the Brethren's dress code. The boardroom was full of very well-dressed administrators and bureaucrats with very good manners. We were introduced to the entire board, as well as the head cupper and other technical people. KPCU officials were excited to meet us and to demonstrate that they were an honest and transparent service provider to the farmers who owned the organization. For the next several hours, we went through the entire range of KPCU operations. First, we went to the receiving docks, where the beans come in from the farmer co-ops and are weighed and cataloged; then over to the mill area, where the beans are cleaned; up to the third floor, where all samples are analyzed and graded; then to the warehouse, where the beans are stored prior to being sold at the state auction. At each step, we reviewed the paper trail. It was very impressive and very complete. There was little chance for a mix-up of beans or grading mistakes in what appeared to be an unbreakable chain of custody.

We were rushed through things a bit, but I attributed that to the officials' desire to get through our visit and get back to work.

Back in the boardroom, I was asked my opinion of their system, and to explain Fair Trade and how it would bring more money to the farmers. I complimented KPCU for their program and went through the Fair Trade system. I also shared my experience from the night before, which might have great portent for KPCU.

That evening I had been invited to a most unusual dinner party. During my research for the trip, I had come across a small project, funded by USAID, to help small businesses in Kenya. The project head was a twenty-eight-year-old Hawaiian-American named David, who cheerfully told me about his project via e-mail and invited me to visit him in Nairobi. I took a taxi to David's apartment, in the upscale neighborhood by the new U.S. embassy. I entered a place full of expensive African art and furniture, fine wines, and a lovely Kenyan housekeeper. *Man*, I thought, *these USAID guys make really good money helping the poor of the world.*

David introduced me to the other guests that evening: a couple from America (the husband worked at the embassy) and another twenty-eight-year-old named Yasuo, who worked as a consultant to the World Bank. The embassy man was clearly a spook—I could tell from the tone of his questions and the job he held at the embassy. (I would reveal his name, but then I could be charged with a federal crime.) Yasuo had a more relevant job—he was doing a "value chain analysis" of the coffee industry. He was looking for the inefficiencies and structural problems within the coffee industry and would make recommendations for change to the World Bank. If the Bank accepted his analysis ("and it certainly will" he cheerfully told me), it would advise the Kenyan government of the recommendations.

"What happens if the government doesn't accept your findings and the Bank's recommendations?" I asked.

"The Bank is holding up 75 million dollars of loan money. If they don't accept the recommendations, they don't get the money."

I was face-to-face with Structural Adjustment. A twenty-eight-year-old had the power to tell the Kenyan government what to do by yanking the international purse strings.

"So what have you found so far?" I asked tentatively.

"Well, there are many inefficiencies in the system here. First of all, there is massive corruption all up and down the line, from the Minister's office to the cooperative management. Then there is the problem with the farmers getting paid. There is a serious lag time between when they give their coffee to the co-op and when they ultimately get paid. Sometimes this can be six months or more. During that time, the farmer has no income at all. We call that the 'hunger lag.'"

I couldn't argue with Yasuo. He was an incredibly intelligent and erudite young man, and he had obviously done his research here.

"So what will you recommend? Shake up the bureaucracy? More transparency in the money transactions?"

Yasuo took a deep drag from his cigarette and shook his head. He released the smoke slowly, so that it curled up past his face. He spoke through the smoke.

"My major recommendation will be to dismantle the cooperative system, get rid of KPCU, and let the farmers sell to whoever they want on the open market."

"You can't be serious?" I nearly shouted. "There may be problems with the system, but the co-ops are what protect all the small farmers from the sharks out in the market. If you take away the co-ops, you invite in even bigger problems and the farmers will have no power to confront them."

Yasuo took another deep drag, his face showing no emotion whatsoever.

"You see, Dean, the co-ops are the problem. They are an anachronism and have no place anymore. They are corrupt and don't provide the services or protection they were meant to. They should be eliminated. I examined the books at the KPCU as well as the computerized records at one of the co-op's offices."

I acknowledged that there was a difference between the state-mandated cooperatives of East Africa and those freely organized by farmers for their own benefit. The story of Ethiopian co-ops proved that. But to dismantle the entire system because of a flaw in the design or because some officials abused it? Wasn't that like throwing the baby out with the bathwater? Yasuo wasn't budging.

I felt the anger rising. *Okay, Buddha-boy, take deep breaths. Observe. I am not the anger. I am not the anger.*

"Yes, co-ops are a thing of the past. They are not efficient and are always corrupt." Yasuo was leaning back in his chair, addressing nobody in particular. The spook looked at both of us in turn, his face devoid of any opinion. *Good spook.* David chatted amiably with the pretty housegirl, who brought more wine to the table.

"Did you talk to any of the farmers about their lives or their problems with the system? Do they want the co-ops eliminated?" *Hold it back, Dean.*

Yasuo looked at me and blinked. He laughed.

"Why should I do that?"

Thus the hopes and efforts of people to live a better life on their own terms, especially in the third world, are dismissed. Peoples' lives and aspirations are marginalized as unquantifiable in an era of economic analysis and efficiency. This arrogant puppy, fresh out of business school, making two hundred grand a year with all the toys. An acolyte of the Chicago School of Economics, he can control or direct the major international resources (including my tax dollars) that flow into these countries. I could viscerally feel the tsunami of self-centeredness and calculation washing over a world struggling to redefine and hold on to a moral basis for behavior and relationship amongst peoples. Don't these guys learn anything about history in school anymore? Had he never heard of the Robber Barons and the excesses of the unfettered market? Hell, hadn't he ever heard of WorldCom and Enron? The needle on my personal safety valve was entering the Red Zone, threatening to burst through the thin veneer of social nicety that kept me in my seat.

"Yasuo," I said with control and determination, "you've got to stop talking like this. I have worked with co-ops around the world for years. There are many, many great ones really making a difference in people's lives. If you say one more disparaging word about things that I know are true or people I respect and care about, I am going to leap over this table and tear your throat out."

Yasuo and everyone else at the table were completely stunned. *Oops, definitely bad dinner etiquette.* The spook appraised me through hooded eyes. David hurriedly downed his glass of wine and Yasuo crushed his butt in the ashtray.

"Why don't we change the subject?" I said with all the affability of Genghis Khan at the gates of Rome.

"Uh, okay" came Yasuo's brief reply.

"So you see," I concluded to the KPCU heads, "it is absolutely essential that I be able to demonstrate that the system is transparent and accountable to the farmers. Otherwise . . . ," (I paused for dramatic effect) "you will probably all be out of a job."

The men were quiet and thoughtful but showed no discomfort or concern. I explained that the best way for me to support their system was by tracing the actual beans from the farmers at Rianjagi and Gakundu through the KPCU and auction systems out to Cooperative Coffees and following the money from Cooperative Coffees back down to the farmers. Once this was demonstrated, the farmers and KPCU could apply for the Fair Trade Registry, and the benefits of that system could begin to flow.

Mr. Munyi, the human resources administrator of KPCU, expressed his appreciation for my work and said that the records of KPCU were open to me, and that all documentation for the Cooperative Coffee transaction would be given to me that afternoon. He seemed excited at the chance to show the integrity of the KPCU system that he helped administer. He asked John Karuru, the head of quality control, and Sylvester Koth, the valuation and marketing chief, to ensure that this was done. All the men in the room murmured agreement. Justus smiled and patted my back. Francis, who hadn't said a word during the entire meeting, looked pleased. Coffee was served.

We rushed out into the midday traffic in Nairobi toward Kiambu, one of the outlying towns, where a new coffee factory was being built. Justus said that the Minister wanted us to see it, as evidence of how much the government was doing for the farmers. I told Justus that although I appreciated the tour, none of the farmers we were buying from were going to use that factory, so it was kind of irrelevant to the investigation. Also, it was to the north of Nairobi, while the big meeting of environmental and organic agricultural groups was to the south of the capital. It was already one o'clock and our meeting was at three. Would we make it?

"No problem, Dean." That sweet, moon-faced smile. "We will be at the factory in a half hour and be back in plenty of time."

An hour later we were still on the road, and I was getting increasingly frustrated.

"How much longer, Justus?"

"Only a few minutes."

A half hour later I was getting pained looks from Francis and Alexia. If we returned right now, we would barely make our meeting. Just a few more minutes . . . just a few more miles.

"Stop the van, Justus. We have to turn around now." It felt terribly rude, but I couldn't blow off all the folks waiting for us. This was the meeting we had planned, not the Minister, and it was incredibly important to our project.

"But the Minister!" Justus pleaded. "He really wants you to see the factory! It is right here on your schedule and there are many people waiting there!"

"Stop the van. We have to go back now." I felt a little self-conscious at this, but my primary responsibility was to our project, which included creating a web of allies and finding technical resources for the farmers. I had to focus on the transactions with Cooperative Coffees and the specific farmers who supplied the beans, not go off on a dog and pony show to see unrelated factories and farmers we don't deal with. The new factory could wait, even if it pissed off the Minister. Justus shook his head sadly. He didn't want to disobey his boss, but he also wanted to respect his guests.

We pulled into the CAB International (CABI) compound in the Gigiri suburbs of Nairobi at four-thirty—an hour and a half late. CABI, headquartered in the United Kingdom, has been in East Africa for ninety years doing agricultural research and demonstration projects. The meeting room was full of unhappy faces representing an alphabet soup of grassroots organizations, international consultants, and agricultural extension folks: CABI, KIOF, ICRAF, CANET, KOAN, KFT, FAO, and more. I explained as politely as I could that we were thrown off our schedule trying to do too much. Justus looked relieved that I didn't blame him or the Minister for our late arrival. Each of the organizations introduced itself and its work. I was disappointed, but not surprised, that most of them had never heard of each other and certainly never worked together. Most large international organizations have little, if anything, to do with small grassroots groups, even when their offices are in the same village and they are working on the same issues. This is pretty typical in the world of international development, where many organizations guard their turf jealously for fear of having to share resources with others, or maybe having funding sources snarfed up by their development competition. Once, in Guatemala, I tried to pull together four major international development groups working in the same small village. After all, wasn't it logical that, if we all worked together, so much more could be done? What a dreamer. None of those organizations wanted to work with the others, as money, turf, and advertising all came into conflict. Sorry, I thought the primary objective was to help the folks in the village.

Ever the optimist, for the next two hours we worked on a plan to pull together resources from all of our organizations to create this new initiative for Fair Trade and organic certification in Kenya. There was a lot of excitement in the room—until we got to the topic of money. Most of these organizations operated on grants that were specific to particular projects assigned by the granting agencies. They did not have generic funds to dedicate to this work. Would Dean's Beans or Cooperative Coffees pay for it? *Gulp!* We started to look for ways to fund pieces of the project. Maybe FAO could fund some of the research on alternative income crops for the farmers or environmental techniques for soil conservation? Alexia would work with Charles of CABI to put something together. Dean's Beans could finance the training of an organic inspector and work with international organic certifiers to do some capacity building for a new East African organic inspection group. Ultimately, the group would fund itself through fees for its work. John Njoroge, the founder of Kenyan Institute for Organic Farming (KIOF), was the logical candidate for the training, as he had been training farmers for a decade through his independent grassroots organization. We would be visiting one of his trainee's farms the next day. John Mutura, coordinator of the Kenyan Organic Agriculture Network (KOAN), said that his group could do public outreach to get farmers interested in the program. CABI had money for disease prevention in coffee—maybe some of that could be dedicated to this specific project under organics? There were a lot of good ideas and energy to do the work. Nobody asked the Kenyan government to commit any resources, as past experience had taught them the folly of that path. Justus was excited about biogas (alternative energy from cow manure) but could make no commitments or comments on behalf of the ministry. We ended the meeting on a high note, with tasks for everyone except Justus, who would keep the ministry informed. We were on a roll. In the morning we would visit the auction.

After the meeting, Justus called KPCU to see about picking up the documentation of the coffee for Cooperative Coffees.

"Oh, it is too late," he said with disappointment, "they have all gone home for the night. We can pick them up on our way to the auction in the morning."

We didn't.

In the morning we called upstairs from the lobby at KPCU, but John Karuru said that they hadn't pulled the papers together. They would be there in the afternoon, after our auction visit. It was just as well, as we would get more information on our transaction at the auction.

We didn't.

The Kenya Coffee Auction is a very sophisticated, computerized auction process. The auction hall is quiet, as all bidding is done electronically on each lot that passes by on the big computer board that dominates the front of the room. An auctioneer quietly announces new lots and just as quietly announces the end of bidding, the sale price, and the buyer's name. Only licensed buyers are allowed to bid and there are only a handful of them, representing major international and Kenyan coffee roasters and brokers. Maybe I was there on an off day, but I was struck by the fact that the only black face among the bidders belonged to the KPCU representative.

I was given an auction catalog for the day's sale. It clearly showed where the coffee came from, right down to the "factory" where the farmers depulped the beans for shipment to KPCU, the date shipped, and the date received, via a long series of marks for each lot, for example: Lot No. 129. 1303005/KIANJEGE/XAD/007/F07. I went into the programming room and saw the full auction data bank. I asked Simon, the technician on duty, if I could get a printout of the actual sale data for our coffee. I figured that since the coffee was sold only about ten days earlier, the data should be readily available. He said that would be no problem, all he needed was the information on the coffee from KPCU so that he could identify the exact lots from the Rianjagi and Gakundu cooperatives that were bought by KPCU and sold to Cooperative Coffees. The KPCU officials who had met us at the auction said "no problem," they just had to get that information from the office; let Simon know and he could print out the specific transaction for us. We would soon be able to trace another piece of the puzzle.

The auction was very straightforward. Sale prices were around $1.30 per pound, which at the time was pretty good as the international commodity price for coffee was around eighty cents. Clearly, Kenyan coffee was commanding a premium. On lots from cooperatives, KPCU as the seller would subtract milling, transportation, and other service charges from this price and return the difference to the co-ops. Unfortunately, Kenyan processing costs are probably the highest in the world—five times those of Colombia and a third higher than those of Costa Rica, according to a European Union report. But according to Kenyan law, KPCU could take no more than 20 percent of the auction price for milling, et cetera. It had to return 80 percent to the co-ops. The co-ops then take their administrative costs and pass the rest down to the farmers. This should have left the farmers with around a dollar a pound to put in their pockets. During the Atlanta talks, the government had made it clear that Fair Trade would have to give the farmers substantially more than the local market price in order to be meaningful. Cooperative Coffees had agreed to pay $1.85 per pound. Ten cents would go to KFT for its administration and its own capacity building. After shipping, milling, and other charges from KPCU, the Rianjagi and Gakundu co-ops should receive $1.60, well above the Fair Trade price of $1.26 for conventional (not certified organic) coffee. After the co-ops subtracted their administrative and other costs, the farmers should receive in hand $1.35 per pound—a substantial thirty-five cents per pound more than the local market.

We wanted to buy directly from the farmers, but legally that possibility didn't exist at that time. So Cooperative Coffees purchased the lots from KPCU, which had already bought the coffee at auction and had stored it in its warehouse. We understood that the difference between what we paid KPCU and what KPCU had paid at auction would be sent to the farmers. I would know what KPCU paid for the lots when I got the auction report, so I would know what should have gone to the farmers. When I visited the farmers over the next few days, I would be able to pull this all together and create a fully transparent and reconcilable financial flow.

I couldn't.

After lunch, we returned to the KPCU offices. Nobody had gotten the documents identifying our coffee. Francis and I were getting very frustrated. Alexia raised a slightly mascaraed eyebrow. Justus looked sad. John Karuru said he was working hard to get the documents and couldn't understand what the holdup was. I explained that my ability to trace the coffee and the money was fully dependent on getting those documents and on identifying the specific lots of coffee we had bought. John was apologetic and embarrassed.

"This afternoon, before you leave for Rianjagi, I promise," pleaded John, but nothing was there by the close of business.

The drive to Rianjagi got us out of the sprawling concrete capital. Along the dry roads beyond the urban zone, zebras galloped in the distance. We passed through Nairobi National Park, a small animal preserve within the city limits. We passed a hippo and her baby in a muddy wallow, as a jumbo jet soared overhead. From a hilltop we watched as a jaguar crawled through the tall grass toward some Japanese tourists who had gotten out of their car (against the rules!) to take photos of a zebra. We left before the dramatic, sushi-filled conclusion.

Back on the main road toward Embu province, colorfully clad tribal boys and girls herded cattle along the road, right through busy intersections.

"These are traditional routes for the pastoralists," Justus explained. "The law allows them to continue herding these paths, even though they go through towns and private property. You can see how we respect our traditions here."

We traveled through many small towns, clusters of one-story cement buildings painted in gay colors and bright lettering announcing the butcher, the baker, and the agricultural pesticide maker. People looked incredibly sad—and dirt poor. The Kenyan countryside was really in a mess. Coffee had been its number-one export earner during the 1970s, but production had dropped by two-thirds in the last few years, as many farmers gave up the crop during the years of low prices, combined with higher processing costs and the ever-present corruption. Most Kenyans lived below the international poverty line of a dollar a day.

The van swung south and we headed up into the mountains. It was bizarre to see the snow-capped peaks of Mount Kenya in the distance while the temperature around us was in the nineties. When Francis commented that this was not the road to Rianjagi, Justus said that the Minister wanted us to see his family coffee farm on the way.

The Minister's farm sat at the top of a hill, commanding beautiful views of the surrounding countryside. His modern stone house was light, airy, and stunning. I asked to use the bathroom and was directed to a series of small, modern guesthouses off to one side, with very up-to-date plumbing. Justus cell-phoned the Minister to let him know we were there. The farm foreman took us around the fields, showing off the plump coffee berries that had been grown using the most modern of chemicals. Oddly, there wasn't another person on the entire farm, including in the house.

"The Minister comes here on weekends," Justus said matter-of-factly. We thanked the foreman for the tour (and the use of the bathroom) and continued on.

The Minister had arranged for us to stay at the Isaac Walton Lodge, named after the great naturalist. Unfortunately, the nice rooms were under construction and the remainder had thin Masonite walls, plywood-sheet doors, and mosquito netting left over from a Swiss cheese trade show. I made a note to contact Isaac Walton's family and let them know what was being done in their name here at the lodge. The buffet was pretty good, all in all, if you like *nyama choma* (sinewy barbecued goat, the national dish). I felt like barbed wire was stuck between most of my teeth and I could only swallow the impossibly tough gristle, silently praying for a peaceful passage.

The open-air lobby (it was under construction) did offer one amenity: In the morning, various national newspapers were left for the guests. On the front page of the *East African Standard* was an article titled "Ministers Conspire to Dodge Land Tax," starring Minister Peter Ndwiga. Apparently, the Minister had acquired a "multimillion shilling plantation . . . in a prime horticultural farming zone in Embu," had used the property to obtain a 40 million shilling ($600,000) loan the day of the closing from the Cooperative Bank of Kenya, a bank under his ministry (and the bank that holds the farmers' payments!), and had received special exemption from the Finance Ministry not to pay the 6 million shilling (90,000) land tax on the purchase. The Minister's response to the outrage was that there was nothing untoward about his actions.

"Any assertions that there was anything underhand is, therefore, just noise by busybodies." Francis had a strong reaction and loudly cursed the corruption in the government.

An article in *Business Week* wondered what had happened to 900 tons of coffee worth $1,300,000 bought by KPCU the year before for which the farmers had never received a shilling. It quoted one major trader as saying that the cooperative movement was stealing from the farmers, who were unaware of how the system worked.

"Now you see why my people are so poor!" shouted Francis.

But his tone died down when Justus entered the lobby, and the articles weren't mentioned again.

John Njoroge from KIOF arrived in time to join us for the trip to Rianjagi. He had trained a local farmer in organic agriculture and wanted to take this opportunity to show the other farmers of Rianjagi the benefits of this system. John was a tireless advocate of organic farming. His organization survived on a low-fat diet of contributions from European solidarity groups and our small donations over the years of money and the occasional camera.

When we got into the van, Justus waved the schedule about.

"First we will visit the mayor of Embu. He is a very respected man and is excited about your project to help his farmers." The town hall was a short hop from the hotel, down the pink-flowered jacaranda-lined main street of the provincial capital. Unfortunately, the excited mayor of Embu was not in his office, and nobody knew where he was.

We drove far into the brown Embu hills to reach Rianjagi Cooperative. Fifteen men and women in their Sunday best, the board of Rianjagi, were there to greet us under a large canvas awning. Nelson Mwaniki, the tall, statesmanlike chairman, greeted us with Coke, Fanta, and rolls. He recited the pedigree of the cooperative and its altitude (5,000 feet), number of members (1,167), and pounds of coffee produced each year for the past five. To the applause of the other officers and guests, Nelson said that Rianjagi Cooperative had won national awards last year for the "Best-Managed Factory" and the "Cleanest Coffee Factory."

I was introduced as the representative of Cooperative Coffees, the American buyer of half a container of Rianjagi coffee. I thanked Nelson for the introduction to the cooperative. I said that I was hoping to trace our coffee from the auction back to Rianjagi and follow the money that they received to ensure they got what they were supposed to. One of the board members said that they had never met a buyer before and had no idea who bought their coffee or where it went. Beecher Kiura, the co-op secretary, said that he didn't know how to connect the money to any particular sale, even though all of that information was supposed to be clear from the KPCU remittance reports. He stood with his hand on a stack of huge, handwritten ledger books, as if touching them signified the truth of his words. Beecher went on to recite the financial statistics for the co-op. Each farmer had received 19.15 shillings for each kilogram of red cherries brought in to the co-op. I took out my calculator and tried to figure out what that translated to in pounds and dollars. It came out to about twelve cents for every pound of cherries that the farmer picked and brought in to the co-op. Since the average harvest of a member of Rianjagi was less than a thousand kilograms, and there were two harvests per year, the average annual income of a farm family here was around $480—considerably less than a dollar a day per capita.

As Mr. Kiura recited more sad statistics, I noticed that further down the hill workers were sorting through drying coffee on raised beds, removing the defective or poor-quality beans. I whispered to Justus that I wanted to go and talk to the workers.

"We don't have time. We are on a very tight schedule today. You can talk to the farmers at the assembly tomorrow."

Alexia overheard this.

"I think we should talk to them before we leave, Justus, for a little while. These are the farmers who grew Dean's coffee."

The board members were surprised that I wanted to talk to the workers. Justus sighed and caved in. First, John Njoroge talked about organics and how farmers could increase their income and the quality of their crops and environment. The audience was visibly but politely skeptical. All of the typical arguments were advanced. Yields would go down without chemicals. Pests would invade the fields. John countered each argument slowly and calmly. One of the board members said that intercropping, an important part of the organic system, could not work in Kenya.

"If we plant other things in our coffee fields, our neighbors will think we are poor. We cannot do that. When we see corn planted among the coffee in the fields of our neighbors, we know that they cannot afford to buy food."

John countered that corn was the worst thing you could grow among the coffee; it devoured the nitrogen and water in the soil and made the coffee plants very weak. I told the board that farmers all over the world used intercropping to fix nutrients in the soil for the coffee plants, diversify their income, and add a range of foods to their own tables. In Latin America, farmers use a dozen or so different crops; in Asia, it can be as many as two dozen. Ginger, vanilla, fruit trees, beans, guava, and all of the tropical fruits grow in this climate zone and soil type. I told them that I fully respected cultural norms, but this "poverty" thing was actually making them more poor, just to keep up appearances. Maybe it was time to let that one go.

John invited all of the board members to join us at the *shamba* (family farm) of John Kabudi, who lived over the hill and had been certified organic after training with KIOF. They could see for themselves the benefits of organic farming. I then gave my pep talk about Fair Trade and how much it could raise farmer income and address some of the problems the farmers were having accounting for money transfers. I heard someone in the audience grumble about the missing KPCU coffee, but she was hushed by her neighbor. After the talks and another round of the ubiquitous Cokes, we trudged downhill to the sorters. Justus stayed at the awning and called the Minister to tell him we were running a little late today.

Usually co-ops hire local women to sort the beans, but here I found it was the farmers themselves—men and women—who bent at the tables.

"I need the extra money to feed my family," said a farmer named Joseph. "I can't do that on coffee farming alone." Joseph told me that he had harvested about 500 kilograms of coffee in the current harvest.

"So if you get nineteen shillings per kilo, you brought in about 10,000 shillings?" That would be almost $145 for half a year's work. At that rate, his annual income from coffee would be $290—less than the cost of the Minister's suit. While I was pondering that comparison, Joseph glanced up the hill and said quietly, "I am supposed to get nineteen shillings, but I do not get nineteen shillings."

"Why is that, Joseph?"

"I do not know. We all have to pay a lot of money for loans of the co-op, and we have to pay for fertilizer and other things." He stopped sorting and flexed his fingers a few times. "All I know is that I do not get nineteen shillings. I don't really know where my money went. I cannot feed my family on the money I get, so here I am."

"Was it always this way?" I asked.

"No," he looked around at the rows of farmers sorting beans. "Coffee used to put us all through school and feed us, but now we can't pay for school fees. Even if one of us can, there is no money for shoes and books for the children. They are embarrassed to go to school without shoes and books."

"So what do they do all day?"

Joseph just shrugged.

"*Twende! Twende!* Let's go!" pleaded Justus. My head was reeling with questions as we walked back up the hill. Where did the money go? How can it be traced? How could we ensure that the money we were sending to the farmers actually got there?

We piled into several pickups and vans and headed to the Kabudi *shamba*. John Kabudi was a member of Rianjagi, but none of the board members seemed to know about his organic experience. And, because there is no formal organic recognition in Kenya, John and his wife, Agnes, received no better price for their coffee.

John and Agnes greeted us warmly at their small wooden house. Attached to the house was a corral occupied by two enormous and healthy cows. Agnes showed us how the cows were fed with the good food from their fields and had their diet supplemented with EM ("enhanced microorganisms"), a Japanese-cultivated beneficial bacteria that was gaining a lot of attention in Africa. I had only heard of the stuff through a New Age-y cultlike organization in the United States, but every one of the farmers here seemed aware of it. To demonstrate its efficacy, Agnes urged me to drink some. She said it would do wonders for my digestive tract, which was experiencing a mini Mau-Mau uprising that morning. Would this cow medicine overcome the *nyama choma*? I took the plastic cup of brown swill, the consistency of an Amazonian tributary. *Well, bottoms up!* I thought; or, more hopefully, *bottoms quiet!*

The group wandered through the *shamba*. It was the first coffee farm I had seen in Kenya that had substantial shade. Here, huge macadamia trees loomed over the coffee plants, fixing nitrogen into the soil and adding another cash crop for the family.

"I sell these nuts for seventy shillings a kilo, almost four times what I get from coffee," John said with a shy smile. Between the coffee trees the ground was covered with squash and bean vines. Here and there an avocado tree drooped its mammary-shaped fruits toward the ground, and pumpkins the size of a banker's butt blocked our way down some of the rows. It was a beautiful farm. John Njoroge kept up a running commentary on the benefits of this type of agriculture as John and Agnes Kabudi walked behind, huge smiles on their proud faces. The board members were stunned. John Njoroge was making a great contribution here. Before we left, John and Agnes insisted that we take photos together holding their organic certificate from KIOF, and I wanted some shots of a smiling Agnes threatening me with the huge machete she carried all day. After she removed the huge knife from my larynx, the short, very round woman grabbed me in a bear hug.

"Nakupenda!" (I love you!) she shouted gleefully.

The next day we headed off to Gakundu Cooperative. We didn't visit the coffee fields but went right to the co-op headquarters in the village of Manyatta. There, in a very cramped brick building, we met the board of Gakundu. The co-op had three times the membership of Rianjagi but paid a considerably smaller sixteen shillings to the farmer for a kilo of cherries (that's ten cents per pound). John Muchuri, the chairman, proudly showed me the computer system that they had been given for being the "Best-Managed Co-op" several years ago. All of the books were computerized, so I was able to see the exact payments from KPCU to Gakundu and the exact payments to the farmers. Bingo! Now maybe I could understand why farmers got so little money at the end of the day.

Joseph M'nthimu, the treasurer, showed me the payment report that the co-op had received from KPCU for the last harvest. It broke down all of the expenses: legal fees, transportation, milling, cleaning, sorting, bagging, "managing," agent fees, and more on the million kilos of cherries delivered by the co-op and sold by KPCU. The average auction sales price for all coffee was $1.30 per pound. But according to the KPCU payment sheet, the co-op received only 75 percent of that back after deductions, not the 80 percent required by law. I asked Joseph about this.

"Well," he pulled his ear and thought, "that is how they calculate the expenses. There is nothing we can do about that. We get what they decide to give."

I looked at Justus, who shook his head sadly. Francis was nearly purple but kept his anger in check. I asked Justus how KPCU could do that so boldly.

"This is something the Minister must look into," came his concerned reply.

Joseph M'nthimu brought up another report on the computer screen. It was the co-op's books of account for the year. It showed that from the money received from KPCU, another 12 percent of the total was gone, so that the money available for distribution to the farmers was only 63 percent of the money received at auction for their beans.

"What is that big deduction for?" My head was starting to spin, trying to translate shillings into dollars and kilos into pounds, let alone trying to understand the logic of these transactions.

"That is to pay back the loans. In 1996 we built a new factory to process the farmers' cherries for delivery. It cost 12 million shillings [$180,000] that we had to borrow from the Cooperative Bank," Joseph reported. The Cooperative Bank is the "farmer's bank" in Kenya. I had read that the bank receives money from the European Union at 5 percent interest to help farmers with projects like this. I asked Joseph if that was correct.

"Well," he sighed, "the loan was written for 5 percent, but then the Cooperative Bank notified us that the interest rate was going up to 15 percent, and that's where it's been for many years now."

"So you see, we sell our coffee and the bank is waiting for us. That is why we have so little money," added John Muchuri.

"That's really high! How can the farmers pay that back?" I asked.

"Well, actually we pay about 20 percent, because we don't have the money to pay the loan on time, so the interest and penalties build up."

"Why don't you have the money?"

"Well," he looked nervously around the room, "we don't get the money from KPCU for five or six months after we deliver them the coffee, sometimes as much as a year. And three years ago, when the Coffee Board was in charge of our accounts, they lost 13 million shillings of our money. That was a very hard year for us. We had less than a shilling per kilo to distribute." He smiled at Justus. "Now that the new government has restructured things, it is much better."

"But if the money is in the KPCU account at the Cooperative Bank all those months, don't you at least get interest on it?"

Joseph looked at me blankly. "No."

"Let me try and understand this. The Cooperative Bank has your money in the KPCU account with your name on it for six months. You don't get interest. But in the meantime, you are being charged interest and penalties by the bank because you don't have the money to pay the loan to the same bank?"

"Yes."

I felt like we were in the Twilight Zone. Alexia and I kept exchanging looks of bewilderment. Francis looked like he had to pee so badly that he couldn't keep still, but he was just holding in his anger. Justus had a pleasant, if vacant, expression on his face. He stepped outside from time to time to call the Minister. John and the other Gakundu board members were politely listening but didn't express any emotion that I could decipher. Why weren't the farmers up in arms?

"Last year, the members of Riko co-op brought these problems up at a public meeting in Nyeri, Wangari Maathai's district," volunteered James Mbogo, the co-op secretary.

"Well that's good to hear," I stated in a huff. "What happened?"

"They were attacked and beaten by thugs. Some of their homes were burned and their coffee trees pulled out. The policemen just watched."

Joseph brought up the next screen, a series of members' pay slips showing how the money received from KPCU was credited to each farmer's account. It showed the total amount of coffee cherries brought in by each farmer and what they were to receive at sixteen shillings per kilo. Another line item was "Previous Advances" showing the "cherry advance" of twelve shillings per kilo that the farmer received when he brought in the harvest to the co-op's factory. I asked the treasurer where the co-op got the advance money.

"Well, we borrow it from the Cooperative Bank at 5 percent interest." But when we tried to figure the interest out, it came closer to 20 percent.

Another entry was entitled "Total Debt." I was afraid to ask, but I did.

"That represents the money loaned to the farmers by the co-op for fertilizer, labor, and other things. The co-op charges 15 percent interest.

When we calculate what to pay each farmer, we reduce the amount by what they have received as an advance, and then we take 50 percent of what remains to pay off a portion of their loan to the co-op."

I looked at the entries for several of the farmers. Munyi Ndia had harvested 549 kilos of cherries worth about $124. He had received a cherry advance of $98. Half of his remaining $26 was used to reduce his total debt of $120. So Mr. Ndia received in hand his cherry advance plus an additional $13, bringing into his household a whopping $138 to live on for half a year. A quick calculation showed that, at the rate of interest he was being charged and with the small harvest, Mr. Ndia would never pay off his debt.

Harriet Gicuku was considerably better off. She had harvested 1,965 kilos of coffee cherries and had no debt to the co-op. Her total income for half the year was $450. This was the highest take-home income I saw on the list, and it translated to roughly $2.25 earnings per day. I never asked how many children that figure had to support.

Clearly, the coffee farmers of Kenya were getting strangled. The co-ops were not providing the strong organization here that they were in so many other countries I had worked in. Here, too, the co-ops were caught in a system that bled them from every direction. The banks were ripping them off. Their own processor and agent, KPCU, was ripping them off. And, according to Yasuo (the World Bank consultant), the cooperative managers themselves were grabbing whatever they could. I shared these observations with Justus, who said I must bring these things up to the Minister, who would want to know my opinion.

"In fact, we must go now, because the Minister is going to meet us at the Embu Coffee Society meeting. We must not be late."

As we left the building, I was hailed by a small circle of farmers seated around an old man near our cars. One of the board members told me not to bother with them. Justus urged me to get in the car.

"You will have hundreds of farmers to talk to at the meeting," he pleaded. We wandered over to the group and introduced ourselves.

"Oh yes," said the elder, "we know who you are. You are the man who is going to give us more money for our coffee." His name was Justus Mwathi. He was seventy-two years old and had been farming coffee all his life. He wore a stained, crumpled brown suit with immense dignity. He sat on a wooden chair and leaned forward on a Victorian cane. He had the demeanor of a teacher in a one-room schoolhouse and a clear twinkle in his gray eyes.

"I have read about your Fair Trade and I have some questions for you." From a dozen yards away, Justus urged me to get in the van. I sat in the circle, opposite Justus Mwathi. He asked me to describe the Fair Trade system. He wanted to know how the Fair Trade prices were determined. I described the meetings in Europe in the late 1980s, where farmers and buyers had come together to find a price that was meaningful for the farmers. I talked about the "basket of goods" approach that had been used to determine the minimum farmers needed to feed their families, pay their bills, and improve their lives. I then described the price Cooperative Coffees was paying, and how it was meant to bring a much greater amount to the farmers here in Embu. He kept a knowing smile. As I spoke, I had the clear impression I was walking into a trap.

"All this is very interesting, sir. But let me ask you, if your 'internationally recognized Fair Trade price' is not enough for us to pay for school and feed our families here in Kenya, can it truly be said to be 'fair'?" He then went through with his cane in the dirt the same calculations I had just done on the computer, proving that even under the Cooperative Coffee price the farmers of Embu would be making at best only a few dollars a day.

The farmers stared at me. Justus Mwathi had a look of triumph on his face. He continued, "I have rapped you on the knuckles, young man, to show you that your system does not apply here. You must pay more money to us than to the other countries."

On the way to the Embu meeting, I churned inside. What does it take to be "fair"? Can it be reduced to some simple, universal equation? In Kenya, thanks to the World Bank structural adjustment policies, people have to pay higher fees for school and social services (where they exist). So now do we have to factor higher school fees into our pricing because the Kenyan government knuckled under to the World Bank? Yes, according to Justus Mwathi. And what about corruption and bureaucracy? If farmers are getting only 63 percent of the sales price instead of the legally mandated 80 percent, do we have to pay higher prices to ensure that the farmer gets enough money to feed his family? Does social justice require us to basically pay ransom for these farmers who are being held hostage by their own government and administrators? These are issues that most Fair Traders don't ever have to consider; just pay the licensing fee, slap the label on your bag, and you've done your part.

The school auditorium was packed with over three hundred farmers. We sat on the stage waiting for the Minister. After a half hour, to Justus's consternation, I went out into the audience and started talking to whichever farmer I sat down with. (It works for Phil Donahue, doesn't it?) I asked them what they thought the biggest problems were. Some said the price of coffee, others said government corruption, some didn't want to talk. Justus kept calling me back to the podium, and after another half hour I relented.

Soon the Minister arrived. We were all introduced by a member of the Embu District Coffee Union Cooperative Society, the umbrella group for all Embu cooperatives. Francis described how Kenya Fair Traders was trying to establish Fair Trade relationships between Embu farmers and buyers in the United States. I gave a short speech on the need to have transparent accounting and to ensure that the farmers got the money they were supposed to.

Then it was time for the Minister to speak. He received a long applause from the crowd; after all, this was Embu and he was the Member of Parliament for this district. The Minister hushed the crowd with hand gestures. He gave a passionate speech on the need to get more money to the farmers. His speech was interrupted several times by applause. He did not explain why so little of the money received at auction made it back to the farmers, focusing instead on the world coffee situation and low prices around the world. Oddly, Kenyan auction prices continued to be higher than world prices, but the farmers were unaware of this, and the Minister made no mention of it. He then motioned my way and thanked me for coming to Embu to help the farmers.

"Mr. Dean is here to bring more money to you. He has presented a proposal to the ministry to buy coffee from Embu farmers at Fair Trade prices. Under his plan, your cooperatives will receive $1.45 for your coffee, and you will be provided with technical assistance and access to new markets."

Well, I thought, *the details are a little off, but at least he is supporting the program.* I was smiling at the crowd as the Minister continued. He turned to me and pointed a finger. His voice took on a stronger tone.

"But this is not enough. I will see that he pays you at least $1.65 for your coffee!" The crowd smiled and applauded as the Minister continued. "No one will cheat our farmers in Embu anymore. I will guarantee that he pays the highest price!"

My jaw dropped! What was the Minister doing? We never agreed to that price. And we weren't the ones ripping off the farmers! Then it hit me—he was setting me up as the fall guy. Now it would be my responsibility not only to pay a higher price, but to take the blame when that money didn't reach the farmers after snaking its way down the corrupt and byzantine channel that I had discovered during this visit. When we didn't agree to any more than we were already paying, and when the farmers of Rianjagi and Gakundu never got a penny more from all the extra money we had already given for the elusive Cooperative Coffee shipment, the Minister would tell the farmers that he had saved them from the dishonest Americans, who had promised so much and delivered so little. He had tried to get us to give more money, and when we didn't, he would send us packing. The sonofabitch was setting me up!

When I got my chance to speak to this group, I would have to be honest about what I had learned about how the system operated here, lay it out in a straightforward manner and discuss what we could try and do about it. I was very skilled at this kind of communication with farmers. I would not let the Minister off the hook and set these farmers up for even greater disappointment. It was time for questions from the farmers. I fully expected them to ask for more details about our program, maybe ask the Minister how he would guarantee them more money at the end of the day. The first farmer rose.

"Mr. Minister, will you tell us about the land deal in the papers?"

The Minister said that he would be happy to explain the very complicated legal situation to his constituents and prove that he was the victim of scandalous attacks by the media and the opposition. But in order to spare our foreign guests discomfort at hearing all of this, he would switch to the Embu language. Francis could not speak the dialect, so we could not understand the passionate diatribe delivered by the Minister on the subject. I spent the ten or so minutes making organized notes for my talk. I wanted to be absolutely clear and wake the farmers up to the whole system.

Suddenly, the Minister stopped. Strong applause. He walked off the stage.

Justus turned to me and said pleasantly, "The meeting is over." I looked out at the audience, which was starting to file out the auditorium doors.

"But wait, I was supposed to talk to the farmers. You've been telling me to hurry up the whole trip because we would have this great opportunity to talk to the farmers at this meeting. There is a lot I have to say." Justus gave me that sad, hangdog look again.

"The Minister had to leave on important business. The meeting ends when the Minister leaves. I am sorry." He motioned us off the podium and out the door. Outside, the Minister's black Mercedes waited. The window cracked open. Justus walked over and leaned inside. He nodded and return to me.

"The Minister would like to offer you a ride back to the hotel."

"I would rather spend some time in town here, talking to the folks who have remained."

"You really must go with the Minister. This will be the last chance you two have to talk. He likes you a lot and he values your opinion." I told Francis and Alexia that I would meet them back at the hotel. Whatever was up, at least I was about to get to the bottom of it.

I sat in the back with the Minister. The black leather was cool in the air conditioning, giving me a little chill down my sweating spine.

"I appreciated your talk," the Minister said smoothly. "I hope that your visit has helped you understand the problems we face here. The farmers need more money to live." Was he kidding? Did he think I didn't get what was going on in there?"

"Well, I must say that I was surprised at your take on things. You know that we have already paid far more for the coffee than these farmers have ever been offered. I think there is plenty of money if it only gets down to the farmers." *Gentle, Dean, this is a Minister with a lot of power, and Heaven only knows where this car is going.* "I still haven't received the paperwork from KPCU to identify the Cooperative Coffees shipment and track the money down to the co-ops. When that has happened, then we can see what else we need to do." I smiled pleasantly.

The Minister looked pained.

"Ahh, you have not gotten the papers yet? I will see that you get everything you need by the time you return to Nairobi. Nothing must prevent the farmers from getting their money."

This was not a simple cultural misunderstanding. We were not living in the same reality. What was going on inside that man's head? One thing zealots, fundamentalists, con artists, and too many politicians have in common is the deadpan sincerity in their voices. I have met some of each, and I still can't tell whether they believe what they are saying or are simply so vested in making others believe.

"So, did you enjoy your visit to my family coffee farm?" He changed the subject easily.

"Uh, well, yes, it was very well maintained. And the bathrooms were very clean."

"That is good. We have an excellent coffee there. Perhaps you would be interested in purchasing our coffee? I can guarantee you a higher quality than you receive from the co-ops." The Minister was selling out his own constituents! "When will you need another container?"

When I got out at the Isaac Walton, I felt like I had to puke. Was it the blatant corruption, the realization of the horrible bind the farmers were in, or the air conditioning in the Minister's Mercedes? The last time I had had this feeling was after a ministers meeting in the Bahamas in the mid-1980s. Obviously, I have an allergic reaction to ministers. I was working with a group trying to salvage a famous treasure wreck. We wanted to do it differently than the usual grab-and-go treasure hunters, so we offered to set up a conservation facility, help establish a maritime museum, and work with the government to create tourism off the project. Jobs and money into the economy, respect for cultural heritage. The room of ministers sat silent. We took a coffee break. I asked the Bahamian lawyer who was with me what the problem was—the four ministers sat attentively throughout the meeting, but they didn't seem excited.

"They are waiting."

"For what?"

"For you to pass an envelope full of money across the table to get the permits you will need."

I was furious. Here I was offering something good for the nation and the people, and all these crooks could think about was lining their own pockets. *Only in the Bahamas*, I thought at the time. And yet, the etiquette of bribery is well known the world over. *Baksheesh* in the Middle East, *jeito* in Brazil, *un petit cadeau* in West Africa, *refrescos* in Mexico, *kitikarogo* in Kenya. In the United States we sanitize bribes as consulting fees, land deals, tips on pork belly futures, jobs for relatives, and fat lobbyist donations—that is, when they aren't straightforward gobs of cash. It is sad and amazing how hard it can be to try and do the right thing when you are surrounded by people and institutions that see everything through the filter of self-interest.

We returned to Nairobi to get the papers from KPCU. No luck, and a lot of blank stares. Not only couldn't they tell me which coffee we had bought, but they had not received the Cooperative Coffees money due to a bank snag, so we couldn't trace the financing either. I was so upset at this turn of events that I canceled the rest of the trip—two days of visiting the Minister's pet projects, which had little to do with the farmers and none of which was in Embu. Alexia and I flew off to Mombasa to decompress on the beach, search for old coins, and find the former hiding place of Osama Bin Laden.

A month later, the coffee arrived in New Orleans by container ship. Cooperative Coffees sampled the arrival and found that instead of the high-quality "84" rating of the preshipment sample, the landed batch sampled out at a miserable "76." Our professional cupper said that he didn't think it was the same coffee as the original batch. Did KPCU switch the coffee?

I e-mailed everyone involved with the transaction, from the Minister's office to KPCU, the farmers, and Kenya Fair Traders. Nobody knew anything about it. There was still no paper trail to identify the coffee, and I was getting no response whatsoever from anyone on following up with the finances. What did the farmers get out of the money we sent? Without knowing which coffee we had, there was still no way of knowing. We had paid $1.86 per pound for inferior coffee that we couldn't trace back to the farmers. Was it laden with pesticides? Did it come from a plantation that used child labor, a documented problem in Kenya? We couldn't tell. Our experimental Fair Trade coffee from Kenya was no different from the majority of Kenyan on the market, and it was not even high quality. I put the full-court press on the KPCU people and the Minister's office, threatening, cajoling, pleading—nothing.

Finally, I started to receive news from some of the KPCU employees.

Several of the people at KPCU who had tried to help us, such as John Karuru, had been fired. There were claims that they had stolen money and cooked books. I found that really hard to believe as they were not in the position to manipulate the books and physically have coffee moved about.

Then I got an e-mail from John Karuru. He wrote that many "junior employees," himself included, had been accused of participating in another big coffee theft. He said that it was obviously a higher-up job, as it would be impossible for 120 tons of coffee to disappear from the KPCU warehouses and get swallowed up in the market "without the knowledge of the top management, including the security staff, who control the collection of all goods from the KPCU warehouses." I thought it seemed like a piece of cake for folks who had walked off with 900 tons the year before. A week later, John sent some documents to KFT in the United States to help us understand where our coffee went, or where it came from. Whatever. The documents got lost somewhere in somebody's care and I have never seen them to this day. Eventually I received an e-mail from a former KPCU worker who wrote that the coffee did not come from either Rianjagi or Gakundu. Rather, it had been swept off the floor of the KPCU warehouse, which would explain the different grades and screen sizes in the lot. Was this true or just a pissed-off ex-worker talking? Who the hell knows?

In the meantime, Cooperative Coffees was stuck with a container of non-organic, non-fairly traded, mundane Kenyan coffee that none of our members could use. The group tried to find a mainstream buyer for the container, but to no avail. Nobody needed another container of mediocre coffee from Kenya. It took an act of God to save us. Almost a year after the transaction, Hurricane Katrina smashed New Orleans. Our warehouse was flooded and destroyed. All the coffee inside was ruined. The insurers paid us the value of the coffee as we had paid for it, including one container of Kenyan.

All during the trip, I kept asking myself, is it possible for good works to be done when so many of the people and organizations involved have a different agenda? Is there some tipping point where good intentions and hard work can overcome systematized corruption and self-interest? And the ultimate questions raised by my coffee farmer "professor," old Justus Mwathi, still lingered: What are the elements of fairness? Are they really a certain price and a set of rules that at the end of the day deliver enough for a quality life? Or are they more of a process that recognizes and deals with each country's on-the ground realities?

The winds of change have been blowing gently through Kenya. Since my visit, there has been a shift. It took more than a year, but the Kenyan legislature finally stood up and broke KPCU's grip on the farmers. Falling somewhere between Yasuo's World Bank "nuke 'em out of existence" prescription and my hope of strengthening the co-ops, the government has eliminated KPCU's monopoly on milling coffee from farmer cooperatives but has not eliminated the co-ops themselves. It also allows cooperatives to market their own coffee and find their own buyers, even though the buyers have to purchase the coffee at the auction (where they may be outbid by others, thereby increasing farmers' income). Members of Kenyan cooperatives are looking to Ethiopian cooperatives for guidance, as the Ethiopians have taken the next step and allowed their cooperatives to sell on the Fair Trade market outside the auction.

As dynamic as this may seem, it is really a very small opening. Only a handful of Kenyan farmer cooperatives have the skills or resources to look beyond the system that has abused them for so long and market their own coffees. I have received many calls and e-mails from farmer groups trying to sell their coffee directly without understanding the intricacies of quality control, sampling, marketing, and prepping for export. It will take years for these farmers to receive and integrate the necessary technical training and capacity building to hold their own in international markets. In the meantime, free-market buyers large and small, the saviors under the World Bank plan, are lining up to give the small farmers of Kenya the back of Adam Smith's Invisible Hand. Yet this is the challenge. We must look beyond the labels to share Justus Mwathi's vision of relationships that deliver for all of us. Only then will we be able to consider ourselves truly fair.

John Njoroge is coming to the United States to receive his organic inspector's certification training in November 2007. Under an agreement I worked out with QAI, that organization will use John and KIOF for East African inspections until KIOF can achieve international recognition as an independent certifier. FAO and CABI continue to work on using macadamia nuts and other intercrops to increase farmers' income. Two farmer cooperatives that have broken away from KPCU have been certified for Fair Trade, but none have been certified as organic yet. The Minister has never been held accountable for the unpaid land taxes, and most Kenyans I talk to just shrug off any talk of serious anticorruption reform. The work continues.

PART TWO

SOUTH AMERICA

3

Bridging the Gap

PERU, 2003

The three Peruvian farmers seemed so out of place in the cavernous Hynes Convention Center in Boston. Dwarfed by the soaring towers of glass and steel, the lone woman in the group stepped toward me, holding out a ziplock bag full of unroasted green coffee beans. "Please, sir, would you like to try our coffee?"

The annual Specialty Coffee Association of America (SCAA) convention is held in a different city each April. It is the only opportunity for the myriad players in the specialty coffee world to get together. Thousands of roasters, importers, exporters, baristas, farmers, and café owners mill about hundreds of booths that hawk the latest Willie Wonka processing machinery, the fastest brewers, and the newest coffee origins. Starched corporate types jostle with café hipsters to ogle the sleek Brazilian espresso machines or the vivacious Gabriellas serving their hot shots. For most of us it is a place to network, to see old friends, and to party. For the small farmers of the world, it is an expensive gamble. Many of these groups spend more than a farmer's annual earnings to send representatives to the convention, hoping to make that one connection, that one big sale that could change the dynamics of poverty in their lives. Unlike the large estates or the groups supported by governments, these independent small farmers don't have fancy booths at the convention. Instead, like the three Peruvians standing before me, they wander the exhibition halls in their Sunday best, armed with samples of their recent harvest and poorly photocopied descriptions of their farms or cooperatives, seeking out potential buyers. Usually their targets take the sample, say thanks, and promise to get back to them. This is the typical industry blow-off. After the convention, the empty hotel rooms are filled with abandoned samples and flyers. The little bags of dreams end up tossed in the hotel dumpsters. The farmers go back to their towns with nothing to show for their efforts except photos taken with potential buyers and receipts for overpriced accommodations, meals, and airfares.

"My name is Esperanza. I am the general manager of Pangoa Cooperative in Satipo, Peru. Please, sir, would you sample our coffee?" she said. Their weathered faces were full of expectation, hope, and fear.

I took the little bag, opened it, and smelled the fresh, earthy sweetness of the beans. "This coffee is very nice. I will be happy to roast it up and let you know." How easily the response came. This was my tenth sample of the day, and it was only the first day of the convention. Esperanza winced visibly. Damn it, I couldn't do this anymore.

"Look, Esperanza, I really don't need any more Peruvian coffee, so maybe you should keep the sample and give it to someone who really might try it. Besides, I buy coffee only from Fair Trade cooperatives. I would be happy to help you apply for the Fair Trade Registry if you'd like."

"Thank you, but we have been on the registry for three years already and we are certified organic, too. But we have not had any Fair Trade sales yet, so we have to sell our coffee on the conventional market." Esperanza was clearly a determined woman, but her slumping shoulders told me that years of disappointment were taking their toll. Her companions looked similarly crestfallen. Fair Trade promises farmers significantly more money than conventional sales, but only about 20 percent of Fair Trade–eligible coffee gets sold that way. Farmers sell the remainder of their harvest however they can, often to local middlemen who pay pennies for high-quality, certified beans and make enormous profits passing them on.

I felt a surge of compassion for their situation that pushed me past commercial need. I also genuinely liked Esperanza. She was one of a growing handful of women leaders in the coffee world. She was short, round-faced, and pleasant, but clearly strong and no-nonsense when it came to business. I took the plunge.

"Okay, my friends, I'll tell you what . . ." How often had new paths in my life begun with those words? "I am going to help you get your first Fair Trade sale. Let me take your sample and check it out. If the coffee is as good as it smells I guarantee that I can find you some buyers."

A container of coffee weighs 40,000 pounds. That's a lot of beans, and one hell of a promise to make to an unknown producer group. We didn't use that much Peruvian in a year, so I had some work to do. Esperanza was startled. Her eyes moistened and she grabbed my hand. Behind her, the two men beamed.

I ran down the halls of the convention, looking for others who might take this crazy chance with me. Large importer from New York over there? Too conservative. My own roasters' cooperative? Not enough data on the growers and not enough members use Peruvian. I walked past some smaller progressive buyers, but I knew that they had their Peruvian relations already. Finally I saw John from Royal Coffee. These California importers were open-minded and adventuresome. We often swapped travel tales and tips, and I had bought great coffee from obscure sources from them in the past.

"John," I said breathlessly, "I've got a great deal for you."

He eyed me with a mixture of suspicion and humor. "Another water buffalo deal in Sumatra?"

I told him about Pangoa and showed him the ziplock bag. Over his shoulder in the Royal booth sat several forlorn samples from other countries.

John shook his head sympathetically. "The market's flooded with Peru. There's not much space for new origins."

I weighed in with the conviction of a gambler in Vegas. "Okay, if you will import a container, I guarantee that I will buy half of it." A cocked eyebrow for a reply. "And whatever you can't sell from the other half, well, I'll buy that too!"

"Are you sure about this? That's a big commitment. But if you are willing and if the coffee checks out, I think we can do it."

The Pangoans were stunned. Even though there would be coffee ready to ship in June, Esperanza told me to wait for the July harvest.

"Each month we harvest a little higher up the mountains. The best coffee is at the highest altitudes. We want to send you the best, so you must wait until July." The little group was delirious. "Then you must come to Pangoa and celebrate. You must see how we live and what we have done to survive."

The coffee came in sweet and smooth. The big beans were picked and processed with obvious care. Like the best Peruvian coffees, these beans had a mild acidity and a creamy body. I began to research Satipo and Pangoa in preparation for my visit. I read the daily newspaper, *El Comercio*, online. I Googled all the right words. There was not much to find, and what there was, wasn't promising. That week, terrible floods and mud slides had wiped out a village and the main bridge from Satipo to the mountains. An infestation of sandflies, formerly found only in Sudan, India, and Brazil, had found its way to Amazonian Peru in time for my visit, the parasites injected by their bites causing 140 deaths in the area in the past nine months. The previous year, Maoist Shining Path guerillas had shot down a government helicopter and ambushed a patrol in the area. Maybe this wasn't a good time to come.

"There are no problems here," came the e-mail reply to my concerns. "Everything is just fine." Of course, this may have been true for people who live through civil war, pestilence, and natural disaster on a regular basis, but I was a little hesitant. Then Esperanza sank the hook in.

"There is a small tribe of Ashaninkas farmers in our cooperative. They live on the Amazonian side of the mountains. We can visit them if you'd like. They have never met a coffee buyer or an American before." Hmm. War, disease, and floods on the one hand. Indigenous peoples, celebration, and adventure on the other. Just enough frequent flyer miles—I'm there!

The plane arrived in Lima at 1 AM. Esperanza and the two men waited at the gate in the same formation as in Anaheim. Esperanza reintroduced me to Don Flor and Don Evaristo, two of the coop's directors. Hugs, handshakes, and celebratory laughter all around. After a short night in a local hotel we began the ten-hour drive to Satipo. Our little rental car chugged happily out of the crowded capital. We sped north and east, past the slums of Lima and past the vast mines that have bled Peru's mineral wealth northward for centuries. I passed out in the backseat from the weariness and the fumes, until the car stopped with a jerk. I opened a bleary eye to see snow outside the window.

"Wake up, Mr. Bean! This is the highest paved road in the world! Don't you want to take a picture?" They were very proud of this piece of pavement, so I stepped out of the car to oblige. My flowered tropical shirt was no match for the freezing temperature and the wind, but I did wake up quickly. My head was spinning and I could barely breathe.

"Oh, that's the altitude," said Evaristo sympathetically. "We must get you a cup of coca tea to clear your head and restore your balance."

"Coca tea?" Let the games begin!

The mildly bitter brew did restore my equilibrium, but it didn't give me the buzz I was expecting. I asked delicately about this. The Pangoans laughed.

"No, that will happen later, when you chew the leaves in the field," Don Flor stated in a matter-of-fact tone. "The tea is only to soothe you."

Coca has gotten a bad rap in the press. It is certainly abused when turned into cocaine with the help of toxic chemicals and when grown by farmers forced at gunpoint to rip out their coffee plants to grow the stuff. But coca has a positive side. It is the plant of the Incan gods. When the leaves are chewed they act as a mild stimulant, which helps farmers work in the high altitudes where the lack of oxygen knocked me for a loop. Even more significantly, coca has one of the highest concentrations of proteins and vitamins of any plant, and it forms the basis of a healthy balanced diet for the people of the high Andes. Where coca is eradicated and forbidden, local malnutrition follows.

We climbed up and down mountains for several more hours, finally arriving at a long line of cars and trucks toward dusk. We had arrived at the washed-out bridge. The steel superstructure was twisted forty-five degrees and came to an abrupt end halfway across. A single wooden lane with a steel cable for a handhold had been constructed to allow people to walk over the powerful, bloated river below. On the other side, another group of farmers waved to us in recognition. Several young men vied for the honor (at the going rate) of carrying our bags across the span, underneath a sign that read "Danger! Do Not Cross This Bridge."

Downriver, a line of large trucks waited. I asked Esperanza what was going on.

"That's how we get our coffee across the river and that's how supplies for the farmers and the towns get over." I watched as two large dugout canoes with huge outboard motors revved up parallel to the shore, their bows aimed upstream against the raging current. Long planks hewn out of jungle hardwoods straddled the two canoes, making a giant platform. Slowly, a full semitrailer drove onto the platform, men on the left and right shouting a flurry of contradictory directions. Once the trucks were on board, the canoes roared forward at full throttle. The current was so powerful that the canoes made no progress, but slowly went sideways across the river. Once across, the canoes were secured to the muddy banks with ropes and the truck disembarked. Another truck loaded on the far shore for the return voyage. I gained a new appreciation for my morning cup of coffee.

"Peruvian engineering," beamed Esperanza.

We finally pulled into Satipo in the dark, and I quickly passed out in the local hotel. The morning poured hot and sticky through the broken window. The manager told me that there were some people waiting for me outside. After a quick, ice-cold shower I looked out the window to see four pickup trucks overloaded with farmers waving at me. I was invited by Esperanza to sit in the cab of the first truck, and away we went to the office of the cooperative. We arrived at the large cinderblock warehouse at the edge of town and were greeted by another forty farmers and their families. After a quick tour of the empty warehouse and the cement coffee-drying beds in the courtyard, we went up to the office on the second floor. An old, wheezing computer sat in a small cubicle next to the main room. The crowd piled in and settled down, proud and expectant faces aimed my way. Esperanza introduced several very old men who had been the founders of the cooperative and were held in the highest esteem. Dons Alfredo, Ninfo, and Fidel had the gnarled hands of a lifetime in the fields. I thought I could tell their age by counting the wrinkles in their leather faces. Each gave a brief speech about the history of their group, the struggles they had overcome during the war (I didn't know which one), the government's obstinence, no money, bad weather, and local middlemen. Finally Esperanza spoke forcefully about how long and hard they had worked, and how much faith the farmers had put in her and the directors when they embarked on this unknown path of organics and Fair Trade. How much time, energy, and money they had spent in hopes of breaking out of the poverty of the current system of selling their coffee to the middlemen and getting hardly enough to feed their families. As she spoke, the crowd became emotional and agitated. She concluded brightly by saying that all the hard work had paid off, they had finally made a sale that recognized the value of their efforts and the quality of their coffee. She compared the Fair Trade sale price we had paid of $1.46 per pound to the other two containers they had sold so far that year. One went to a New York broker for eighty cents per pound, and one to a Lima exporter at fifty-three cents. Several of the older men began crying softly, placing their faces in their hands.

"Now Mr. Dean Beans is going to speak to us." I long ago gave up trying to explain the difference between my name and the company's name. I am known as Dean, Mr. Dean, Mr. Beans, Mr. Dean Beans, and more. It could be worse. I was once acknowledged by a Maori elder at a public ceremony after working with his tribe in New Zealand for almost a year this way: "We'd like to thank Greg here for all the hard work he's done with us."

I thanked Esperanza and everybody for inviting me, and I took out two green foil bags of Pangoa coffee, roasted and packaged with a label that read "Pangoa's Pride." Like most growers, these folks had never seen their own coffee roasted and packaged for sale, nor had many of them tasted their own beans. Instead, the farmer delivers the beans to the co-op still surrounded by the pulpy red fruit, or maybe in *pergamino* (depulped, but surrounded by a paper skin that is milled off later). We sent the beans off to be brewed by Beatrice, the office manager. I told the co-op members that, even though our company was far away to the north, we knew who the people of Pangoa were, and we respected them. One way to demonstrate that respect was to pay a fair price for the coffee. I also took out an envelope containing twelve hundred dollars. I explained that we have a six-cent-per-pound profit-sharing program with our farmers that they could use for whatever their co-op deemed appropriate. I described how other co-ops had used their Fair Trade premiums and our profit share to finance businesses, provide health care, build roads, and pay for schooling for the kids. I congratulated them on their incredible determination and their wonderful coffee.

The aromatic Pangoa's Pride came in and an incredibly noisy coffee break ensued as the directors and the members discussed ways to use the money. During the break I wandered into the office. I noticed a letter from the U.S. Food and Drug Administration (FDA) regarding the need to register each shipment due to the new bioterrorism regulations. The letter recommended using a company that could file the forms for a mere four hundred dollars per shipment. I took a closer look at the letter. It was not from the U.S. government but from a company called FDA, and it was clearly designed to confuse the farmers and get them to pay an outrageous fee for a simple one-page notice. I told Esperanza that any importer could file it for her, and that Royal and I would take care of it. She told me sadly that they had already sent the money for the first container.

It took about four hours for the overstuffed pickup trucks to reach the first coffee village. During the drive I learned a lot about my hosts. In the early 1980s, Esperanza had been the first female agronomist to work in the coffeelands of Peru. I asked her if it was hard to work with the male farmers at that time.

"No," she stated matter-of-factly. "They had to listen to me. I knew more than they did." She worked with the co-op throughout the era of terrorism, when the Maoist revolutionaries of the Shining Path murdered villagers and kidnapped their sons and brothers for conscription into war and madness. The 1970s and 1980s were hell for rural Peruvians, as the violence of revolution and the heavy response by the government left few villages untouched. Esperanza helped manage an unbelievable debt load of a half million dollars run up by inexperienced managers at a time of plunging prices for coffee. Finally, she was asked to manage the co-op in 1993 by a unanimous and grateful all-male board of directors.

We navigated a series of rickety wooden bridges that groaned beneath the wheels. The farmers sang happily in the back, screaming like kids at the fair when we hit a particularly nasty pothole. Crushed in the cab with the driver, Esperanza, and two elders, I decided that I would spend the next leg of the trip back in the economy section, which looked a lot more roomy than here in first class. We pulled into an open field bordered by a scattering of dull, weathered one-room wooden houses. The farmers lived here, while their coffee plots were high above on the slopes that surrounded the village. A dozen farmers and their families emerged from the houses. They were shabbily dressed and looked as if carved from mahogany. My shoulders were patted with sledgehammers and my hand gripped by iron as they welcomed me. We made our introductory speeches as a flock of agitated turkeys and highly amused children ran around us.

In order to visit Paco Moreno's plot, we had to climb inordinately steep slopes, grasping exposed tree roots and slipping on the crumbling earth. The forest was thick with hardwoods and vines. The treetops chirred and chirped while the understory thrummed with beetles, frogs, and a million unseen creepy-crawlies. Halfway up my bad knee started to complain and I was a little short of breath. One of the farmers pulled a few leaves off a low bush and told me to chew them, packing them into my cheek but not swallowing the bitter juice. I realized that this was coca and that the forest was bursting with the plant. After a few minutes I was energized and we continued to climb. Forty-five minutes later we emerged into a grove of enormous and varied flowers. We were encompassed by surreal splashes of color. Long, drooping stamens awaited their dusting of pollen from the hummingbirds and bees that made the air vibrate. The danglers lined both sides of the path ahead like an honor guard of horny satyrs, welcoming local maidens to the dance. The forest was dotted with the deep green serrated leaves of healthy coffee plants, the branches drooping low under the heavy load of a ripening harvest.

We visited Paco's processing area, comprising an immaculate, steaming compost bin and a raised-screen coffee-drying bed. Most coffee farmers dry their beans on cement patios or hard earth surfaces. I was stunned by the sophistication of the raised screens on wooden frames, which looked like they came out of the pages of *Popular Mechanics* magazine. Esperanza stated that the co-op researched all of the modern methods they could and that the farmers of Pangoa readily adopted new methods. Paco chimed in proudly that he had much more to show me, but first we must have a small celebration. A five-gallon diesel can appeared, along with a box of colorful plastic cups. A viscous white liquid sloshed around in the can. Paco announced that we would all share *chicha*, the mildly fermented corn drink used ceremonially by the Incas, but socially by the farmers. The fermentation process gets a flying start—the corn is chewed by the women and spit into the mash to get it going. Unfortunately, the proper custom is to drink the whole cup, fill it again from the can, and pass it on to your neighbor. Sort of a salivated version of a Japanese sake session. It took about twenty rounds to empty the can, by which time I had the immediate urge either to pee or to puke. "Coca leaves will calm your stomach," said a solicitous farmer.

Farther up the mountain we came upon a series of man-made ponds. The ponds were ringed with beehives. Frederico, the owner of this plot, told me that he raised tilapia here. I peered into one pond and saw the red and white backs of the fat carp swimming languidly through the dark water.

"We sell the fish in the market in Satipo, and the overflow of the pond fertilizes Paco's trees down below," Frederico said simply. "The bees pollinate the coffee trees, but we haven't figured out how to sell the honey yet."

I looked over toward the hives and saw Carlos, the agricultural extension agent for the co-op, standing very close to some hives. I started to shout that he should get away from the openings, as bees freak out when there is something blocking the hive entrance. Before the warning was out there was an explosion of angry, buzzing, stinging bees from two hives. They swarmed on Carlos and darkened the sky above us. We ran for the little shed on a nearby hill as the bees attacked us relentlessly. Finally, the bees retreated, having ensured the safety of their hives.

"Coca leaves will take away the pain," said a farmer.

In the morning, our three-truck convoy carried on over the mountains. This was the Amazonian side, where the mountain streams drained into that incredible river and flowed on to its Brazilian and Ecuadorian tributaries. The roads were considerably worse here, and what towns we passed were miserable and small. We were headed to Boka Kiatari, an Ashaninkas settlement of about sixty families. All of the cooperative's directors and office staff were in the trucks, as well as many farmers from other towns.

"It's really wonderful that all of the directors came along," I remarked.

"This is the first time for any of them to visit Boka Kiatari," Esperanza replied.

"They haven't visited their own members' lands? Just because it's so far from Satipo?"

"No, they are not allowed by the Ashaninkas. They might get shot if they came uninvited. Thirty years ago, *colonos* invaded the territory with the approval of the government. They really tore up the land. They logged all of the oldest trees and dammed some rivers. So a lot of the Ashaninkas sided with the Shining Path rebels up here. It's kind of a dangerous place."

As we rolled into the first hamlet within the indigenous territory, ten short, stocky men stood in the road. They were barefoot and dressed in red ocher-colored shrouds. The bottom half of their faces was painted a deep red and their straight black hair was covered with feathers. Some carried rifles, others had bows and arrows.

Esperanza, Evaristo, and I got out of the first truck. Nobody else moved. Esperanza waved hello to the oldest man and introduced him as Don Nyako, the village leader. He patted my shoulder warmly and welcomed me to the land of the Ashaninkas. He introduced his sons, Fredi and Adolfo, and the other men. Then Don Nyako looked long and hard at the trucks. After an excruciating silence, he nodded and walked back toward the village. Esperanza told everybody it was safe to come out now. The Pangoans piled out of the trucks and walked quietly behind the Ashaninkas men. The village was a small compound of ten three-sided huts arranged in a semicircle. The walls and roofs were made of saplings strapped together, and the walls were adorned with skins, feathers, bows, and arrows. In one of the huts, five women and several small girls worked over a huge metal pot plunked down onto a well-stoked fire. Don Nyako called to the oldest woman, who came grudgingly over to his side. She wore the same maroon shroud, the lower half of her face a dark red. Her eyes were black, but they burned with the intensity of the coals in the wood fire.

The men and women of the co-op and the tribe were talking in small groups, getting to know each other. Occasional bursts of laughter or shouts of approval rang through the compound. Cameras appeared and group shots were organized. One of the directors, a large man named Armando, roughly grabbed Don Nyako and pulled him to his side for a photo. The old man nearly fell over, and some of the younger men looked sharply at Armando. But Don Nyako's good nature and laughter prevented the incident from turning ugly. After the photo, Don Nyako called everybody to sit for the formal greetings. He invited Esperanza to speak first. She recited the long and painful struggle of the cooperative, ending with the good news of their first Fair Trade sale to Mr. Beans. She passed around the little green foil bag of Pangoa's Pride. The Ashaninkas fondled it lovingly, sniffing the aroma through the gas valve in the bag. Esperanza explained the description on the bag. The men smiled and nodded approvingly. She also told the crowd that I had delivered the profit share to the co-op to fund needed development projects.

Don Nyako spoke next. He told the history of the Ashaninkas and how they had resisted Spanish colonizers and kept their culture into this modern age. He spoke evenly about the land invasions of the recent past and the damage done. He ended brightly that it was a new day, as the *colonos* and the Ashaninkas were gathered together for the first time. Don Nyako turned to his wife and asked her to speak. She looked at the ground, shook her head, and mumbled something sharply. Don Nyako asked her again and a third time before she finally consented to speak. She walked into the middle of the assembly and stood next to me. I smiled at her. She looked slowly around, her eyes burrowing into each face she focused upon. We waited expectantly. She took a deep breath and spoke.

The words exploded out of her fiery red mouth. "You people stole our land! Now you are here to steal our coffee! Get away from here!" She looked straight at me. "Get away from here now!" She folded her arms and glared at Don Nyako.

The crowd was dumbstruck. Esperanza turned to me and said pleasantly, "It is now your turn to speak."

Although I was taken aback by her accusation and the intensity of her short speech, I recognized that she was right.

"My friends, Dona Nyako is correct. In the past, people came and stole the land and abused the people. And we come here with promises that it will be different. So I ask Dona Nyako not to judge us on our words, but to judge us on our deeds."

Dona Nyako stared at me for a long time. Then she grunted, turned, and stomped off toward the cooking hut. Don Nyako smiled at me. "She really likes you."

A collective sigh of relief arose. A soccer ball appeared and some bottles of local firewater made the rounds. Some kids brought out a small mammal skull attached to a stick by a foot of string. They showed us how, with a flick of the wrist, the skull could be balanced on top of the stick. I gave up after five tries, hounded out of the hut by the hoots of my seven-year-old tutors. I wandered over to the cooking hut. Dona Nyako supervised several younger women in the preparation of a feast for thirty. Two girls about six years old were poking the coals of the fire and adding more wood. I looked into the cooking pot, watching a scaly foot bobbing up and down with the stirring current.

We sat along the walls of the biggest hut. Don Nyako brought me the first plate. It looked like a week's worth of grub for the village. The banana leaf plate was burdened with several large yams, two ears of corn, a gray gruel, another unnamed vegetable—and a scaly foot.

"Armadillo," said Don Nyako brightly.

I looked at Esperanza. The group looked at me. I felt the hot, greasy juice of the armadillo leg running through the plate and onto my lap. I ate what I could, gnawed the little leg a bit, and washed it all down with some ancestral rocket fuel. I prayed silently for peaceful digestion. The gods were kind.

Fredi invited me to walk through the coffee fields, hidden deep within a dense overstory of bananas, tangelos, pineapples, and broad-leafed hardwoods. Along the way we plucked at coca leaves for better digestion. Fredi led me past the coffee and down a winding trail into the forest. The tension of the meeting and the noise of the gathering faded with each step. We stopped at a massive tree. Fredi put a hand on the ancient trunk and spoke over his shoulder.

"This is a Grandfather. It is a *tornillo* tree. So many of the Grandfathers were cut down by the *colonos*. But this Grandfather survived. He gives us seed to plant and we scatter them in this valley. Many of his children are coming back."

He told me that he was being trained as the village healer and had been taken into this forest since he was six to learn all the plants and their healing and helpful properties. It was a lifelong learning, he said, as there were thousands of plants and they acted differently in different combinations. He bent down and pulled gently at a small fuzzy frond.

"This is *ajomacho*. If you chew the root, it will ease any pain in your stomach."

For the next hour or so, we wandered through the forest. Fredi stopped here and there to point out a plant and describe its qualities. He talked about the government complicity in the theft of the land, allowing logging companies and *colonos* to invade in direct contravention to the law. He also talked about the co-op's efforts to help the Ashaninkas regain title to the land and the health care and educational assistance that Pangoa made available to its members. I asked Fredi about the shroud he wore. I had seen the Cofan wearing similar clothing in the Ecuadorian Amazon. Did the ocher color and shape symbolize the relationship of the people and the forest or some other spiritual connection? He looked at me in surprise, then down at the shroud. He smiled broadly.

"We used to be naked in the forest. Then the Jesuits came about two hundred years ago and forced us to put these on. I guess it just caught on over time."

Esperanza met us when we returned to the village. A meeting was in progress to discuss the use of the profit-sharing money. The directors had decided to divide it evenly among the five communities of Pangoa. The Ashaninkas had already decided that their share would be used for reforestation of the degraded lands with *tornillo* trees, which they consider the anchor of the ecosystem. Reforesting would also allow the Ashaninkas to heal their relationship to their injured lands, reclaiming a sense of stewardship that had been severely damaged. Esperanza said that the renewed forest, if carefully managed by the Ashaninkas, would also provide "a social security system for the future." The co-op directors voted to provide transportation and additional technical assistance to the community for this project. Dona Nyako grunted at me. It seemed a friendly gesture.

We got in the trucks for the quick trip to the main Ashaninkas settlement at Boka Kiatari. Thirty or so huts surrounded a huge field, used intermittently for soccer or as a landing strip for small airplanes. A celebration was under way even before we arrived. I was immediately taken aside and dressed in an off-white shroud. A bark hat with feathers was screwed to my head. My hosts ushered me over to a small gathering, where an archery competition had begun. The Ashaninkas versus the *colonos*. A young man put a wooden bow into my hands and pointed thirty yards away at a target. I looked at the bow and tested it. My dad was a bow hunter and I used to do archery as a kid. *I can do this*, I convinced myself. The young man then handed me a long, pointed stick. I noticed that it had no nock, the little slit at the end to hold the arrow on the bowstring. Nor were there any feathers to guide the arrow in flight. *These guys could learn a few things from the Iroquois about making arrows*, I thought. I watched some others let fly and noticed that they were holding the arrow against the string with the tips of their fingers. None of the archers came anywhere near the target. I wondered how these people could find enough slow-moving (or sleeping) game to hit. My turn.

Well, I said to myself, *I'll just hold the arrow like I ordinarily would, even without a nock.* I lifted the bow high, slowly brought it down, and pulled back the bowstring in a rather theatrical gesture. The crowd waited. I sighted the target and raised the bow a touch for the proper arc. You are the arrow. You are the target.

I let fly with intense concentration, holding the pose to follow the trajectory of the arrow. Where the hell did it go? The crowd doubled over with laughter. The pointed stick lay at my feet. *Next time I'll try it their way.*

Several rounds later, two champions were declared. Only one Ashaninkas and one *colono* had managed to come anywhere near the target. The grand prizes were presented: a garish plastic wall clock and a baby armadillo. I gave thanks for my lack of skill.

As twilight dropped, several flute players appeared from the village and entertained us. Next, two women from the co-op got up and sang a screechy love song in Spanish. The *chicha* flowed, and the event quickly turned into a homespun version of "Peruvian Idol," with everybody getting up and doing what they felt moved to do. I sang an old favorite, "Bubbles of Love," by Juan Luis Guerra. The women howled when I sang "I wish I was a fish, so I could put my nose in your fish tank and blow bubbles of love wherever, passing the night together, slipping around in you." Frederico, the carp farmer, smiled dreamily, no doubt thinking lovingly of his own ponds.

There were about thirty very young children there, sitting at the feet of the adults and blowing bubbles from the little wands I had brought for them. They didn't understand the song but cheered me on nonetheless. I asked if I could tell them a story. They gathered around me by the fire. I told them about the Man with the Golden Arm (with apologies to the Boy Scouts of America for my Peruvian adaptation).

"Once there was a man in Satipo who had lost his arm in the war. The government rewarded his courage by giving him a golden arm. He wore it proudly during the day, but at night he took it off to sleep. Some of the local children, just your age, took his arm one night as a joke and hid it in the forest up here somewhere. [The kids sitting around me were drawn in like moths to a flame.] When the man woke up and could not find his arm, he ran through the streets yelling, '*Quien robó mi abrazo de oro?*' ('Who stole my golden arm?') He went crazy, and he began to roam the forest at night looking for his arm. 'Who stole my golden arm?' He finally went into the forest one night and never came back to Satipo. But sometimes on a dark night like this, you can hear him in the forest. 'Who stole my Golden Arm?' [The kids' eyes were like saucers. Their mouths hung open and they edged ever closer to me and to each other.] 'Who stole my GOLDEN ARM?? WHO STOLE MY GOLDEN ARM!!!'"

I turned suddenly and pointed straight at one small boy. "*YOU DID!!!*"

The kids all screamed in terror and delight, joined by several adults, who then composed themselves and smiled with great dignity. Old stories never get stale; they just need new audiences.

It is never wise to leave an isolated mountain village in the dark or in a torrential thunderstorm, but we did. The pickups slid along the muddy roads up and over the mountains. We stopped several times to push one out of a deep rut. Wet, cold, and sore, we pulled into Satipo well past midnight.

We held an all-day workshop the next day at the co-op warehouse. First, we created a marketing package to help Pangoa get greater visibility at the next show and have materials to hand out to any potential buyer. We gathered good photos of the coffeelands and the farmers at work, including the Ashaninkas in their traditional clothing. I gave them a copy of the cupping report that Royal had done. This demonstrated that the coffee was of a very high quality and had desirable characteristics for the specialty market. I added a letter on our company stationery extolling the virtues of the coffee and the reputable nature of the organization. We sketched out an effective brochure to complete the presentation.

Next, we explored business options for alternative income generation.

Their biggest concern was the honey. They had tried to sell it in Lima in five-gallon glass jars and had not succeeded. I asked if they knew about *chupas*, little straws filled with sugar or sweet jellies that kids suck on. Could they make honey *chupas* and sell them in the market in Satipo or even Lima? The directors were very excited. Sure, they could find the straws. They knew all the small markets in Lima where a stall could be had for a little rent. Okay, but are there enough people passing by to support a stall? What would the rent be and how many *chupas* would you need to sell? We quickly evolved a business plan. Esperanza and Don Flor would check out the location when they took me back to Lima. We also looked at increasing the sale of cocoa. Several of the farmers had been growing cocoa for years without a ready market, selling the unprocessed beans to middlemen for nothing. We looked at the structure of cocoa processing and discovered that there was a co-op in Lima that processed cocoa for export. They determined to explore that path.

We took a final trip into the countryside, stopping at a large field before a hill covered in heavy brush. The directors looked at the site longingly.

"This will be our new processing facility, our *beneficio*," said Don Flor proudly. "Here we will dry and process all of our beans for export. We will get our own export license and we will never have to sell to middlemen, those *coyotes*, again." The others murmured in agreement. This was one of the most powerful ways for coffee farmers to raise themselves up economically. By controlling the whole process from field to export, the farmers would keep much of the upstream value of the coffee, instead of seeing it gobbled up by layers of processors and exporters up the chain. But all I could see was a nice plot of thickly overgrown land.

We walked through the field up onto the apparently undeveloped hillside. As we cut through the brush, foundations began to appear, along with parts of old machinery. I felt like the guy who had stumbled upon Machu Picchu back in 1911. Kids rushed past me laughing, trying to be the first to find certain machines and climb on top. Farmers congregated in groups, discussing this machine or that drying patio.

"Hey! What's this place about?" I asked in surprise.

Esperanza smiled. "Years ago, this was a *beneficio*. The man who owned it cheated us all the time. He abandoned it, and now we will buy it and repair it." I looked about at the rusted machinery and the broken cement. This was a dubious venture, but I didn't have the heart to douse their passion.

"It will be ready in about a year and a half," Don Flor said firmly. What should I do? Be a supportive friend to a clear fantasy? Gently bring some reality into the equation? I was here to give them advice, and they trusted me to be honest. *Okay, here goes.*

"Esperanza, Flor, my dear friends, this is a great idea, and I fully support your desire to control your own processing. But wouldn't it be better to start from scratch, get newer machines that already work? Maybe locate your *beneficio* closer to the warehouse? It looks like a lot of work and a huge amount of money to get this old plant started again." *Whew, that was as gentle as I could make it.*

The directors looked at each other. Don Alfredo, whose gnarled hands were indistinguishable from the thick tendrils of a vine he was uprooting, stood up and stretched his back. He shook a finger in the direction of the town.

"It will take hard work and money, yes, but we must heal this land from the abuses of that other guy. We have to show our children how to stand up for themselves and reclaim their land and their pride. And we can make those old machines work again, right, Flor? Don Flor can twist the rusty nuts off a priest!"

I left Pangoa loaded up with a five-gallon jar of honey, an ocher shroud, and some tree pod jewelry. Since my flight was not until midnight, I treated Don Flor and Evaristo to a boat ride around the historic harbor of Callao in Lima. Neither man had ever been to sea. My tales of sharks in the harbor attacking small boats didn't help. I think they were happy to see me off at the airport.

Several months later I received a letter and a package from Pangoa. Esperanza wrote that they had sold three more containers under Fair Trade contracts to European buyers, thanks to the marketing materials, the cupping report, and the letter of reference. The co-op was working on the reforestation project with the Ashaninkas and the *chupas* were flying out of the stall in Lima. Enclosed with the letter was a large promotional calendar for Pangoa. A green foil bag of "Pangoa's Pride" was featured prominently on the calendar. And there, buried among the monthly grids and photos of farmers, was a short American wearing an off-white shroud and a crown of sticks and feathers. The caption beneath the photo read "Honorary Member of Pangoa."

By the end of 2005, Pangoa had sold nine out of the ten containers it had produced that harvest as Fair Trade. It is now processing all of its own coffee at its new beneficio, *rusty nuts and all. Esperanza gave a speech to a full house of roasters, importers, and farmers at the 2006 SCAA in Charlotte, North Carolina, followed by a stirring talk to 3,500 teachers in New York, where she received a standing ovation that easily surpassed that of the prior speaker, Hillary Clinton. She is also mentoring several young women leaders from nearby cooperatives. The co-op has used its most recent social equity premium to start a women's credit fund.*

Our reforestation project caught the attention of the Green Development Fund from the Netherlands, which granted the Ashaninkas over ten thousand dollars to expand the important work of healing their land.

4

Global Warning: Climate Change, Conflict, and Culture

COLOMBIA, 2007

The Intergovernmental Panel on Climate Change (IPCC), government officials, and scientists from more than one hundred countries wrangled for weeks in Brussels in early 2007 as to whether global warming was a man-made or a natural phenomenon. They argued over droughts, air circulation patterns, snowfall, ice caps, and a thousand other indicators of whether global warming was "likely" or "directly" our fault. In spite of the strong belief in the scientific community that all of our cars, factories, and other activities were speeding up global warming at an alarming rate, the politicians managed to get the official word to be "likely."

High in the Sierra Nevada (Snow-Capped Mountains) of Colombia, indigenous Arhuaco coffee farmer Javier Mestres had no such doubts. He did not see things in parts per million. He had never heard of the global circulation model that tried to measure increments of change in the temperature of the ocean or dynamics of the atmosphere. He was unaware that the IPCC report stated that Colombia would heat up dramatically in the next twenty years and lose 90 percent of its glacial snowcaps by 2050. Javier saw the results of a warming planet clearly in the premature flowering of his coffee plants on his four acre family farm in the slopes above Nabusimake, the capital of the Arhuaco nation. He showed me the smaller, weaker berries that dotted the stems and wondered why the outside world wanted to harm these beautiful plants. Why were we changing the world?

For centuries, the Arhuaco spiritual elders, the Mamos, known in their language as the "Elder Brothers," have carried out monthly rituals in sacred sites throughout the Sierra Nevada, which they call "the Heart of the World," to ensure that the planet is kept in a geo-spiritual balance. But for the past two decades, the Mamos have been observing rapid changes in the Heart of the World. They have watched the snowcaps on their sacred peaks shrink over time and have seen the plant life change. They have felt the lower moisture levels in the air and soil and noted the changing migration patterns of the birds and butterflies. They have shared these observations with the tribe, and increasingly with the outside world, with us—the "Younger Brothers."

I was in Colombia to learn about the impacts of global warming on the Heart of the World. I was there to assist the Arhuaco in their struggle for self-determination, supported (and challenged) in part by coffee. I was also there to heal the wound in my heart from the kidnapping and murder in 1999 by the leftist rebel group FARC (Armed Revolutionary Front of Colombia) of my dear friend, renowned indigenous rights activist Ingrid Washinawatok. It was a visit that had been delayed many times by war, weather, or fear.

I have had a troubled relationship with Colombia since the beginning of my work in coffee. During the 1990s and until very recently, it was nearly impossible to buy directly from small farmers, as the Colombian Coffee Federation, a powerful parastatal organization, had a near monopoly on exporting. It was difficult to have direct relationships as well, as the decades-old war between the government, the FARC, and the increasingly active right-wing paramilitary groups made farmer visits virtually impossible. A near breakthrough came in 1998, when I received a telephone call from a young Arhuaco leader, Moises Villafanes. He had heard of my work with

indigenous peoples in different countries through what some American
Indian activists used to call the "tom-tom telephone." Would I be willing to
come to Colombia and work with the Arhuaco on territorial recognition?
Also, the Arhuaco were thinking of exporting coffee for the first time by
themselves, instead of selling for pennies to local middlemen who reaped
the profit for themselves. Could I work on that? I was very excited at the
prospect, but each time we scheduled a trip to the Sierra Nevada the war
turned hot.

Then, in February 1999, Ingrid, Lahe Gay (an indigenous Hawaiian),
and Terry Freitas (an American environmental activist) were kidnapped in
Colombia while working with the U'wa people. The U'wa were trying to
protect their territory from the massive ecological and cultural disruption
spilling over from oil exploration and development by Occidental Petroleum
and had even threatened a mass suicide if the drilling did not stop. Terry
had worked with the U'wa for two years on this issue. Ingrid and Lahe were
there to help the U'wa set up schools taught in U'wa and incorporating U'wa
culture into the curriculum. This was necessary to confront the erosion of
the tribal fabric brought about by television, globalization, and the influx of
miners, colonists, geologists, and roughnecks (oil workers) into U'wa lands.

Upon hearing of the kidnapping, I went to New York to work with
an impromptu group of activists, family, and friends to find Ingrid, Lahe,
and Terry. It took days of back and forth with the Red Cross, the Cuban
government, several churches, and the FARC representatives in Geneva
before we could confirm who had grabbed them. Just when things were
looking up, we were told that our friends' bodies had been discovered in a
farmer's field over the border into Venezuela. They had been murdered by
their FARC captors. It took a shocking six days to bring our loved ones
home. Six days of dealing with a turf war between the State Department and
the FBI, six days of fending off corrupt coroners, six days of unfathomable
grief as I spent days and nights on the phone with countless government
officials in three countries, FBI agents, Air Force colonels, and White House
liaisons. Six days of hearing how the White House would do everything
possible to bring them home—provided that the families would agree to let
the government wrap the caskets in flags for the world to see our grief and
to bolster support for the war against drugs and terrorism. Six days that were

ultimately resolved with the greater assistance of my local travel agent and the magnanimous anonymous charter of a private plane so that I could get Ingrid home.

There were people in the U.S. diplomatic corps who worked very hard to expedite their return, and I am being unfair to them. They live in a world of regulations and funding priorities that limit their ability to get the job done quickly, despite what they themselves felt personally. Such is the nature of large organizations, although it was hard for me to keep that perspective through the pain. Ironically, it was the Venezuelan military that broke the bureaucratic logjam, sending helicopters to ferry the necessary paperwork from outpost to courthouse to capital for processing, and sending troops to stand down the local officials looking for bribes before they released the bodies.

The trauma of the deaths and the struggle to bring Ingrid, Lahe, and Terry home made it impossible for me to deal with Colombia for several years. And yet, as a coffee roaster and an activist, I was very aware of the ongoing struggles of the indigenous peoples and coffee farmers there, including the growing participation of our government in the civil war and drug situation. I wanted to be involved, but I could barely mention Colombia without crying.

At the SCAA fair in Anaheim in 2002, I met a group of young farmers from the Cauca region of Colombia who had formed a cooperative, Cosurca, to take control of their lives amidst the war and chaos of the times. Like so many other small producer co-ops around the world, Cosurca had a deep social mission to improve the quality of life for the farm families through the economics of coffee. The general manager was Rene, who (like me) was a lawyer and community organizer. When I told him Ingrid's story he held me and we both cried. The healing had begun. But when I tried to talk to Rene about buying coffee at the SCAA, we were quickly surrounded by big, well-dressed businessmen—the representatives of the Colombian Coffee Federation. They basically squeezed Rene out of the circle as they informed me that if I wanted Cosurca coffee, I had to take conventional as well as organic, in spite of my insistence that my company bought only organic coffee. Cooperative Coffees, our roasters' cooperative, did buy several containers, as we had members at the time who would take conventional coffee, but it was difficult to have a direct relationship given the export control by the federation.

I quietly began to assist Rene in obtaining an export license for Cosurca—a potentially dangerous maneuver for the young farmer group. Over a two-year period, however, Cosurca was successful and was able to set up its own direct export office in the capital, Bogotá. I also bought coffee from Fondo Paez, a small cooperative made up of indigenous farmers from several *resguardas* (indigenous reserves) along the Cordillera Central. Yet I was always drawn to the Sierra Nevada, the Heart of the World where the Elder Brothers kept the earth in balance. During the early years of the new millennium, the Arhuaco Mamos were sending young men and women, like Moises and his sisters, to a university to train as lawyers, economists, and ecologists, hoping to create a strong corps of professionals steeped in their own traditions. In this way, the Mamos would educate the Younger Brothers and defend the Sierra Nevada from the onslaught from the modern world. They also created several organizations, such as the Gonawindua Tayrona Organization and the Tayrona Indigenous Federation (CIT), to present a united front to the outside world and coordinate community activities. The Mamos traveled to the World Bank in Washington, to the European Commission in Brussels, and elsewhere around the globe to bring their message—their warning about the imbalance in the ecology of the planet—to the Younger Brothers. They sat stoically after each chance to speak while the fate of the world was politely and dispassionately discussed at wine and cheese affairs, and while the power brokers of the Western world grabbed a quick photo opportunity with these curious prophets. Moises came to New York and Massachusetts in 2003 to share the message with university students. We reconnected briefly when he stopped at our beanery. He shared my sadness about Ingrid and hoped that we could work together someday to heal that pain and the pain of the Arhuaco, as the assault on the Heart of the World heated up.

In 2006 Cooperative Coffees was approached by a nonprofit group in Colombia called Caja Herramientas (Toolbox). They were working with the Arhuaco to commercialize their coffee and equip the Arhuaco over time to become direct exporters. Their project, Café Tiwun, was certified organic but had failed to get on the Fair Trade Registry. There was some debate inside Cooperative Coffees as to whether to buy from a group not on the registry. As I dug deeper into why the Arhuaco group hadn't made it onto the registry, I found that the reasons were more cultural than substantial. The Arhuaco had developed the coffee project as a part of CIT, part of the broader movement for tribal national sovereignty. They did not organize a formal "cooperative," which was a requirement for the registry. Yet they were transparent, the money went back to the farmers, and the goal of the project was clearly to support and empower the community within a culturally appropriate design. This type of organizing for self-determination was happening all over the globe but did not fit neatly into the European-based categories recognized by the registry. Cooperative Coffees made a decision to buy their coffee, and we were happy with it. But as the new crop was coming in, the samples were uneven in quality. We needed to know what was up: was this a seasonal anomaly, or was quality control a serious issue? We couldn't continue to buy from a source that proved unreliable. Someone had to go to the source and check it out. After a sober talk with Ali and John (Ingrid and Lahe's husbands) and a similar conversation with my own family, I decided that it was time to reengage with Colombia. I contacted Caja Herramientas and arranged a visit right after Semana Santa (Easter Week).

Joel, a Dutch man who was working with Caja on the commercialization project, met me at the airport in Bogotá. On the ride to the hotel, I asked if he knew a young Arhuaco man named Moises, whom I had met years ago. Joel looked surprised.

"We live in the same house in Bogotá. I think he's there now." Joel dialed his cell phone and spoke with Moises. "He wants us to come right over."

We arrived at the house and argued with the taxi driver, who wanted more money for the shorter trip ("Colombian taxi logic," chuckled Joel). Inside the one-story, white cement building stood a stocky man with long, jet-black hair. He wore a white woven cone-shaped hat (representing the snowy peaks of the Sierra Nevada), a white tunic that went to his knees, and white leggings. A *mochila*, a woven bag with a geometric design, hung at his shoulder.

"Dean, *nu junakanah* (my close friend), *nu guiya* (my brother)," Moises said, smiling warmly. "You have finally come to Colombia."

Moises was enrolled in law school, focusing on indigenous rights and international law. He was still on the path. We went into his room and he showed me photo albums of his work. Moises in Washington with Bill Clinton. Moises in Rome with Deepak Chopra. Moises in Bogotá with Shakira. All the notables in politics and culture were there in the photos. He had been a tireless advocate of his people, trying to educate the Younger Brothers about the Law of Origin—the Arhuaco worldview—and its relevance to our behavior today. I was soon to learn that Arhuaco men, like Hassidic Jews and the Torah, like Tom Cruise on *Oprah*, liked nothing better than to urge you to change your ways and see the world as they do.

Moises was not surprised to have me show up at his house unannounced after several years of silence. He knew that we were both working in our own spheres, in our own ways, to heal the world. He wanted to know why I came to Colombia at that moment. I explained about the coffee situation and the need for me to assure Cooperative Coffees that the coffee would be good and that the organizations, Caja and CIT, were truly working in the best interests of the farmers and were transparent and inclusive. He was happy for me to be doing that, as an outsider's eye would lend an impartial view.

"When you visit our territory and meet the people, you will be satisfied," Moises assured me. I mentioned my desire to understand the impacts of a warming planet on the Heart of the World. Moises talked for a long time about the drying up of rivers due to the lessened snow at the peaks and the erratic rainfall of the past few years, and the movement of plant species up the mountains as a result of greater heat and less water at the lower altitudes.

"It is as if you can see the plants trying to run from the sun and the heat, which should not be so strong in the lower zones." Moises spoke with a combination of scientific awareness and poetry that made things incredibly clear. "But you should not hear these things from me, you should hear them from the Mamos."

"That would be great, Moises, but I can't hike up the Sierra Nevada ten thousand feet to meet the Mamos. I know that they don't welcome outsiders easily, especially on short notice. And, frankly, my legs aren't strong enough for the journey and I'm afraid to go deep into the mountains because of Ingrid." Moises smiled and put his hand on my shoulder.

"You won't have to make that trip, my brother. One of the Mamos is right here, staying with us in the next room. He can answer all of your questions about the changes in the Mother, and you can talk to him about the pain in your heart."

I was stunned. It was another of the magical moments in my life where my calling out for help was answered with the speed of spiritual e-mail. Actually, so was finding Moises again. So was this whole trip.

Moises went into the back of the house and reappeared after a few minutes. He was accompanied by an older Arhuaco man in traditional dress, with a full head of flowing black hair in tight ringlets. My initial thought was that he had a perm, but I later found out that there were several Arhuaco hair and body types, depending on where in the mountains they lived. Moises introduced him as his uncle, Fambautista Villafanes. The Mamo shook my hand with a powerful grip. Up close, I saw that he was a muscular man, his skin tight on his well-defined arms. The Mamo was eighty-three years old, but he looked to be in his late forties. *Man, do I need to start doing sit-ups,* I thought irreverently.

I noticed that the Mamo was staring at me intensely. I held his gaze, ultimately relaxing and drinking him in. He turned to Moises and nodded brusquely. Moises said that he had told the Mamo the reasons for my visit and now the Mamo had approved and was ready to talk. I thanked them both for the honor. I told the Mamo that I had read some articles and books about Arhuaco society and the role of the Mamos in keeping the world in balance, but I was aware that these were only secondhand reports from anthropologists and other outsiders with their own agendas and worldviews. Would the Mamo help me understand their ways better, so that my work with the Arhuacos could be better informed? He agreed with another sharp nod of his head.

When Fambautista Villafanes was five years old, the Mamos came to his family. It was probably 1929, the beginning of the Great Depression in our world, maybe even the day the stock market crashed. In the Sierra Nevada, it was but a moment in the seamless cycle of the world that the Mamos protected. They had chosen him and some other young boys to become Mamos, a great honor in Arhuaco society. He was taken high into the Sierra Nevada to the small village of stone huts with thatched roofs where the Mamos lived and trained. He was put into a dark hut without windows and kept there for the next sixteen years. Every day the Mamos came in and taught him the Law of Origin, the Arhuaco understanding of the creation of the universe and the role the Mamos play in maintaining the necessary harmony between the spiritual and material planes. He soaked these teachings into his pores, using his mind to imagine the world into being as he was deprived of a literal view of the world outside. He was taught the rituals for balancing the worlds and the "payments" needed in ritual offering to correct imbalances. He was taught the proper use of the *poporo*, the hollow gourd that Arhuaco men receive upon maturity that will carry the calcium of crushed seashells from the ocean at the base of the Sierra Nevada. The men take a chew of coca leaves, then plunge a stick into the mix and put a small amount of the shell into their mouth to increase the saliva for chewing. The stick is then rubbed on the outside of the gourd, depositing the thoughts of the man in a yellowish accretion, a lifelong record of his mind. When the Mamos felt the student was ready, he was taken out into the bright, clear sunlight of the high Sierra Nevada. His senses were so heightened that he could hear the beating of a bird's wings and see a plant growing. He was taken to the sacred sites, the places of power throughout the Sierra Nevada, where his blinded visioning of the world could find expression in color and sound. It was his time to take his place in the order of things.

I asked the Mamo what changes he had noticed over his lifetime.

"The Younger Brothers have come here, to the Heart of the World, and are cutting out the Mother's heart. They dig out the gold that we need for our rituals. They cut down the trees that hold the earth in place and destroy these homes for the birds. The Younger Brothers pollute the water with chemicals from mining and are making drugs from the plants, from the sacred coca!" While he spoke, he rubbed the stick onto the *poporo* in a hypnotic rhythm, the pain and confusion caused by the foolish actions of the Younger Brothers etched in layers. "They have invaded our land. They destroy sacred sites to make mines and farms. They are making it difficult for us to do the work we must do to keep the world in balance. What would happen if we stopped keeping the world in balance? If we didn't make the payments, would the trees still grow?"

I was taken aback by this last comment. I agreed with the need to stop the destruction, but did he really believe that the world would stop if the Mamos weren't able to perform their rituals? Did they really believe that they held the world together? To my rational mind, it seemed a quaint and romantic notion. But maybe it was true. Maybe there is a tipping point where the whole thing comes down. It certainly happens on the micro level, where localized ecosystems and plant and animal communities crash when the balance is disturbed beyond repair. Ecologists tell us about "trophic cascade," when the crash of one system leads to the crash of another, and then of many related systems. Is the critical point on Earth located here in the Sierra Nevada? Are the spiritual rituals the prime focus of energy, the "seams" that hold the world intact? The Mamos believe so.

"So what must be done to control this destruction?" I asked respectfully. The Mamo looked piercingly into my eyes.

"All the white men must leave the Sierra Nevada."

"Uh, I know that would be ideal, but what can be done practically?"

"I told you. All the white men must leave."

Maybe that was the most effective way to protect the sacred lands, and maybe that will ultimately be the solution—create a Heart of the World International Sacred Landscape. This is the underlying dynamic for the concept of *totem* or *taboo,* the recognition that there are places or actions that must be safeguarded for the benefit of the whole. Maybe we need to recognize and protect sacred spaces, beyond the multiple-use designations of national parks and forests, so that they can be accessed only by the ritual keepers. Whether or not the keepers actually hold the world together, their ritual activities keep the need for balance between the sacred and the profane within our collective psyche.

"But there is more," the Mamo continued. "Beyond the Heart of the World, the Younger Brothers are changing the whole earth. I don't know everything they are doing, but they are changing the whole earth."

"Are you talking about global warming?" I asked.

"I don't know what you call it, but yes, the Mother is getting warmer. The rain falls differently than before. It is later, but it falls harder. It is destructive sometimes when it should be nurturing. Many of the rivers are dry before they reach the sea. And the snows on the peaks that replenish the rivers are less each year. Even the bees are disappearing, and that affects the flowering of the coffee and all other plants."

I asked the Mamo how he knew there were fewer bees.

"I can hear them. Their sound has lessened," he replied. "It is all happening very quickly. First you took our gold. Then you took our land. Now you are taking the water and the air itself. The Younger Brothers are waging a war on the earth and it must stop!"

While the Mamo spoke, Moises sat thoughtfully, chewing and rubbing, creating in calcium an indigenous response to the IPCC findings. I wished that the bureaucrats arguing in Brussels about global warming could read the record in the *poporo*. I wished I could hit them over the head with the hardened gourd.

Moises changed the subject. He asked me to tell the Mamo about Ingrid. I told him the story, opening the wound anew. The Mamo watched the hot tears roll down my cheeks as I let out the darkest details of the tragedy known only to me, things that I had never shared even with the families. The nausea and pain ebbed a little as I finished. The Mamo sat quietly for a moment, then spoke curtly.

"Mamos are not counselors for your personal problems. We guard the earth from imbalances. What you are saying cannot be fixed by talking; it must be dealt with spiritually!" He stood up quickly and left the room. I turned to Moises in a panic.

"Did I say something wrong? Did I insult him? Why did he leave so abruptly?"

Moises smiled, his face full of compassion. "No, he left because he needs to begin work on your healing. Go out to the mountains and do your work. When you return to Bogotá, come see the Mamo. *Eh gui anachuqua*. He will be waiting for you."

Valledupar sits like a supplicant at the foot of the Sierra Nevada. It is a friendly, clean town where the Arhuaco and the colonists mix freely. The FARC does not have a presence here, and the right-wing paramilitaries seem to have vanished in recent years. Only the occasional military roadblock remains to remind citizens that the bloodbath of civil war had washed over this area, leaving mass graves, forced conscription, and kidnappings in its wake. I felt no fear in Valledupar. The biggest conflict seemed to be whether to listen to traditional indigenous music, the folkloric Vallenato rhythms, or the latest global top forty. The town was abuzz with preparations for the annual Vallenato Music Festival, a three-day, nonstop hoedown of accordians, guitars, and percussion traditionally opened by the president of Colombia.

"But lately it's the vice president," noted my host, Caja Herramientas cofounder and lawyer Nelson Guzman. "He really knows how to live. The current president works too hard and doesn't know how to play." We were entering the Casa Indigena, the official headquarters of CIT and the Café Tiwun project. Here I would meet the Arhuaco leaders who ran the political and economic functions of the resurgent Arhuaco nation. I would also, hopefully, get formal permission to go up into the mountains and visit the farmers who grew our Colombian coffee.

There were a few Arhuaco men and women in the large courtyard as we entered. The men were scribing their thoughts on their *poporos* and the women were doing a similar action by drawing out long strands of cotton by hand into thread for weaving. It was a peaceful scene and nobody seemed to take notice of my entrance. Nelson introduced me to several people, but all I got were indifferent glances or limp hands to shake.

"Don't take it personally, Dean," Nelson offered kindly. "Remember that the Arhuaco think of all outsiders as the Younger Brothers. It's not that they think you are inferior or anything, but they think you don't know much."

"That's okay. I'm used to people thinking I'm an idiot, but it usually happens after they get to know me." I meant it as a joke, but Nelson shook his head knowingly. Another man approached us. Nelson introduced him as Wilber Mestres. Wilber was a young man who, like Moises, had been charged by the Mamos to use his Western schooling and organizational skills to help his people. Wilber was the coordinator of the Café Tiwun project. Like the others, he didn't seem terribly interested in meeting his first coffee buyer. *Maybe a customer relations course would be helpful here*, I fumed, my undies in a bit of a bundle.

We entered the office rooms at the back of the courtyard. Inside, a handful of middle-aged men in traditional clothing were seated around a laptop, gesturing at the symbols and designs on the screen. They were having a discussion of the Law of Origin, which someone had outlined graphically on the computer. They stopped as we entered, greeting Nelson and giving me the hairy eyeball. Nelson introduced me as a representative of Cooperative Coffees, who had bought their first exported coffee, and also as a lawyer with years of experience working with indigenous peoples. No reaction. *This was not going to be an easy crowd*, I thought. I was asked to introduce myself and talk about the reasons for my visit. The men worked their *poporos* as I spoke, the rubbing giving off a small, still voice. They were pretty indifferent as I talked about my background and coffee work. They weren't very moved by my concern for the consistency of the coffee samples we had received, either. However, when I spoke about specific situations—fighting land invasions, arguing treaty rights, and observing how coffee could be a very divisive force in a community at times—the men took a keener interest.

The general secretary of CIT, Jeremias, took out a large paper drawing of the Sierra Nevada. He showed me how the mountains were divided into the lands of the four tribes that lived there, the Arhuaco, the Kogi, the Wiwa, and the largely assimilated Kankuamo. Jeremias told me with great pride that the Sierra was a very unique mountain system that contained every major ecosystem from ocean and mangrove swamp to desert, rain forest, and glacier—all within roughly twenty-five miles as it soared upward from the coast to reach nineteen thousand feet above sea level. It was the tallest coastal mountain formation in the world. Jeremias's fingers traced the routes of the thirty major river basins that take fresh water down the mountains to the sea. It was the whole world in miniature, and its high peaks were truly the Heart of the World.

Unfortunately, the views of Jeremias and the Mamo were not the only ways in which the Sierra were perceived. To generations of colonists, the mountains represented fertile farmland to support their families. To the FARC it was a rich recruiting grounds and an easy place to hide. To the various churches it had been a place to harvest new souls. To the multinational mining companies it was a new place to dig up for private wealth. I showed the men a memo from Proexport Colombia, an industry group for mining companies, exclaiming that the mountains had "attractive geological potential for mineral extraction" of gold, tin, and other ores. I gave them a copy of the new mining law that extended licenses from five to fifty years, with another fifty-year automatic renewal. Clearly, the white man was not going away.

In fact, there was another insidious invasion going on. Jeremias explained that there were two other coffee export projects starting up besides Café Tiwun. Café Nacer was a cooperative of Arhuaco and colonists all living closer to Valledupar and farming the lower slopes. Café Ney was all Arhauco farmers, but it was owned privately; the farmers got paid, but the profits went to the owner/manager.

"Are these projects part of the larger movement toward Arhuaco nation building?" I asked. The men looked at each other before Jeremias replied.

"Well, not exactly. They don't coordinate with us at CIT or other Arhuaco organizations. They are privately run."

"So coffee is introducing the concept of private gain into your communal culture?"

This led to a deep conversation concerning the values that lie hidden within any system, and how important it is to be able to identify those values to understand whether they are coherent with or contrary to what you are trying to accomplish. In this case, privatized group operations may not help to strengthen Arhuaco identity as a group, even though they bring more money into the region. Further, the Arhuaco grow food and trade crops in a very distinct pattern on their farms. The pattern was evolved by the Mamos as providing the proper balance between family, community, and the outside world. Sixty percent of the land is dedicated to food for the family and communal obligations, and up to 40 percent for trading up and down the mountain and to outside markets. But the introduction of coffee as a cash crop for export was putting pressure on farmers to dedicate more land to coffee, threatening the age-old balance. Private ownership, competition among family groups, changing patterns of production, increased reliance on export earnings—was this the path ahead?

After that honest but sobering discussion, I was given permission to go up to Nabusimake, the Arhuaco capital. Wilber left the room. Nelson told me that he had another meeting.

"But isn't he going into the mountains with us?" I asked in surprise. No, we were going with a young Arhuaco driver and an agronomist. That was that.

The ancient Toyota Land Cruiser smelled of leaking gas, which was not alleviated by the many holes in the chassis. We drove through the streets of Valledupar to pick up water for the five-hour trip and to retrieve our driver Seykarin's *poporo* from his house. Seykarin had short hair and wore Western clothes. He also preferred pop salsa and Vallenato music, which blared out of the speakers incessantly. A few miles out of town we were stopped by a military roadblock. The four heavily armed soldiers peered through dark glasses at the inhabitants of the Land Cruiser, walked around the car, and held a private conference. The youngest, a pimply-faced warrior, looked past Seykarin toward me in the passenger seat.

"Habba nice day!" he chirped, and waved us on. Seykarin said that the FARC and paramilitaries were no longer a problem around Valledupar and the military was a calming, if not entirely welcome, presence.

We turned off the main road and started to climb to Pueblo Bello (Beautiful Town) where a wealthy rancher, who was a local paramilitary commander, had ordered the abduction and murder of forty-three villagers a decade earlier in retribution for the theft of forty-three cattle from his ranch by FARC soldiers. The villagers either didn't know or were too afraid to say who had stolen the cattle. Outside of Pueblo Bello, a road sign advised careful driving.

Slow Down
Indians and Animals in the Road
Welcome to Pueblo Bello

"We still have a long way to go around here," Nelson noted pensively.

Beyond Pueblo Bello the road turned nearly vertical. It also lost any semblance of being a road. I congratulated Seykarin as a representative of his people for having the worst road I had ever been on in my life. The road was gutted deeply by trenches from heavy rain. There were thousands of refrigerator-sized boulders everywhere, as we bounced and bottomed out toward Nabusimake. We had to stop often to reconnect the speaker wires, which vibrated loose, and to find the car keys, which kept jiggling out of the ignition and headed toward the holes in the floorboards. The going was so slow that at one point we were passed by a little boy on a mule. Neither the kid nor the mule returned my friendly wave.

"The Arhuaco at Nabusimake decided not to repair this road anymore. They wanted to keep strangers out and discourage tourists," Nelson informed me.

"Most indigenous groups are trying to create respectful tourism to bring economic benefits that honor the culture," I volunteered.

"Not here."

We arrived at the large cleared field that surrounded Nabusimake at dusk. The town was a collection of thirty-six stone buildings with thatch roofs. This far up in the mountains there was no electricity, so the close cluster of thatched huts took on the appearance of a herd of woolly mammoths in the dying light. The whole town was surrounded by a waist-high stone wall that created more of a psychic than a physical barrier to entry. But it clearly said "stay out." We climbed over and wandered up the cobbled paths between the buildings. The town seemed empty.

"Nabusimake is the capital, but it is used only for assemblies and other meetings," Nelson told me. "Each of the twenty-eight Arhuaco communities in the *resguarda* has a house here, and there are communal buildings for meetings, a jail, and the houses of the *comisario* and the *cabildo*. That's the constable and the governor." Nelson also told me not to feel bad that there was nobody there to welcome me to Nabusimake.

"One time a large delegation of international diplomats, including the French and Dutch ambassadors and some European Union people, came up here by helicopter to visit Nabusimake. There were only a few people here to meet them. They were never even offered any food during their visit. I told you they don't generally welcome strangers here, no matter how important they are in the outside world."

We found a house with an open door. Inside sat six men, encased in almost total darkness except for the glow of a dying fire. This was the house of Gregorio, the *comisario*. It was his job to keep order in Nabusimake, which didn't seem like a tough job since nobody lived there. Gregorio motioned us in and Nelson told me to sit down next to the last guy, who was in no hurry to move over for me. I sat with half my ass on a log, which at least made it easier for me to turn the other cheek if I got insulted. Nobody seemed interested in my visit, despite Nelson's eloquent introduction. We did, however, get the *comisario*'s permission to take a few pictures of Nabusimake the next day. I had wanted to bring my sidekick cameraman David on the trip, as much for companionship as for filming, but the Arhuaco said no in clear, blunt language.

As we walked out of the village, I noticed a tall belltower next to a deserted stone church. Nelson told me that was the former church of the Capuchin order. (The espresso drink cappuccino was named after their brown cowls.) The Catholic Church had been awarded a contract by the government to provide education in Spanish and math to the Arhuaco in the early 1920s— about the same time as the Mamo Faumbautista Villafanes had gone away for his Mamo education. In essence, the Capuchin priests had bought the tribe from the government. This was going on all over the Americas (including the United States) during that era. Different churches bid for the right to mine the souls of the indigenous peoples, and the mining concession went to the highest bidder—or the one with the best connections. To the Capuchins, a real education meant abducting the children from their families to live at the school, forcing the schoolchildren to cut their hair and wear Western clothes, and punishing the kids for speaking Arhuaco or practicing their own religion. One of the stolen children was Wilber Mestres's mother, Dona Faustia. She had been grabbed at age four and brainwashed into Catholicism. At ten, she ran away into the mountains. Dona Faustia had recovered her language and is a strong advocate for her people today. But she is still a practicing Catholic. She is an example of what is called "the lost generation" in indigenous North America. These are the tens of thousands of kids who shared Dona Faustia's fate and grew up estranged from their own culture, their own language, and all too often their own families.

The Capuchins had another method for breaking the culture of the Arhuaco. They tried to breed them out of existence. The priests brought in dark-skinned converted Christian men from the desertlike Guajira region of Colombia. They forced the women to marry these non-Arhuaco newcomers and breed children who would not be fully Arhuaco. They would not have to be reprogrammed away from their culture because they would grow up speaking Spanish and learn the history of Colombia and the Church, not the Law of Origin. This was the story of Dona Ynes, who rented us a room during our stay in Nabusimake. She was a squat, dark woman who wore plain dresses and an apron every day. At a young age, she been married off to a Guajira man and had several daughters. The daughters were in their early twenties and still lived in the house. But Dona Ynes was less interested in sharing her own history than in the fact that I didn't finish the dinner she prepared for us, in spite of my insistence that I was not hungry. I had eaten a steak the size of a football that afternoon in Valledupar with Nelson, but Dona Ynes would not have me in her house without her version of nutrition. She brought out a large plate of potatoes, rice, and bread for me—enough carbohydrates to choke Dr. Atkins. When I didn't finish one particularly mountainous potato, she glared at me and asked why I didn't like her cooking. Nelson and Scykarin beat a hasty retreat, and I was left alone to explain myself to this iron-willed chef. I got my revenge in the morning, however. After Nelson had cleaned his carb-filled plate and left the room, I switched plates, leaving him with the half-eaten corn Frisbee that sat on mine. I went into the kitchen and proudly proved myself an esteemed member of Dona Ynes's clean-plate club, but shook my head sadly as I glanced at Nelson's remaining food. She stormed into the guest room and berated Nelson for not finishing. Let's call it Fare Trade.

In 1983 the Arhuaco got the government to remove the Capuchin order from Nabusimake, which the Church had renamed San Sebastian de Rabago as part of their ethnic cleansing campaign. The Mamos took back their own name for the capital. The traditional government was restored, and it took over the school and closed it for one year to educate the students in traditional knowledge. They hired teachers who could teach in Arhuaco and restructured the curriculum to be more culturally appropriate. That was the first year Wilber Mestres, son of the kidnapped Dona Faustia, began school in Nabusimake. A new generation was born. *Ingrid would have been proud of this*, I thought.

In the morning we caught up with the *comisario* and the group from the night before. They were in a more receptive mood. One of the men asked me what indigenous groups I had worked with in Central and South America. He was very aware of the issues facing each group I named. He knew about the Zapatista struggle for autonomy in Chiapas, the Secoya battle with Occidental Petroleum in Ecuador, and the Ashaninkas attempts to resuscitate their sacred lands in Peru. I felt like I was being tested, and the animated discussion that followed comparing the Arhuaco situation to those of other indigenous peoples told me that I had passed. As we walked around Nabusimake, the men pointed out things I should know. Those two doors in that windowless building? Those were the men's and women's prisons. Any infraction of the law between two Arhuaco came before the *cabildo*. Minor theft or drunkenness for more than three days landed the offender in the dark clink for several days. A serious crime would be brought before the whole Arhuaco community assembly, which met annually. The community would hash out the facts and mete out an appropriate remedy. If an Arhuaco committed a minor crime or breach of the peace in Valledupar, the case would probably be referred to the *comisario*, who would come down and cart the offender back up to Nabusimake.

Gregorio pointed out a round stone building used for day-to-day administration. It had a small solar panel on the thatched roof to power a radio transmitter. This allowed the community to keep in touch with the government in Valledupar in case of emergencies or important news that couldn't wait for the next bumpy rider between the two worlds.

"Inside that building, we decide on what land to buy back from the colonists," Gregorio said. The Arhuaco had embarked on an aggressive campaign to buy back land that had been stolen or sold to colonists. Most of this land was on the lower slopes of the Sierra Nevada. The *comisario* told me that traditionally the Arhuaco had planted different crops at different altitudes and traded between the ecological zones. This ensured a wide variety of foods and nutrition for the people. But since the colonists came with tobacco, coffee, and cattle, the old patterns had been disrupted. The Mamos had instructed the people to buy back the land in order to restore the communal harmony needed to balance the earth again.

"So in this way coffee has disrupted the community?" I asked. Gregorio must have thought it an odd question for a coffee buyer to ask. He looked at me curiously and responded.

"Yes, but now we must use coffee to provide money to rebuild the nation. It can be used to buy land back and to educate our young people."

At the coffee farm of Javier Mestres, we walked through beautifully pruned patches of plants, interspersed with small groups of yellow coca bushes. Nelson pointed out the importance of coca in Arhuaco culture. Coca was in the *mochila* shoulder bag of every adult Arhuaco man, for use with the *poporo*. It was also part of the greeting between men, as they exchanged a small handful of coca leaves instead of shaking hands. Coca was a sign of the deep cultural connection among all Arhuaco and between the people and the earth. Javier told me that many Arhuaco had suffered loss of their coffee harvests and food crops as a result of the aerial coca eradication program. He described the high-pitched whine of the small planes as they sprayed toxic poisons on the coca, and how the clouds of murder drifted wherever the wind took them. He said that the Mamos were very upset over the spraying, which often killed plants and poisoned water at sacred sites as well as crop fields. Javier never mentioned that the spraying was funded by the U.S. government under Plan Colombia. I didn't know if he was being polite to a guest or simply didn't know the complexities of our government's War on Drugs. I didn't mention that some organic farms in Colombia were losing their certification because the aerial sprays drifted onto their coffee plots. Many of these were farms that had given up coca for coffee and other crops to break away from the cycle of violence and ecological damage related to cocaine production. I stroked the leaves of one plant. They were firm and deep green. The stems were thick and flexible, apparently very healthy. But to Javier's knowing eye, there was a problem.

"The flowering comes too early and drops off before the berries can take hold. My harvest has been going down steadily over the last five years. The rains come too fast and not when they are supposed to." Javier turned over a leaf to reveal a small brown patch of *royo* (bacterial rust). "The rust is stronger, too." This was one strange impact of global warming: the toxics in plants were getting more concentrated, and diseases were getting stronger and harder to control. The studies I had read concerned poison ivy, but it was clear that this subtle change was occurring in other chemical and bacterial forms that had been kept in check by cold nights and shorter growing seasons.

"Is this why the quality is different this year?" I asked, hoping to clear up this problem.

"*No, señor*, the yields are down but the quality is the same. We pick out the malformed beans before we send them to the processor in Valledupar. We are very proud of our coffee."

We visited farms further up the mountain, hearing the same stories about the impact of weather changes on the coffee and other crops. The farmers were confused and frustrated about these changes that they could not control or manage. One group working a field together welcomed me from a distance in that good old Elder Brother way.

"*Beca na zoyano*!? Where do you think you're going? Go away!"

I took their picture just to piss them off. It was childish, but it felt good.

We made it down the mountain and back to Valledupar by late afternoon, just in time to visit Coopcafenor, the cooperatively owned processor that milled, graded, and bagged the Café Tiwun for export. The manager, Pedro Plata, was very open and friendly. He showed me the processing plant and explained all the record keeping. Both the handwritten and computer records clearly demonstrated that the farmers were receiving the money they should and that the beans were handled professionally. I traced one shipment from a farmer in Nabusimake all the way through the Cooperative Coffee contract from the previous season. We talked about the problem of uneven samples this year. Pedro was perplexed. Nothing had changed in their system since the last year. As we dug deeper into the books together I asked him about the quality differences between the lower- and higher-altitude farms. He said that he was aware of changes in quality over the past few years, especially with the lower farms, but didn't know if it was due to the changing weather. I asked him how they segregated the coffee for export. Was it by altitude or by local region? Pedro said they mixed it all together. It was all Café Tiwun.

"That's it!" I shouted. "That's why the samples were so different. The coffee we got last year probably came from different farmers than the ones who grew the samples this year." I explained that it was really important for them to segregate coffee by altitude and region if they wanted to have a distinct coffee in the marketplace. That way a buyer could be guaranteed a similar taste and quality profile each year, instead of the luck of the draw that happened when everything was mixed together. That is what differentiates specialty coffee from whatever comes out of a supermarket can. Pedro and Nelson were very excited. The project was only two years old and had never received this kind of input. They were taking the first steps to ensure that Café Tiwun would bring real money consistently back to the Arhuaco community. I asked if we could get samples from different regions and altitudes and choose which one we liked the most.

"*Seguro!* Sure!" Pedro replied with glee. "We can do that for you and we can do that for everybody! Now let's go celebrate with a beer and some Vallenato music!"

By the time we showed up at Casa Indigena early the next morning the room was full and buzzing. Apparently the word had gotten back to the CIT leadership that my visit was a success. We had figured out a way to improve their coffee project and shown knowledge of and respect for their culture (except for that last photo op). They were the same men as at the first meeting, but the atmosphere was totally different. We had further deep conversations about coffee, culture, and global warming. We talked about how they would use the $1,100 profit share I had for them from our last year's sales. In keeping with the Arhuaco ethos, they split it between the spiritual (buy more land) and the material (begin to build their own processing plant). Jeremias and Julio unrolled that large piece of paper and began to draw symbols and animals around the geography of the Sierra Nevada. They began to explain the Law of Origin to the Younger Brother. They had welcomed me in.

Back in Bogotá, the Mamo beckoned me to enter and sit in his small room. He was ready to help me heal the tear in my heart from the death of Ingrid in Colombia. We sat together on the mat on the floor of his tiny room. He took out a piece of paper with her name on it. In his other hand, the Mamo held a small glass vial of gold dust.

"Gold from the Sierra Nevada has always been a medium between the worlds for us," he said softly. "Close your eyes and see your friend, find peace with her." He began a low, murmured chant. It was soothing to me as tears flowed freely. The Mamo opened the vial and poured a small amount of the precious dust into my hand. "Blow it into the air. Release your fear and your pain. You will be at peace with this land. You will be at peace within yourself."

I prayed that peace would come to the Arhuaco and their sacred mountains, as well.

CIT and Caja Herramientas representatives came to the 2007 SCAA trade show and conference for the first time. Their increased attention to quality has resulted in over fourteen containers of coffee—well over half a million pounds—being sold this year. The Mamos and their advocates, such as Moises and Wilber, continue to roam the world, trying to enlighten the Younger Brothers as to the profound danger we are in as a result of global warming and other grievous injuries to the Mother. Many more people are listening.

PART THREE

CENTRAL AMERICA

5
—

The Flickering Candle of Freedom

GUATEMALA, 1993

The crushing grip of General Rios-Montt had been eased. The army had pulled back to its heavily fortified bases. The guerillas had laid down their arms, or at least hidden them in the thickly forested countryside. The appalling massacre of whole villages had ceased. In the world markets, the price of green coffee had risen to almost a dollar a pound—high enough to keep food on the tables of the coffee farmers and keep the bankers from repossessing their lands. The whole country seemed to emit a collective sigh as "the dark times" began to fade.

It was time for a new beginning. Time for a national election, in which even the guerillas urged participation. The first free and open election since 1954, when the democratically elected Jacobo Arbenz was overthrown by the CIA, big business, and large landowners pissed off at Arbenz's redistribution of coffee and other agricultural land to peasants.

International election observers from around the globe were flooding

Guatemala City ("Guate" to the locals, pronounced "GUATay"). Rigoberta Menchu, the gentle yet tenacious advocate of Guatemalan indigenous rights and Nobel Peace Prize laureate, asked me to observe and help ensure a fair election. I had been part of the organizing committee that had brought Rigoberta to the United States in 1980, when she was a young, timid activist. Being an openhearted guy, I stepped up and gave her a big hug and a kiss on the cheek, much to the shock of Rigoberta and the chagrin of the rest of the group.

"And that's the last time I let him kiss me," she says whenever the story is told.

Since I had worked for many years in the indigenous coffee communities around Lake Atitlán, and because I was a lawyer, Rigoberta felt I would do a good job.

"We need you to be the eyes of the indigenous peoples in that region," she said, adding with a twinkle, "just keep your eyes on the voting, not on the women."

According to the rules, all electioneering was to be suspended during the week before the election. This was meant to envelop the process in peace and dignity and relieve some of the tension surrounding this historic event. But when I landed in Guate five days before the vote the streets were awash in rallies and marches. The flags, banners, and pamphlets of the parties were piled like snowdrifts against the buildings and curbs. It was a tide of participation that no regulations would stem.

I checked in at the office of CUC (United Peasants Committee), a small but powerful indigenous organization allied with the left and probably the guerillas. CUC was my official sponsor. The baleful brown eyes of Che and Jesus stared down at me from opposite walls as I waited in the anteroom. Roberta, the energetic head of the organization, greeted me. Her traditional *traje* (clothing), a red and blue woven *huipil* (blouse) and black *cortes* (skirt), made a strong statement as she accompanied me to register as an observer at the modern downtown office of the Ombudsman for Human Rights. Our timing was good; the ombudsman was wounded the next day by right-wing gunmen.

Pressing my new credentials into my hand, Roberta wished me luck in Solola, the department capital for the Atitlán region where I would

Above: Young nomadic herder in Ethiopia shows the fresh milk she will sell to the local coffee shops that dot the most remote villages. Right: Dean, with Oromo elder, takes the first cup in the ritual blessing of the new water supply system at the Haro cooperative in Jimma, Ethiopia.

The well-dressed Minister discusses the plight of Kenyan farmers over a cup of coffee with Kenya Fair Traders representatives…

…while children of impoverished Kenyan farmers pick coffee instead of going to school.

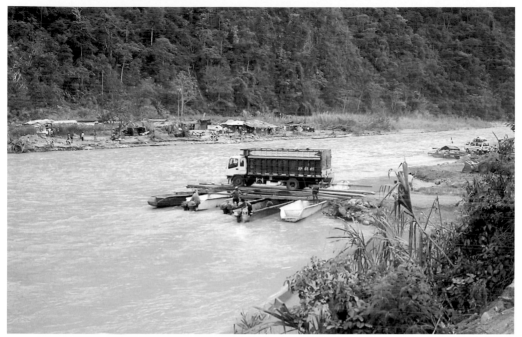

Peruvian engineering at work! Farmers float coffee trucks across a swollen river with logs and motorized canoes.

Ashaninkas women in Peru prepare a feast of Amazonian fruits, vegetables, and assorted forest creatures.

The first credit Julia has ever received. Julia affixes her thumbprint on her loan agreement from the new women's bank we started with Guatemalan women around Lake Atitlan.

Dean observes indigenous farmer voting in first free election in Guatemala in four decades. Colored ballots for different parties help illiterate voters make their choice.

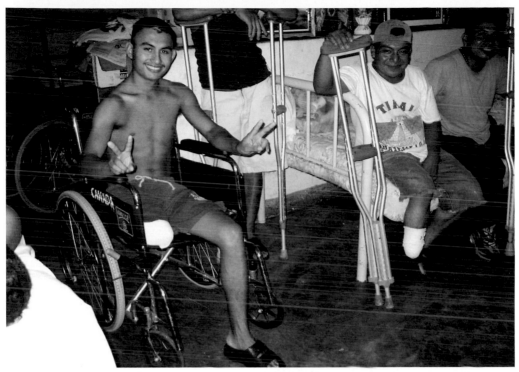

Death Train victims Wilmer, the coffee farmer from Honduras, and Manolo, the shoemaker from Guatemala, hope for a better future.

Maria Magdelena in her new home and store, reunited with her kids, after we successfully repatriated her to El Salvador.

The mystical painting on the door of the Zapatista headquarters in Oventic, Chiapas, representing the connection of indigenous peoples and the Earth, as well as noting that corn originated in this region.

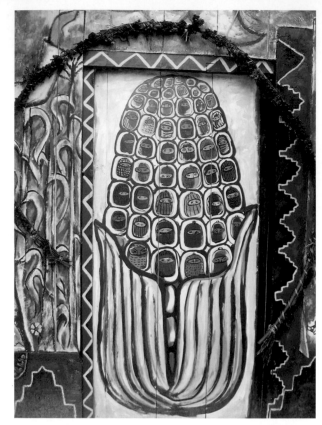

Arhuako leader Jeremias explains the Law of Origin, the indigenous worldview, and the significance of the Sierra Nevada in Colombia.

Left: Paman Dean takes a munch break from fertilizing and weeding the Sumatran coffee fields.
Above: Loading coffee on the in-famous Bugi schooners in Jakarta. These hundred-foot ships are built without power tools on the beaches of remote islands.

The Gayo widows, whose farmer husbands were killed in the civil war in Aceh and North Sumatra.

Java jivin' with the Asaro Mudmen in Simbu Province, Papua New Guinea.

This simple hand depulper immediately increased the quality and value of the coffee produced by these indigenous PNG farmers.

be working. We had so much to talk about, but Roberta had to balance the needs of her people with the needs of her ten-month-old daughter, swaddled in the black-and-red-checkered *rebozo* (shawl) slung across her breasts and left shoulder. To the knowing eye, the colors and small patterns of her *traje* would mark her as coming from Chimaltenango, high in the mountains beyond Guate. The army had used indigenous designs as a tracking mechanism—they knew what patterns belonged where. They assumed that a Chimaltenango or Huehuetenango pattern outside of those geographic areas meant a guerilla messenger, or worse. The wrong pattern presupposed wrongdoing, and thousands of indigenous men and women had "disappeared" during the dark times for nothing more than this. No questions asked, no excuses heard.

Roberta and the CUC were known quantities to the government. I wondered who was watching her. She left me at a café across from the ombudsman's office and disappeared behind a large banner in a street march. She knew how to get lost in a crowd quickly. The café was full of foreign election observers proudly displaying their blue armbands. There were representatives of international labor unions and teachers organizations, United Nations staff, Swiss parliamentarians, and countless human rights and democracy NGOs (nongovernmental organizations) workers enjoying their last latte before heading off to the hinterlands. I sat with a small Swiss delegation—a lawyer and two labor leaders. They had already been in Guatemala for two weeks watching the electoral process and had mixed reviews. They noted the enthusiasm and hope felt by the population in general but had observed some ominous signs.

"In Santa Lucia the army was right in the middle of the town," noted Charles, one of the union men. "They are supposed to be in their garrison locked away from the voters. But there they were, guns and all. And a bunch of ex-military commissioners—the ones that were dismissed for violence and corruption—were right there with them."

"It sends a clear message of intimidation to the people," observed Brigitte, the lawyer. She took a sip of coffee and added thoughtfully, "But you know, there have been so many decades of harassment and intimidation, even where people weren't being murdered. It would be unrealistic to think it would just stop because of the election rules."

When they heard that I worked in coffee regions they described their meeting with some coffee workers from Huehuetenango. The farmers told them that they couldn't vote without forgoing two days' pay, plus having to pay for food, transportation, and lodging to vote. It wasn't worth it.

Bernard, the other union man, stated, "And then there's the kidnapping of Rigoberta Menchu's two-year-old nephew yesterday. What a mess, eh?"

"What?" I exploded. "What happened?"

"Three men with guns grabbed the boy from his mother's arms right outside of Rigoberta's house. They must have been waiting." Bernard paused for a minute. "There is such a culture of violence here. What do these people have to go through to find some peace? I hope these elections begin to crack things a little."

At five AM I stumbled through the public bus terminal. I wanted to visit the coffee farmers of Lake Atitlán before reporting to Solola. I had worked with these Tzutujil people around the lake since the late 1980s, creating women's banks and health projects through Coffee Kids, the nonprofit development group I had cofounded. We were introduced to the area by Garth Smith, an intrepid Javatrekker who owned Organic Products Trading Company (OPTCO). Garth didn't just buy coffee from these folks. He worked to help them organize, to increase the quality of their harvesting and processing, and to get their coffee certified organic.

I boarded the bus to Los Encuentros (the Meeting Places), a dusty commercial intersection parading as a village, where the major roads of the country come together. From there I could get a local bus to the lake. Within an hour of leaving Guate, the sun was rising over the huge and fertile valleys that allow passage between the country's massive mountain ranges. The valleys were bursting with agricultural abundance. Shocks of yellow corn, deep blue broccoli, and white cauliflower spread across the fields with a dozen other colorful crops. It was a deceptive landscape. These exquisite crops were grown for export by poorly paid workers who often suffered from malnutrition. This was the Valley of the Jolly Green Giants, the huge multinational food processors that controlled the land. Dole, Del Monte, Chiquita, and Daishowa from Japan grow snow peas, broccoli, cauliflower, melons, cut flowers, and more, in what Chilean poet Pablo Neruda described as "agro-imperialism."

I had decided to take a detour to San Lucas Toliman on the southern end of the lake on my journey to Santiago Atitlán. San Lucas is where we had set up our first village banks with Coffee Kids. It was also where I had met my first coffee farmers, visiting several small, poor plantations on that part of the lake. I saw the absolute squalor of the workers' housing—tin shacks without water, electricity, or windows. There was no schooling for the workers' kids, so there was no future for them beyond working the coffee fields next to their aging parents. The workers taught me the owners' "tricks" to keep from paying even the meager wages required by law. The owners forced the workers to spend sixty hours in the field but paid for only forty. The sad housing and pitiful field lunches were taken out of their pay. They were fired before working long enough to be considered more than "seasonal workers" with few legal rights. Years later, I would understand the bitter irony of international certification groups that claimed that "abiding by national labor laws" was sufficient to declare a plantation as treating workers "fairly."

It was clear to me that these farm owners wanted Coffee Kids to feed, house, and educate "their" workers so that they wouldn't have to. When I returned to the States I told the folks at Coffee Kids that this was not development. Instead, it was supporting and maintaining the very abusive structures we'd hoped to alleviate. I also determined that if I ever roasted or imported coffee, I would buy beans only from small farms and cooperatives, where the people had some possibility of bettering their own lives.

The bus to San Lucas Toliman was a recycled yellow school bus from El Norte (the United States); the words "Northern Valley Regional School System" were still visible through the thin yellow repainting. I had seen our old yellers throughout Latin America. Discarded in the States, they were born again as transportation for churches and schools, their origins always readable through the unprimed paint-overs.

There was no back door on the bus, and most of the seats were no longer bolted to the floor. Diesel fumes whiplashed into the open rear. Half a dozen kids hung out the doorless back, laughing at the jolt of each gear change. We passed the main army base for the region. The gatehouse was a bizarre structure, a one-story-high pair of army boots topped by a giant helmet. It would have been a cartoonish site but for the chilling message it sent: "We see you and we crush you. We cannot be stopped."

The bus sputtered and chugged its way along the mountain roads toward the lake, depositing metal-flecked gear grindings along the roadsides. As we topped one long slope the lake came into view. Lake Atitlán is stunning. In fact, Ernest Hemingway, when taking a breather from fishing and booze, stated during a visit that "Lake Atitlán is the most beautiful lake in the world." It is huge for a mountain lake, seven miles long by three miles wide. The southern shore of the lake is dominated by the three enormous volcanoes El Toliman, Atitlán, and San Pedro, which rocket ten thousand feet above sea level. The volcanoes provide fertile slopes for great coffee, but several three-thousand-foot sheer faces await the unwary or the undercaffeinated. The lake is actually the remnant crater of an extinct volcano that covered the entire region and blew its massive cone skyward some eighty-five thousand years ago.

There are only eight settlements of varying sizes around the lake. From this high vantage point, eight distinct plumes of pollution emanate from the towns into the lake. From the smaller towns the light brown of soil erosion and some agrochemical runoff seeps out. From Santiago Atitlán and Panajachel ("Pana"), the two largest towns that face each other across the lake, the thicker dark brown of sewage oozes and spreads from their shores. The lake looks a lot prettier from down below. All but Pana are overwhelmingly indigenous, while Pana is the international traveler and tourist mecca of the region. Frankly, once in Pana is enough, and I would pass through later, on my way from Santiago Atitlán to Solola.

The bus roared away, leaving me alone on the outskirts of San Lucas Toliman. I walked around a bit as more memories flooded in. This was the first place where I had spent significant time in the homes of traditional Mayan peoples. It is where I experienced the heavy smoke of dung and firewood stoves in their adobe houses. The smoke attacks the eyes of the women while they prepare the meals, eventually causing blindness for many. It was here that I learned the lesson that, even in a small town where everybody is related by blood and custom, different groups can have profoundly different priorities concerning community development. The organization that goes into a village with a preset plan and few options will not leave a sustainable legacy. Their work must be rooted in the express needs and dreams of the people, not the funding priorities of the donor or the developmental flavor of the month.

It was early afternoon, time to move on to Santiago. The road from San Lucas to Santiago was a long and winding dirt thoroughfare—and incredibly dangerous. The only safe route to Santiago was by boat across the lake from the other towns. Since I had chosen this trip down memory lane to San Lucas I had placed myself in a needless predicament. Because of the poor conditions, the road had to be traveled slowly, making escape from the many bandits who preyed on its travelers problematic. Like the locals, I waited at the edge of town for a newer-model pickup that looked like it might survive the journey. A bright red Toyota pickup came four-wheeling down the road. I flagged it down, and the driver agreed to take me to Santiago for five *quetzales*. There were stretches where the tall hardwoods created a thick green ceiling high above the road, blocking almost all of the light. We slowed to a crawl through one deeply rutted patch. Right in the middle, the driver stopped to light another cigarette. The silence outside the truck was eerie. Harry Potter wouldn't have stood a chance in this Dark Forest.

We emerged from the forest into the fields at the edge of Santiago Atitlán. Just ahead, five pickups blocked the road. Fifteen rough-looking Ladino men signaled us to stop. *Uh-oh*, I thought, *this is it.* They greeted the driver by name. I leaned out the window.

"Hey! What's going on?"

One of the men approached me. "Hello, mister! There were a couple of murders on the road yesterday. A tourist and her guide. Nobody's taking any chances. We were waiting for the first car to come through, then we'd know that the bandits were gone for a while and it was safe to travel. Thanks a lot!" The men piled into their trucks and sped away toward San Lucas. The driver turned to me and shrugged. We put the truck into gear and entered Santiago Atitlán.

The driver kindly took me close to Diego's small house. The steep slope and narrow alley to the house forced me to walk the last quarter mile. The one-story adobe house was typical Atiteco. A small front room served as a living room and meeting place with a few chairs. A doorway led to the kitchen and two bedrooms. A small courtyard with a papaya tree and a few scratching chickens shielded the bathroom and washing area. Diego's wife, Maria, greeted me at the door. She wore the traditional Atiteco white *huipil* with horizontal red stripes. Small roadrunners and plumed quetzals stood proudly between the stripes. The neck was brocaded with flowers. Maria had woven this on a backstrap loom, one end tied to a tree while the other looped around her hips on a leather strap. The beautiful blouse represented eighty hours of hard work and enormous pride. Maria sent one of the kids for a "Coca," as the ubiquitous soft drink is called here, and we sat together on the front step. She updated me on the progress of the women's bank in Santiago. Maria was the president. All of the women were wives of coffee farmers and each had started a small business with the loans from their village bank. Maria and four other women had pooled their loans to buy thread in bulk at a substantial savings. This allowed them to sell their weavings reasonably and bring needed income to the household. She proudly pointed upward at the new tin roof that her savings had purchased since my last visit. I asked her if there was any resentment among the men when women bring good money into the house. She laughed and said not at all, the families were strong here and everybody pulled together.

Diego arrived from the field wearing an incongruous, sweat-stained Budweiser T-shirt. We greeted each other with a traditional handshake and pat on the shoulder. The lengthening shade had dissipated the intense afternoon heat. Since our farmer meeting would be over dinner, we had time to visit the coffeelands high above town on the slopes of the Atitlán volcano. The altitude, along with the volcanic soil and the incredible husbandry of the farmers, accounts for the unique taste and high quality of the coffee from this region.

The road became less passable as we rode higher. Along the margins, men and women carried large sacks of red coffee cherries on their backs, supported by straps across their foreheads. Almost all of the people wore traditional *traje*. Occasionally, kids would lead a donkey down the road with four or six sacks balanced on its back. The farmers would carry these sacks for as much as three hours to reach a local weighing station for their group. Here they would get a receipt for the weight of the cherries. They would present the receipt for a payment of two or three cents per pound at their group office in town. This was an advance against the ultimate sale of the processed beans. The harvest had not started in earnest, so these cherries would be from the lowest altitudes and would not be the highest quality.

We stopped at one of the weighing stations to talk to Marcos, a member of the board of directors. Marcos backed one of the farmers up to a hanging scale. He put a big hook through the sack and the farmer loosened his headstrap. The sack hung suspended while Marcos took down the weight from a rusting spring dial. No thumbs here. Diego and I loaded this and six other sacks into the pickup and drove on.

We passed the newly rented hillside and watched a dozen farmers digging out weeds and clearing small patches among some ancient hardwoods. Other farmers were planting bananas and papayas to give the young coffee plants needed shade. They planted pumpkins, beans, and squash to fix nitrogen into the soil around their coffee plants and to supplement their tables or income. Others carefully placed the seedlings into their holes, composting deeply with rotted manure, leaves, and grass clippings.

We drove on to the established plots further up. Here the broad-leaved hardwoods stood forty feet tall, dwarfing the human-sized mature coffee plants. Their leaves floated down like paper plates, covering the soil against weed invasion and providing nutrition as they decomposed. Diego looked up at the sound of a Baltimore oriole.

"Listen, Dean." He strained his eyes to find the bird. "There he is! That one comes from your part of the world. He's a typical tourist. He flies down here, eats our food, enjoys our land, and shits on us." Diego laughed at his own joke.

"Did you hear about the new Smithsonian program to certify farms as migratory bird habitat?" I asked.

"Yeah, one of those guys came down here to tell us about the birds we've been living with all of our lives. We know all that stuff and we told him some things. But we're not gonna pay money to that museum to tell the world what we already know."

"Well, I think the broker or importer pays the licensing fee, not the farmer."

Diego gave me a "don't-you-know-anything" look. "Dean, you know if the importer has to pay something extra, he figures out a way to pass it on to us."

"Diego, not all the brokers and importers are like that."

He laughed. "No, just nine out of ten." We talked about the brokers and importers who came down here, who was up-front and who was ripping them off. Always the same players.

I tried to be cheerful. "Well, my friend, we're working on that. Someday things will change."

Diego smiled ruefully. "I know. I just hope that day comes while I'm still around. I'd really like to see it."

We walked the plot for a while, looking at the health of the plants, noticing the small patches of *royo* (bacterial rust) on the underside of a leaf here and there. Although *royo* is the parasitic enemy of coffee, a healthy organic plot can keep it under control. It was a remarkable patch of earth. These farmers were truly stewards, balancing their need to make a living with a deep knowledge of the needs of a healthy ecosystem.

Diego noticed that the sun had dropped below a crest of hill. "Time to go. We've got to meet the farmers and these roads aren't safe after dark." On the way down the mountainside we dropped the sacks at the *beneficio* (processing plant). Here the cherries would be soaked, stripped of their fleshy fruit, and dried in the sun until all that remained was the *pergamino*, two coffee beans nestled together and surrounded by a thin parchment. The *pergamino* would be shipped to a mill, the parchment stripped off, and the beans cleaned, graded, and bagged for export.

By the time we returned to Diego's, most of the board and many of the members were there. Sprinkled about the crowd of twenty red woven shirts were a handful of freshly scrubbed Dean's Beans T-shirts. My cartoonish face beamed out of the logo. Even Diego had swapped his Budweiser shirt in my honor. At first I was a little embarrassed by the gesture, but then I remembered that the other guy on the T-shirt with me was one of them, and that the mountains in the background were Atitlán. To the farmers, wearing the shirt was an act of solidarity.

The dinner was a typical Atiteco spread of tortillas, beans, and chicken. A squash, pumpkin, and onion dish graced the table, all of the ingredients picked fresh that day. The only drinks were warm Cokes, Sprites, and Fantas, not a Pepsi to be seen. For dessert, some cake, an amorphous sweet corn dish, and two packages of Twinkies.

After prayers in Spanish and Tzutujil, Diego, Maria, a few farmers, and I made opening speeches. I always soften the crowd with the Tzutujil greeting "*Utza quesh!*" (Welcome!), but I have to say it three or four times before the farmers realize that I am speaking their language. It's not just that my pronunciation stinks, but they are not used to hearing their language come out of a white face. Not many people speak Tzutujil beyond this side of the lake. In fact, more people ride the New York subway on a Monday morning than speak Tzutujil. I ended my speech with the traditional closing *"Maltiosh a Dioss!"* (Thanks be to God!), pointing to the heavens to get this one across.

As I gave the speech in Spanish I had to wait and let Maria translate to Tzutujil every so often, as few of the farmers spoke the national language. Most of my jokes fell flat given the translation lag time and the cultural differences. But there was no misunderstanding when I talked about the election. Usually, indigenous crowds don't go in for the question-and-answer format with foreigners, sitting instead in polite silence. Yet this night was different. Lots of questions, lots of concerns. Do we have to pay to vote? Will they steal our ballots? Will they watch us and know who we vote for? This was a sadly realistic assessment given the climate of fear and suspicion that had permeated the land for decades. It was a prelude to the unspoken question: will we disappear after the election if we voted for the wrong candidate? Someone asked hopefully, "Can you arrest someone who bothers us?"

Reginaldo, a very funny guy, broke the tension in the room. "Hey, you gonna pay for us to get over to Solola and vote? It costs a lot of money and then we gotta have a big lunch and stay in a nice hotel!" Some people laughed; Diego seemed embarrassed; others looked at me expectantly. In fairness, it is not unusual for an organization that calls a meeting here to pay for food and transportation. I had done so on other visits when we had coffee or development to discuss. But that was ten or twenty people in Diego's house on their home turf, not three hundred with travel and per diems.

"You are such an idiot!" bellowed Reginaldo's wife, Gracia, as she whacked him on the head. "Mr. Dean is not here to feed your fat face. He is here for the election." She turned to me and pointed a muscular finger, greasy with the chicken fat from the paper plate on her lap. "You will be our eyes over there. You're gonna make sure everything is fair, right?" I felt the weight of their hopes, fears, and expectations.

After the meeting, Diego and I walked down to the Hotel Tzutujil. This is the high-end business traveler's hotel in Santiago Atitlán. Actually, it is the only hotel in town. Each small room has bare cinderblock walls and a lone naked light bulb suspended above the bed. The communal shower at the end of the hall has a "flip-on" (switch) for electric hot water on demand, taped haphazardly together about an inch from the watering-can spray head. Cold showers would do, thanks. I always take a high outside room with a balcony, as the slight breeze from the lake at night helps break the swelter and encourages the mosquitoes to take a break from the new ethnic cuisine now and then.

When he left, Diego patted my shoulder.

"Get a good night's sleep, my friend. Tomorrow we will visit Maximon. He knows that you are here and wants to help you with the election."

Down the block an Evangelical church had opened since my last visit. Holy rock and rollers jammed for Jesus on electric guitars 'til the break of day. By 5:15 AM I was ready to testify or kill. At the same time, the misty morning view of Lake Atitlán from my balcony was stunning.

Maximon is the syncretized saint who meshes the Mayan god Mam with the Catholic Saint Simon. His name combines "Simon" with *max*, the Mayan word for sacred tobacco. Tobacco is used throughout the indigenous world to open a channel between earthly existence and the realm of the spirits. Syncretization is a strange accommodation. It allows colonized peoples to continue their own religious beliefs and practices by wrapping them in the cloak of the colonizer's religion. At the same time, it affords the colonizer a foothold in the spirit of the community. In Brazil the lusty, busty Yemanja, goddess of the rivers and seas, morphs into the Virgin Mary in many churches. In Wiccan Europe, syncretization gave the nascent Church a chance to overlay its festivals of Christmas and Easter onto earlier ritual celebrations of seasonal change. Whether syncretization is the natural outcome of cultural coexistence or an early example of globalization is debatable, but few major religions have been untouched by the phenomenon.

We approached the house of Andres, the *ak-jun* (priest) of Cofradia Santa Cruz (the Brotherhood of the Holy Cross). Since the sixteenth century, the brotherhood (it's all men) has been in charge of caring for the effigy of Maximon. Each year the Cofradia selects one of its own to be the *telinel* (dresser/attendant) to Maximon, to care for the Mam or the Old Man, as he is variously known, in his home. It is a great honor, but comes at a cost. The *telinel* is required to keep his home open for supplicants and visitors for a full year and must keep the house supplied with the candles, incense, tobacco, and alcohol that Maximon requires. Most often these are brought as offerings. However, it is the responsibility of the *telinel* to keep the house stocked, which can mean a considerable outlay for a poor villager.

The house was shrouded in strings of Christmas lights (the intermittent blinking ones), Guatemalan flags, three crucifixes, and little wooden Day of the Dead skeletons. I knew that this was a stage set for getting visitors into the right headspace, but it looked so damned tacky. It didn't help that of the four *ak-jun* on duty outside, two were sleeping or drunk.

Even though it was early morning, we couldn't enter the house because it was jammed with people. We sat on the bench outside. Eulelio, one of the *ak-jun*, told me that Maximon was helping a young man return to the community. It was Jorge, one of the farmer's sons. He had been forcibly taken into the army at age twelve and had participated in the massacre of an entire village.

Thankfully, those days were gone. All over Guatemala, communities were performing similar purifications for their returning sons, or mourning the ones who would never come back. Eulelio sighed deeply. "That boy's been gone a long time. The Mam will cleanse his soul and take away his shame. He'll come back to us whole."

After an hour or so the people filed out of the house. I nodded respectfully to Jorge's father, who had been at the meeting of coffee farmers the night before, as he walked by with his arm around his son. The young man was ashen and weak, but he looked relieved. Maximon had been there for him.

Eulelio told me to enter the house. Andres and three other *ak-jun* sat inside. The top half of the room was lost in an acrid fog of cigar smoke and incense. One *ak-jun* was standing and chanting. He looked like he was ascending into the heavens, as half his body was in the clouds. Andres stood and walked toward me, cutting a swirling pattern through the smoke. He greeted me with a firm handshake and a pat on the shoulder.

"Have you come to pay respect to the Old Man and seek his help in the election?"

I shook the smoke and judgment from my head. "Yes. Diego told me it was time to visit Maximon."

"You must know the Mam to see into our souls if you wish to help the people here. You know the Mam was here long before Christ came, even though they are brothers? Come, sit and let me tell you."

Andres described Maximon as the "spiritual heartbeat of our people." "He survived the Mexican invasion, he survived the old Christians and the new ones"—the Catholics and the Evangelicals—"but he has had to change, sometimes to hide. They tried to kill him many times, but he can't be stamped out like a bug, you know?"

I tried to follow him. "You mean they tried to kill him by preventing worship?"

"Oh sure," Andres replied, "but sometimes they really tried to kill him. When I was younger a crazy priest tried to burn the Mam like he was some witch. We chased the guy away but he came back with a gun. We wrestled with him and the gun fell down. Some bullets spilled out of that old revolver, and we keep one of them up there with the Old Man. The Mam took the power of the bullets for himself." The others chuckled and nodded.

"But you know that son of a bitch came back and snuck into the *ak-jun's* house and chopped off the Mam's head. Then he ran away across the lake with it. They hid him in a museum in Europe. But the Mam came back. It took thirty-five years, but the Old Man's head came back here."

"So things have been okay since then?"

Andres sat back on the couch next to me and thought about it. "Well, there's been a lot of pressure on the Mam. When I was a kid the Mam was brought out as part of our Holy Week procession, and he sat up there right in between Mary and his brother Jesus in the Church. Then, during the bad years, the Catholics stopped the Old Man from entering the main part of the church and sitting with his family. Now he sits in a side room, and all of the other saints and holy things are taken out of the room first."

"Doesn't sound very respectful to me."

"Ahh, these things come and go. The most important thing is that the Mam is here with his people. He is here to give us his strength and guide us. Are you ready to see him now?"

"Sure, let me just sit here a minute and clear my head. I want to be fully present to receive his wisdom." I sat on the couch and took a long, slow breath. I began to understand the role of Maximon as a symbol of Mayan resistance as well as the representative of whatever spiritual path had its roots here. Jimenez, probably the oldest man, offered me a glass of rum to "cleanse" me for the visit. I hate the stuff unless it's in a tall glass with tropical fruit juice, ice, and maybe a little umbrella, but I wanted to respect the ritual. It burned so bad it must have killed every living organism in my system.

Andres gave a long prayer with one hand on my shoulder. He held some red nut beads and a piece of crystal in his other hand. He held the crystal against his forehead, then against mine as he concluded the prayer. He stood up and went to the far end of the room. He and another man pulled a rope attached to the ceiling and down came a folding ladder.

"Come on. The Mam is waiting for you."

Andres went ahead, then I climbed up. The low attic of the house was filled with religious icons, statues, cloth, and paintings. Candles burned in the four corners of the hot, musty room. Andres took the nearest candle and crawled across the room. He lit two more candles and an incense burner. As my eyes became used to the shadows and half-light, I saw that Andres was kneeling and chanting next to a prostrate figure. He beckoned me closer.

"Maximon welcomes you," he intoned. Andres lifted a bottle of rum and poured another glass. He drank it and poured another for me. I politely declined, telling Andres that I would rather sit respectfully than throw up on a deity.

"That's okay," Andres said thoughtfully. "You come to the Old Man with respect. That's the most important thing. Come closer. He won't bite you." He laughed, "But he might jump up and snatch your notebook!"

I crawled to the left of the supine saint. Maximon lay there, his wooden face wearing a slight grin that seemed to move with Andres's chants in the candle flicker. A big cigar stuck out of his mouth at a jaunty angle. The Mam wore a cowboy hat—no, he wore *five* cowboy hats. Andres drank more rum, his prayers ratcheting up in intensity. He stroked the Mam's face imploringly, he patted his shoulder empathetically. I saw Andres's shoulders jerk as he sobbed quietly. I noticed with a start that Maximon was only about three and a half feet tall. He had on a traditional Atiteco red shirt, and his neck and shoulders were covered with woven scarves and modern neckties. Out of this fabric sprawl leapt a Mickey Mouse tie, with the World's Most Famous Rodent and his sidekick Goofy smiling upward. On his legs, Maximon wasn't wearing the traditional white pants with woven bird patterns. Instead, he sported a new pair of blue jeans and a little pair of cowboy boots. I couldn't resist the impression that he was one of those evil dolls that comes alive in cheap slasher movies. The tie could have been an expensive and precious gift from a villager, or it could have been a playful gesture. After all, Maximon is known to have a great sense of humor.

"Dean," Andres interrupted my thoughts, "the Mam wants you to talk to him now. Tell him what you need. He can help you. Get closer so he can hear you. He's old and doesn't hear so good anymore."

I leaned forward. "Closer," implored Andres. My face was inches from that cigar. Maximon, Andres, Mickey, and Goofy waited.

Now, I am not a great person to judge the spiritual veracity of any group's practices or deities. Sometimes the pathway to my soul is so direct and searing that I have to turn away from the intensity; other times my spiritual channel is more clogged up than the toilet in a Montana bikers' bar on a Saturday night.

First, a little small talk. I asked Maximon about the harvest: would he ensure a good one for the people of the lake region? Then I moved on to the big issue—the election, about what I could do. Is my role merely to observe? Is my presence heartening to some who might otherwise be afraid? Is there something more proactive I could be doing? Whether I was talking to him or myself didn't matter; it felt good to process my own concerns. I really opened up to the Mam, and I waited. I looked expectantly at the ancient spirit. But all I saw before me was a Pinocchio-sized wooden dummy with funny clothes and too many hats.

"How was your visit?" Andres asked at the bottom of the ladder.

"I really appreciate the time Maximon gave me and I am honored to have met him. But to be honest with you, he didn't really speak to me."

Andres laughed. "What were you expecting? The Mam would jump up and dance for you? I told you, he's an old man. He doesn't do that very often anymore. And boy, is he tired from his work this morning. But he does what spirits do. He takes your prayers up into heaven and finds ways to answer them. So whatever you prayed for, know that the Old Man is up there working on it right now, or maybe he passed it off to some other saint up there. They all work together. Of course, you have to be sincere and ask for a reasonable thing, but then you make your prayer and let it go. Whether or not it is answered is up to him. But I can tell you this, if you don't ask for the help of the spirits your prayers can never be answered. You know what I mean?"

The election was the day after tomorrow. I needed to get to Solola and check in. I took the boat across to Pana. The small boat was filling fast with day-tripping tourists and travelers, returning to the safety of Pana with their swag. Huge backpacks on broad shoulders, fanny packs on broad fannies, and arms full of local paintings, clothing, hats, beadwork, and instruments made it feel more like the evacuation at Dunkirk than a sweet twilight ride across the placid lake. The boatman was charging thirty *quetzales* to cross, but he charged me eight. I looked at him quizzically.

"My sister is in your village bank," he said with a wink. "You get the local rate." Ah, the Good Karma discount.

Pana is an international tourist outpost in the wilds of indigenous territory. It was only a sleepy little hippie hangout in the sixties and seventies; now it hums with Internet cafés and vegan restaurants, discos and shops, hawkers and panhandlers. Andean flute bands, folksingers, and rockers vie for a brisk busker's trade at night. Pana reflects the commodification of indigenous culture, too. Woven traditional patterns and animals embrace water bottle sleeves, halter tops (nice peccaries!), and cell phone cases. This stuff can be bought in a swanky boutique or for less from a barefoot, snot-nosed eight-year-old on the street. For the less adventurous, faux Mayan prints are available on Western-style shirts and dresses. Many are made in China as part of globalization's dive to the bottom of the labor pool.

A yellow school bus (Evanston School District) juggled me over to Solola in twenty minutes. Solola is a bustling town of fifty thousand souls, 90 percent of whom are indigenous Cakchiquel. The streets are littered with discarded newspapers, food, and plastic bags. Diesel fumes laden with dirt swirl down many streets. At the same time, there are many small parks, a very active weekly regional market where almost all of the buyers and sellers wear traditional clothing, and a thousand small businesses that cater to local needs, not tourist whims.

I walked back to the town square and took a room at a quiet, one-story boardinghouse. It had an inner courtyard, beautiful plantings, and wiring that didn't threaten my immediate execution. After a glass of Chilean wine at the bar across the street, I was out like a light.

It was easy to get up in the morning, as the very air seemed to buzz with excitement around the election. Actually, it was the buzz of the flies on the garbage in the alley outside my window, but the effect was the same. I was the last observer to arrive at the municipal building, although the Guatemalans were nowhere in sight. A contingent of observers from Global Exchange (GX) in San Francisco were gathered around a table in animated analysis of a town map. Across the room, a French couple lounged in chairs, blowing smoke rings that seemed to spell "screw you." The man was unshaven and, if the statistics are accurate, hadn't changed his underwear in five days. The woman had that long, languid look of French *femme* travelers everywhere. She wore khaki shorts, a black camisol, and a slight smile. Frankly, they were drop-dead gorgeous. The lone Dutchman, Jan, was tall and thin and sported a bit of a Mohawk (or did he have a bad case of pillow hair?). He was walking around the room energetically, reading everything on the walls and desktops.

It dawned on me that this was it—the whole observer contingent. No international labor groups, Nordic female lawyers, or official U.N. delegations for dusty little Solola. Just our motley, good-hearted crew.

Gregorio, a local artist who was the head of the Electoral Commission for Solola, marched in with four other well-dressed Guatemalans, three men and a woman. All were Ladino. He apologized for his lateness and the meeting began. We took turns introducing ourselves. Many of the GX'ers had previous observer experience in Nicaragua and were raring to go. The seventy-year-old couple was from Minnesota, active in Latin American solidarity work through the Lutheran church. Two Quakers and four plain vanilla activists rounded out their contingent. Jan was a first-timer in Guatemala and was very excited to talk to the voters, especially "the Indians." Jean and Adrienne were from Paris. He had done this many times in many places.

"She is with me" was the extent of Jean's introduction of Adrienne. I was the lawyer/coffee roaster who had been asked to observe by the international indigenous rights community. The Ladina woman looked at me suspiciously, probably wondering what mischief I was up to with the natives.

Gregorio introduced the other commissioners and gave a brief speech of appreciation, and we plunged into the mechanics of election observation. "Remember, you are here to observe, not advocate," Gregorio said sternly (the Ladina gave a pursed-mouth glance my way). "You can document but not interfere with anything you see. We expect copies of any formal reports you produce."

We went over the map of Solola, identifying the ten polling stations throughout the town. We decided to rotate through the locations to give us all an occasional break and to cover the terrain. After all, it wasn't just Solola voting, it was all of the outlying towns throughout the department. We were to use public telephones to keep in touch. Here were the numbers of the polling stations, the Electoral Commission—and the police.

"I won't have any problems," Jean stated smugly, his feet on a desk. He pulled at his Galouise from a long arm that wrapped around Adrienne's slender neck and back to his mouth. "I have done this all before."

"But what if I have more questions?" asked Jan in a slight panic.

The commissioners took us around to the polling stations and to the headquarters of the six major parties. PAN (National Advancement Party) was the neo-liberal party of the modern businesspeople. They had a swank office in the newest building on the main square. The FRG (Republican Front) was on the opposite side of the square. This was the party of the deposed dictator, Rios-Montt, and obviously had plenty of money behind it judging from the bank of faxes and telephones in the office. These two representatives of money, power, and oligopoly seemed to square off against each other, as the indigenous presence (which had never voted before en masse) swirled around them. All of the other parties were housed in traditional, one-story adobe houses far from the city center. Each house was aging and weathered, but freshly painted with a large party logo. They were also well guarded by armed men from the left or right, depending on party affiliation. The AN (National Alliance) office was empty, which seemed to reflect the internal divisions of this coalition of right-wing and right-moderate groups. The UD (Democratic Union), a moderate-left group, had a lot of literature espousing its commitment to governance "by the poor, for the poor," but the office was inhabited only by one poor man during our visit. He was very nervous, and I got the impression that maybe he had snuck in the back door to rob the place seconds before we had arrived.

When we arrived at the one-room building of the FDNG (National Democratic Front) the place was filled inside and out with indigenous men and women. They were organizing information kits, making armbands, and preparing tortillas and beans on a small charcoal stove in the courtyard. The polls showed the FDNG in last place, but the energy and organization of the party portended greater support. We introduced ourselves as we had done at all party headquarters. I could see the shift of attention in the room when I mentioned that I was there specifically to ensure indigenous rights at the polling places. They asked me many questions about my background, who I had worked with at the United Nations, in other countries, and in Santiago Atitlán. I mentioned my visit to Maximon. Hiderico, the office manager, seemed impressed. Although he had met coffee buyers before, he had never met a gringo who had spent time with the Mam.

As we left, Jan turned to me in exasperation. "Why did they ask you all the questions?" I told him that maybe they felt more comfortable with me because I am the same height as they are, and he was so tall. Jan thought about that.

"Jah, maybe I should slouch a little bit."

After a very long hot day of hoofing it all over Solola, we returned to our hotels. Gregorio wished us a good evening and said we should reconvene at 5 AM so that we could be at our polls before they opened at 6.

I had just dozed off, *Journey to Ixtlan* open and resting across my nose, when I heard people outside my door speaking in Cakchiquel, then a polite knock. Hiderico and four other men from the FDNG crowded my doorway. He stepped forward with his white hat gripped to his chest.

"Please, sir, we are having a dinner tonight to prepare for the election. We would like you to come."

"Wow, my friends, this is an honor. But I can't show favoritism. I'm not sure I should go." I really wanted to, but I was very aware of the conflict.

Hiderico smiled shyly. "Well, it is true that we are all members of FDNG, but this is not a party dinner. It is a ceremony to pray for peace and reconciliation. Many of our brothers and sisters will vote for other parties, and they will be included in our prayers."

He looked at his four companions. "This will be the first time any of us has voted at all. There is fear about this. We are asking for strength and protection."

The integrity and hopefulness in those faces brought an unexpected lump to my throat. I nodded and smiled. "Okay, my friends, let's go."

We left the hotel and crossed the square. We wove our way through the busy market, emerging into an area where the cobblestones and hardpack of the streets gave way to rutted dirt roads. The houses were one-story adobe or daub-and-wattle with the building sticks exposed. Some were painted, some were earthen.

I could hear voices raised in song a few blocks away. The deep call of the *tun*, a local drum made from a hollow log, pulsed the night air. The twilight had disappeared by the time we arrived at the little community center. The usual three or four "guards" slouched on benches outside and nodded to us as we approached. The guard nearest the door stood up and smiled, his two front teeth outlined in gold. "*Señor* Observador, please enter." As we crossed the threshold, a hundred brown eyes turned my way and I could hear the whisper "Observador."

Although only two naked light bulbs suspended from the ceiling illuminated the thirty- by forty-foot room, the place was absolutely on fire from the hundreds of black and purple candles that lined the walls. Hiderico told me that these were especially powerful, as they were made from the honeycombs of wild bees. The long table in the center of the room was adorned with a riot of bougainvilleas, orchids, and a host of perennials I could not recognize. Corn, tobacco, dried fish, breads, black pepper, and coffee beans lay as offerings. Thick, acrid incense obscured the ceiling, creating halos around the light bulbs and opening the path for prayer (or, in my case, making it difficult to breathe).

We sat on benches along the walls. I was careful not to lean too far back for fear of setting my hair on fire. At the far end of the crowded room, three older *ak-jun* quieted the singing. They began to implore the spirits to come join the feast and hear the prayers of the people. They called them by name. Jesus, Joseph, Mary, George, Hunab Ku and the Bacab (the creator and his sons), Yumil Kaxob (the maize god), and, of course, St. Simon Maximon. The oldest man began a long chant. Most of the crowd murmured along.

Hiderico whispered to me, "He says we are coming out of the dark times. It is the turning time when the light will come back. He says we must take in this light and fill the world with it or the darkness will return."

"How long will the light last?" I asked, thinking that this sounded like the Eastern concept of light and dark, good and evil in constant tension, each taking its turn at the wheel.

"Well, maybe a hundred years, maybe a thousand. Maybe the light won't return just yet." Hiderico sighed. "We've had a lot of false starts."

The three priests walked around the room, leading a call-and-response chant. They stopped in front of me and one of the younger priests pointed and spoke.

"We have a friend here who was sent by the spirits to help us!"

Uh-oh, I thought, *this is a pretty heavy responsibility to lay on me. I'm just here to be an observer.* People smiled and some clapped. The other young priest had taken a big swig of rum. He walked up to me and put his hand on my shoulder. I looked up at him and smiled. Suddenly, he spit out the rum, drenching me from head to foot. More applause and smiles. I had been cleansed for the work ahead.

On my way back to the hotel I passed a small coffee shop on the square. Jean and Adrienne were seated outside. Jean looked me over and sniffed. "You have been out drinking? You smell like hell."

At 5 AM we assembled sleepily at the Town Hall. We wished each other luck and headed to our assigned posts. My first polling station was inside a huge gymnasium. A marimba band tapped out an upbeat tune on the front steps. The lines of hopeful voters wound their way for blocks outside. They snaked through the big entrance and in a swirling pattern around the gym. Each of the lines ended at a table, where election officials checked national identity cards. The voters were given their ballots and directed to little cubicles to mark their choices. The candidates were organized by party on the ballot. Each party was identified by its chosen logo and a separate color. This was a creative and fair way to deal with the low literacy rate among rural Guatemalans (only 20 percent of rural women can read). After marking their ballots, the voters went to another table and put their votes in a clear plastic garbage bag under the watchful eyes of the election monitors. After voting, people sat in the bleachers or went outside and peered in the windows, content to spend their day watching other people vote for the first time.

I walked along the lines, my blue *observador* armband in clear contrast to my white shirt. Many people nodded. The whole thing seemed straightforward and fair. I chatted easily with the people in the bleachers, while children in *traje* ran around the gym using the lines for a Mayan version of hide-and-seek.

At 10 AM the word came to move to the next station. I passed some GX'ers in the street. They reported that things were going smoothly. But before reaching the next station, I was accosted by some very agitated FDNG supporters.

"*Señor* Observador, you must come!"

We walked quickly down the block. As I turned the corner, four big trucks came into view. Men were pouring out of the backs of the trucks and heading towards my next station.

"What's going on?" I asked.

"These guys are all workers from the coffee plantations. The owners gave them the day off plus ten *quetzales* to come in and vote for the FRG. See! They get the ten *quetzales* as they get off the truck! You've got to stop them!"

I knew that few plantation workers would be given the day off to vote. Even if they were, they could ill afford to give up a day's wages when they could barely feed their families on full pay. The owners were clearly buying votes, but all I could do was observe. I remembered the impotent anger of the Swiss delegates that first day and I understood the frustration of the FDNG men. I could only take photos, write this down, and add it to my report.

The FDNG men were bitterly disappointed. I didn't think it would help to tell them that I had seen this same kind of blatant vote buying on American Indian reservations, where elders were given buffalo meat or a "special allowance" to vote for the incumbent. Yet hadn't I also seen it in New York and Washington, DC, where the promise of a pork-barrel project or "special appropriation" brings the votes in? Isn't the promise "Vote for me and I'll get you a tax break next year" just a step removed from cash in hand? Seeing a man handing out ten *quetzales* seemed more obvious and somehow more egregious than the other situations. But when you get right down to it, I thought, this is politics as usual. At least no one was getting beaten up or shot.

There was a lot of tension in the room as I entered the new station. It was the town hall where we had met that morning. The hall was jammed with the plantation workers. They didn't seem to care about what was going on. The voting "booths" were very open cubicles located in the broad lobby of the building. I noticed that a balcony ran along three walls of the room. It acted as a hallway for the upstairs offices. I saw some surly-looking men watching the vote below. Was that one of the truck drivers? Was this intimidation? These guys could clearly see what was being marked on the well-organized colored ballots. Can't interfere, just observe.

Well, I thought, *no reason I can't observe from up there.* I took the stairs American-style—two steps at a time. My camera was in one hand, my notebook in the other. My badge and demeanor screamed "Observador on patrol!" I said nothing to the men on the balcony—that would be breaking the rules. I merely stood next to each in turn, took their photo, and scribbled in my book. The balcony cleared out quickly and I spent the next few hours alone on that lofty perch.

We all reconvened at Gregorio's for a quick lunch and to swap notes. I warned the others about the balcony. Everyone but the French seemed agitated about that one. Jan talked about his frustration.

"Nobody wants to talk to me. I am here to help!"

The Minnesotans weighed in with typical Midwestern thoughtfulness. "You, know, Jan, there is so much fear just below the surface on this otherwise beautiful day. We have to be considerate of these people. They have gone through so much." It helped.

My last two stations were far from the town center. Although both sites were peaceful enough, I experienced the same cold shoulder that Jan had. People didn't look at me. They generally didn't want to talk to me, even to exchange pleasantries. In these outlying areas it was only until recently that talking to the wrong person could mark your family or your whole village as "sympathizers" or "collaborators." I felt deeply saddened that these people had to carry such a heavy psychic burden. Yet here they were, determined to vote in the hopes that this election would put an end to the fear and the violence. I spent the rest of the day cloaking my exuberance in a respectful silence.

The voting ended without incident at 6 PM. We met again with the electoral commission to talk about the vote count that night. Did we want to observe that, as well? Jean, Adrienne, Jan, the older couple, and I readily agreed. I was surprised that some of the younger GX'ers felt that this part of their Reality Tour was over and that they were ready for their final celebratory assault on Pana. Yet it had been a very long day. We had done our jobs well and the election had passed smoothly. What could go wrong now?

A catnap, a cold shower, a quick *tipico*, and back to the town hall to observe the vote count. Representatives of most of the parties milled about while the clear plastic bags were piled up in front of the commissioners. Each bag was brought forward and a judge would pull out a ballot and mark the master vote sheet. The ballot was then passed to a second judge for confirmation and placed in another big bag behind the judges—very transparent and efficient. The party reps and the observers moved around the judges, watching the counting and often watching each other. At first the room was full of excitement, the air tinged with tension. Over the next few hours, however, it became monotonous. Our movements were now dictated more by the need to keep awake than to monitor the process carefully.

The count droned on past midnight, with most of us falling asleep on the comfortable bags of colorful ballots. Suddenly, a loud "bam!" jolted everybody to their feet. The lights flickered for a moment, then died. The room was engulfed in blackness. Immediately, Gregorio pulled out a Bic lighter and clicked out a morsel of light. Adrienne leapt out of the darkness and across the counting table, smothering the open ballots with her lanky frame like a lioness protecting her cubs.

"Do not touch the votes!" she roared. I realized that it was the first time I had heard her speak, and it was exquisite. The rest of us followed her lead and walked up to the table, shielding the open ballots and the unopened bags from anyone else in the dark room. We instinctively reached out and held hands to form a chain that arced around three sides of the table, with the judges forming the fourth barricade. It was so dark and still. I heard a man sobbing gently in a black corner. I wondered what experiences, what demons, the sudden darkness had triggered for him. Someone opened the front door and told us to hang on. An explosion at the generating station had knocked out all of the lights in Solola.

"Was it sabotage?" asked a voice in the darkness. The front door closed without a reply.

We all stood there. Sometimes a comment, sometimes a hand squeezed in the dark, but mostly that bottomless silence. The room was getting hotter. The several Bics in the room ultimately died as we waited. What else could we do?

A low murmur seemed to approach from outside. It got louder and louder, until it evolved into the sound of a chant. The door opened. The light of a hundred black and purple candles came slowly through the door, as a column of chanting, traditionally dressed people filed into the room. We broke our chain to let the first five or six candles in, as their bearers placed one reverently before each pair of judges. Soon the room was bathed in that hot, familiar light. The chant dissipated as the marchers sat throughout the room, placing their candles before them. Even the balcony was ringed with candles. I could recognize Hiderico and many of the faces from the night before. They would not let the darkness return.

Gregorio looked around slowly. His eyes glistened in the candlelight. He announced in a strong voice, "We will now continue the count."

I returned to my hotel around 4 AM and slept until noon. I didn't see the other observers again. As I packed my bag I could hear excited voices in the courtyard. The FDNG had swept all the seats on the Municipal Council, putting local offices squarely in the hands of the indigenous majority for the first time since before the Spanish invasions. On the national level, the first indigenous woman had won a seat in the National Congress. Rigoberta's nephew had been released unharmed this morning.

I picked up my bag and opened the door. The light was returning.

The struggle for indigenous and basic human rights continues in Guatemala. Recent elections have seen a slow shift toward the center-right, as the national desire to integrate into the global economy draws more voters toward candidates promising jobs and money. Ex-combatants have settled down, many forming coffee cooperatives, such as Santa Anita la Union. Rigoberta may run for president of Guatemala, which shows how indigenous politics have continued to evolve and strengthen. She still won't let me kiss her.

6

Tracking the Death Train

MEXICO/EL SALVADOR, 2005

For the coffee farmers of the Americas, 2000 was not the New Millennium, it was the Perfect Storm. Coffee prices to farmers were at historic lows (well below the cost of production). The World Bank was forcing governments to cut back social services under the sterile name of "Structural Adjustment." Free Trade was flooding Central and South America with cheap, subsidized corn from the United States, taking away local markets and jobs. By hundreds of thousands the farmers left or were thrown off their coffee farms and migrated to the bloated cities. Yet, unlike in the perfect world of economics, there were no jobs in the cities either. Many farmers headed north, crawling past borders, wading rivers, and hiding from cops and robbers in the hope of making it to El Norte, the fabled United States, where they would get jobs and be able to send money back to their impoverished families. At the same time, coffee companies throughout the United States were making the grossest of gross profits. They could buy the beans for so little, without dropping their prices to customers who were so unaware of the economics and true human cost of the trade.

Thus was created a human wave that surged north with the power and intention of Katrina at the levees of New Orleans. Much of this stream of refugees washed up on Mexico's southern border with Guatemala. Here, in the small city of Tapachula, they waited for the massive freight train of the Chiapas Mayab Company that hauled sugar, oils, and cement from this depot all the way to the U.S. border. It was a free ride north for many, but some paid a terrible price. They called it *El Tren de Muerte*—the Death Train.

I had heard stories of the Death Train in the coffee villages of Nicaragua and Guatemala, yet there was little publicity in the United States. There were three possible outcomes for those who rode the train. You made it to the U.S. border but still had to get across. You fell asleep or got thrown off the train by gangs preying on the migrants and died. Or you were sucked under the wheels of the train, losing arms and legs. These people ended up in a little shelter in Tapachula run by a remarkable woman, Dona Olga, who has dedicated her life to the *amputados*, the amputees who end up in her care. Michael Lundquist of the Polus Center for Social and Economic Development in Amherst, Massachusetts, had also heard of the victims of the Death Train. The Polus Center is a a nonprofit organization dedicated to supporting people with disabilities and other vulnerable groups not only in the United States but throughout the developing world. We have worked together in Nicaragua and Ethiopia, forging public/private partnerships that make meaningful change in the lives of disabled peoples in coffee communities. Michael wanted to take a look at Dona Olga's shelter, El Albergue de Buen Pastor Jesus (The Refuge of the Good Shepherd Jesus), to see if there was anything Polus could offer given its expertise in prosthetics and social services. I wanted to understand how coffee farmers from El Salvador, Honduras, Nicaragua, Guatemala, and beyond could end up in this place, and what we and the coffee industry could do about it. I headed south with Marta, a twenty-three-year-old Ecuadoran who worked at Polus and whose native Spanish put my street Spanglish to shame. This was Marta's first trip for Polus. It would also be her last.

When we checked into the small hotel off the main plaza in Tapachula, the guy at the desk looked at my business card.

"You a coffee importer? We got a lot of great coffee here in Chiapas. My cousin has a farm . . ."

"No thanks," I interjected quickly. "I am a *tostador*, a coffee roaster, and I already work with some Chiapas cooperatives. In fact, we'll be visiting them next week."

He seemed to lose interest until he noticed Marta near the luggage. He leaned over the counter and said in a conspiratorial whisper, "She your wife?"

"No, my companion."

"Oh, your *companion.*" He nodded knowingly, his eyebrows moving up and down rapidly in some international symbol of sleazy male solidarity.

"Really, we work together. She is with Polus Center. See? It says so here on her card."

"So what kind of work do you and *your companion* do?" Emphasis and eyes again.

"We're here to look at the Death Train, and to see what we can do to help the *amputados* at Dona Olga's shelter. So we're going to the Death Train tonight and . . ."

"Tonight? You're going there tonight with that lady? Don't be crazy, man! You know about the bad cops and the *Mara Salvatrucha*, the gangs?"

"Well, yeah, I've read about . . ."

"Well, reading isn't going there, man. Don't go alone. Be really careful. Don't take no wallet, no watch, don't even wear good shoes. And maybe she should stay here."

"Thanks for the tips. We just want to see the train, talk to some of the migrants, see how many were coffee workers, maybe see the *Mara* . . ."

He was completely exasperated. "You'll be lucky if you *don't* see the *Mara*. But if you're so hot to meet one, maybe we can help."

"Yeah, well, thanks. I'll take you up on that. Can we have the keys, please?"

I got a note from Dona Olga sometime during the early evening. It said that she wouldn't be available to meet tonight, but she had arranged for BETA, the migrants' protection agency, to take us out to the train. Around eleven o'clock a red pickup truck pulled up to the hotel. Three khaki-clad, burly men got out and knocked on my door. Francisco is the head of BETA, and he explained that they are a federal agency that polices the migrants' ranks, helping with legal or logistical problems and delivering food to the depot every evening.

"Many of these folks haven't eaten in a day or two. They need food to stay alert on the Death Train," says Francisco. Good cops. BETA also acts as a counterweight to the black-clad state police, who "protect" the migrants when they are not shaking them down for cash or sex. Bad cops.

The desk clerk seemed satisfied that we were in good hands. He knew these guys.

It was raining pretty hard when we arrived at the depot. Half of a big, black train was waiting to be coupled with the Death Train, and already there were a hundred people between the cars or sitting on top. The uniform of the day was black plastic garbage bags for ponchos and baseball hats. The only light came from a gas lantern at a food stall, where maybe fifty people crowded beneath its rusted corrugated awning to escape the downpour. Francisco pulled up to the tracks, his headlights cutting through the blackness as people swarmed the BETA boys, waiting for food packets.

"Here," Francisco said bluntly as he shoved a bunch of food packets into my gut. "Start tossing." We frisbee'd the packets out into the darkness. The atmosphere became surreal and festive as people caught and shared out the food. When the food was delivered, Francisco announced that I was there to talk to coffee farmers about their experiences heading north. Some of the crowd took their food packets and scurried away to eat or hide the food, while several young men came forward. We wandered off toward an embankment where we could all sit together. The food stand threw enough light to keep a confidential shroud over the faces.

I explained that I was trying to understand the situation of the coffee farmers in these hard times, and that I wanted to take this information to the United States to make people more aware of their plight.

"So where did you guys come from?" I asked tentatively, aware that these young men needed anonymity and stealth to get north successfully. Two brothers were from Nicaragua; a sixteen-year-old from El Salvador; an older man from Honduras; and two others remained silent.

"We are from Matagalpa," stated Benny, as he put his arm around his younger brother, Pablo. They appeared about sixteen and thirteen but I couldn't be sure, as the rain, the darkness, and the Houston baseball caps kept me at a respectful distance. "Our dad lost the farm a year ago. Pablo stopped going to school to help out. We couldn't pay his fees anyway and he liked to play hide-and-seek with the girls instead of studying." Benny whacked Pablo affectionately on the back of the head. The water from the brim of Pedro's hat splashed me in the face. Benny continued, "We protested to the government most of last year, marching around the country with other farmers. But nothing happened, so we came north."

Benny had participated in the Landless Farmers March, where tens of thousands of dispossessed coffee farmers walked the roads of Nicaragua to protest government and bank land seizures and the loss of livelihoods. It was a peaceful march that had lasted fourteen months. Yet like so much about the coffee crisis of the new millennium the march had received no attention from the U.S. press. I knew about it only because our Nicaraguan farmers requested that we send their annual profit share to the marchers to pay for plastic sheeting (housing) and food. The march gradually petered out amidst exhaustion, the need to feed their families, and ephemeral government promises to find land and jobs for the dispossessed farmers. I had also tried to visit one encampment in the town square of Matagalpa, but by the time I got there government trucks had carted the camping farmers off to other parts of Nicaragua to work on large farms.

Julio, the older man, had been a shopkeeper in an impoverished coffee village in Honduras. He shared a lesson in Survival Economics 101.

"I have only fifty *pesos*. I am hungry but I can't buy food. I need the money to give to the gangs, the *Mara*. If I don't have money to give, they might throw me off the train. Even those police in the black clothes steal from us if we look like we have something worth stealing."

My education was disrupted by a deep rumble that shook the ground. We turned and saw a huge black shape edging up the tracks toward us. The Death Train had arrived.

The migrants scrambled to pick up their backpacks and near the train. In the dull light it was difficult to see the details of the train—but it was easy to feel that looming, menacing presence. The train screeched and banged as it backed up to grab the waiting freight cars. They came together with a loud pneumatic finality. Men and women scrambled to get in between the cars, the best place from which to hang on and not get hit by branches. Others climbed to the top and straddled the middle of the cars. I ran to the train and tried to talk to some of the new riders, urging them to hold on and care for each other, warning them about the gangs and what could happen if they fell off. They were all aware of the risks, but each thanked me for the advice. Other voices of counsel came out of the night.

"*Ten cuidado!* Be careful!"

"Watch out for the cops!"

"Jump on!"

"Climb up here!"

The train lurched forward with a sudden and loud jolt. People screamed; some laughed. A few fell off amidst scolding or laughter from their companions, then jumped back on. The rain was pounding, bouncing off the black garbage bags like a shower off a curtain. The metal gleamed wet and slippery where the migrants would be grasping or stepping. The steel wheels, three feet in diameter, sharpened themselves on the tracks like a razor on a strop, waiting like a butcher's slicer for the unfortunate. The train began to pick up speed, slowly, inexorably. In a minute it was swallowed up by the black night.

We entered the hotel lobby wet, cold, and unnerved. Marta grabbed her key and went straight to her room. I talked with Francisco for a minute before he drove off. I trudged through the lobby, vaguely aware of a seedy-looking character off to the left. The desk clerk called me over.

"It's all arranged," he said conspiratorially. He pointed to the man. "He's over there."

"Who?" I didn't know what he was talking about, and I really didn't care. I wanted to go to bed and let this awful night go.

"The *Mara Salvatrucha*, man. You wanted to meet a *Mara*, so I got you one."

I've gotta work on my Spanish, I thought. I don't remember asking for this. But when opportunity knocks . . . I rushed back to the room and hid my wallet and passport. I thought about Julio, the fifty-*peso* man on the train. I grabbed an American twenty ("Green looks good on everybody," my mother used to say when she gave us money as a present) and went back to the lobby.

"I've got twenty bucks. We can drink until it's done, but that's all I've got."

We sat at a small Formica table in a dimly lit bar down the block from the hotel. There were a few others in the bar. The lighting was low but garish.

A small television at the other end of the room showed some Mexican soap opera while Los Lobos sang on a radio.

I tried to have a little small talk in Spanish but I am not sure what I said. Neither was he.

"What the hell you talking about?" he snarled.

"Uh, can we speak in English?" (I didn't want to chance calling him a big whale, like I did to the pretty dancer in Cuba—*baillena, bailerina*—the stakes were a lot higher here.) He agreed with a grunt. A couple of Tecate *cervezas* later and we got down to it. I asked him how I could be sure he was a member of *Mara Salvatrucha*. He showed me a number of tattoos on his arms and a set of numbers on his gums. Tattoos. For all I knew the guy was lying through his tattooed gums to get the beer money.

"I don't mean to be rude, but anyone can get a tattoo, even one that's supposed to be a gang's colors or markings."

"Okay, you want to go out with me and rob somebody at the train yard?"

"No, I'll take your word for it."

He told me that his family had immigrated illegally to Los Angeles in the mid-1990s. He had sold drugs in his public school "just like everybody else," had gotten caught, and was sent to prison. In the slammer, he got hooked up with the *Mara Salvatrucha*, learning such valuable skills as breaking into a car and hot-wiring the ignition, and a total disrespect of anyone who was not a member of the gang. INS was waiting at the prison door when he was released, and he was put on a bus and dumped over the border into Mexico. He had no contacts, job prospects, or 401(k), so he found his social security in the network of ex-inmate gang members who reconnect on the outside. Apparently, there are several hundred thousand deported Latin gang members terrorizing Central America, so finding friends was no problem.

"So what are you, a reporter or something?" Twenty bucks goes a long way in a skanky bar in Tapachula. He was ahead of me four to two. I told him that I was trying to learn more about the coffee farmers who rode the Death Train and that I wanted to figure out how to help.

"Why do you want to help them?" he asked.

"*Asi es lo que haga.*" (That's what I do.)

"Yeah, well, my family rode that train, that's how we got to the States."

I let the beer get the better of me and got overly philosophical.

"So your mother rode the train, and now you rob people who are in the same situation as your mother was?" *Wrong question!*

His eyes flared at me. He gripped his bottle really tightly.

"Hey *bendejo*! (Asshole!) I gotta make a living! You got a problem with that?" His attitude seemed to go downhill fast, so I decided to feign Montezuma's Revenge and go back to the hotel. I let him keep the change, thinking maybe it would keep him off the tracks at least one night. I felt sorry for the way his life had unfolded, but at the end of the day he was still a predator, and I had learned enough for one night.

Taxi drivers are usually the pulse of conventional wisdom. I asked ours what he thought of the Death Train and Dona Olga.

"Those poor bastards. They are just trying to get a better life. That woman is a saint."

We left the main roads of Tapachula, crossed over the tracks and drove down toward the Coatan River. This is the border between Mexico and Guatemala. There was a guard post on the bridge, but the action was below. The taxi stopped by the bridge so that we could watch the homemade rafts burdened with people, backpacks, and boxes of meager belongings poled or pulled across the slow-moving, brown Coatan. These were the "people's ferries" that brought over the illegal immigrants, *los indocumentados*, right under the noses of the disinterested border police. The flood of illegal immigration was no secret here. A few miles up from the river sat a square cement building, wedged in between other, equally dilapidated one-story structures. There was no sign to indicate it was the Albergue, but it was obvious from the three amputees who leaned against the wall, their faces toward the sun.

We entered the small, cramped building and were immediately assaulted by the swirl of sweat, infection, and antiseptic. It hit me like a punch in the stomach. Marta put her hands over her nose but quickly took them away before the residents could see her reaction. The four small rooms were jammed with wheelchairs, crutches, and old medical equipment. Twenty-six men and women lived here. They had a few things in common. They were all desperate economic refugees, they had tried to go north to earn money to send back to their families, and they had all lost arms, legs, or both to the Death Train. Some were waiting for prosthetic limbs that Dona Olga had purchased or got through donation. Some were learning how to walk or manipulate objects. Others sat in wheelchairs or lay on the messy beds, staring blankly toward a dark future. Dona Olga was not there. As usual, she was running around Tapachula looking for donations of food and supplies or meeting with foreign groups that might offer some assistance. We were greeted instead by Donald, another victim of the Death Train, who seemed to be second in command to Dona Olga. Donald gave us a tour of the small refuge, introducing us to the residents. Some were not interested in talking to us, while others were desperate for conversation, new faces—anything different from the daily routine within these four claustrophobic rooms. Most of the amputees were not wearing their prosthetics, including Donald, who had lost both legs. Several scrambled to strap them on and to pull on pants instead of the revealing gym shorts they all wore. A small stab at dignity. I had been accustomed to being with people with limb loss through my prior work with Polus Center in Nicaragua, where we had set up a café/roasterie manned by disabled people as an income generator for their prosthetic clinic. But this was new to Marta, and the tight quarters, the smell, and the palpable pain completely smashed through her defenses. She trembled constantly and was not able to focus on translating. I thought she was going to puke. She went outside for a breather, returning after she had regained her composure.

Donald Ramirez was twenty-three when he left his family home in Honduras to take the ride north.

"I tried to jump on the train three times while it was rolling, and twice I missed. On the third try, I fell under the train. I thought I was okay, but when I pulled out, I saw that my legs were mashed up. They took me to a hospital and amputated my legs there."

Donald was a smart young man. In a different time and a different place, he would have had a good life and been surrounded by loving family and friends. Here, he felt he had only Dona Olga and God. He saw his path as predestined and viewed the world through his newly found Evangelical lens.

"God has led me here," he said humbly. "I ask for nothing more. I was punished for the life I led. Too many people want money and the things of life, but it was the search for those things that brought this upon me." He went on nonstop about God and Dona Olga. I listened to it all but felt a growing discomfort about his analysis and conclusions. I asked him if he wanted to go home. He looked startled, taken out of his comfortable revelry.

"No. I can never go back. What could I do except be a burden on my parents? No, my life is here."

Here? I thought. Here in these shitty four walls? He's only twenty-three. Will he spend his entire life here?

Dona Olga swept into the refuge. She was wearing a white robe, like a nun or an angel would wear. She had a large cross around her neck and a peaceful, if determined, demeanor. We talked about Polus Center's desire to help out here and its expertise in prosthetics, wheelchair access, and activism for the rights of the disabled. I described my concern about coffee workers and the Death Train and my hope that the coffee industry might participate in any projects we created here. Dona Olga appeared polite, but only mildly interested. She told me about her work saving the victims and the horrible path that brought them to her door. She didn't have time to talk, as she needed to go to the hospital and deliver medicines to two new victims.

"The patients at the hospital have to pay for their own medicines," she said. "I get donated medicine or buy it and have to deliver it every day, until the clients are ready to be transferred to my care." She asked if we wanted to go to the hospital with her and see for ourselves. We agreed.

The hospital in Tapachula was modern and clean. Dona Olga breezed past the security guards with Marta and me in tow. We headed straight for a first-floor room, where two men lay semiconscious in beds. The first was a fourteen-year-old boy named Willy, who had lost his arm two days earlier. He was sleeping, so Dona Olga gave the medicine to the nurse and we moved on to the second bed. There, a twenty-something man with no legs was just waking up. He had been found by police the day before during their morning sweep of the tracks looking for victims of the Death Train. He was heavily drugged. As he opened his eyes, his first sight was the white-clad Dona Olga smiling down at him. He must have thought he was in heaven. I didn't think he was aware that he had lost his legs. Marta and I both felt uncomfortable being at his bedside at that moment. It was weird enough for the man to fall off the train to blinding pain and wake up in a hospital with an angel at his bedside, without having to comprehend what two gringos were doing there. We left the room. Dona Olga came out shortly and told a nurse that his shoes and pants had been stolen during the night. This was not unusual, she said to us.

Marta and I were bruised by the experience. We took a taxi back to the hotel. We didn't speak during the ride. This whole thing seemed a horrifying dead end. What was at all possible to do here besides make a donation and run screaming home? The despair was really sinking in. Marta cried in the taxi. I sat stoically, but my Great White Hope veneer was cracking. When we got out I decided to walk around downtown Tapachula. I had expected a sleazy, down-and-out border town. But Tapachula was a happy place. On the main streets the shops were open and full. Well dressed couples strolled down the sidewalks. Kids in school uniforms and backpacks wandered by in pairs. In fact, Tapachula was second only to Mexico City in income and living standard. It was a strange oasis of relative plenty in the middle of Chiapas, the poorest state in Mexico. Yet not a mile away, the victims of the Death Train sat unnoticed. I stopped in front of a bookstore and realized that I had seen no books or magazines in the refuge. I went in and bought *Harry Potter*, *Treasure Island*, a collection of Greek myths, some math and word puzzle books, and some magazines. That night I stayed in the hotel room drinking beer and watching American movies with Spanish subtitles. At least I could get my mind off the day and get some language practice. Marta just slept.

We went back to the refuge in the late morning, after buying food, men's underwear, and cleaning supplies. We got the big picture the day before; I wanted to get to know the residents better and try to find some meaningful contribution to make. As we helped make lunch, I noticed that a handsome man with one leg named Nelson wasn't wearing any shoes. I asked him where they were.

"Well, I lost the right one when I fell off the train. I gave the left one to Manolo. He had no shoes but he has a left leg. I can find some other shoes when I get out of here, but he isn't going anywhere soon." Manolo was a short, middle-aged man from Solola, Guatemala. He held up Nelson's shoe and laughed.

"I need to fix this shoe, but that's easy. I used to fix all my family's shoes." He looked dreamily upward. "If I could ever go back, I could open up a little shoe store and fix everyone's shoes in the whole town!" Others in the room laughed as well. I thought about what he had said.

"Hey, Manolo," I asked softly. "If you had the chance and enough money, would you really want to do that?" His face lit up.

"Sure. I would pack my bag and go tomorrow." More friendly laughter from around the room.

After lunch, an Evangelical preacher came in. All of the wheelchairs and crutches were moved aside and an impromptu altar set up. A brief service was held. I had forgotten it was Sunday. Afterward, I asked Dona Olga if we could talk. We went outside and I explained to her that I wanted to learn what all of the people would do if they could get their medical and prosthetic needs met. She was very protective of her clients.

"Don't give them false hope," she said sternly. "They have had too much disappointment. They have been betrayed by this world enough. They are happy here."

"But they can't stay here forever. What is your intention about helping them move on?" Dona Olga sighed and said she was too busy just dealing with their daily needs to think about that. It was very clear that Dona Olga, for all of her good works, did not have an "exit strategy." There was no thought given to what these people would do or where they would go after leaving the refuge. They couldn't get back on the Death Train and go north. They couldn't stay in Mexico, as they were *indocumentados* here, too. They couldn't work or even go to school here. They didn't want to go home, as they carried so much shame about failing to care for their families and feared being a lifelong burden to their own poor kin. Would these people never find a home again? I told Dona Olga that I was thinking of how to provide some kind of technical training or other skill support, but I couldn't go very far down that path without knowing what people wanted to do with their lives. I just wanted to talk to them in a friendly way. No promises, no crazy plans.

Dona Olga was not convinced, but she relented. "After dinner you can have your meeting. But you buy the dinner."

Everyone agreed that getting pizza and a mountain of tortillas delivered would make for a festive Sunday dinner. They also wanted Cokes, globalization's quick fix for happiness. They put their personal gear away and straightened up the main room. The place looked and felt brighter when the pizza delivery boys came. I called a meeting of everyone in the shelter, with the exception of some of the newer men who couldn't or wouldn't leave their beds and kept turned to the walls. We sat in a circle—a room full of stumps pointed my way. I began.

"So I want to ask you to dream a little. I know that is difficult, but that ability has not been taken from you. Would you share your dreams with me and with everybody in the room?" They looked at each other questioningly. I continued, "If you could leave here and get a new start, what would you do?" Silence and self-consciousness. This was too much too soon.

"Hey, Manolo! Why don't you start? Tell us about the shoe repair shop." All eyes turned towards Manolo. He fidgeted in his wheelchair for a minute and then told his dream. Everyone in the circle looked startled. *Yeah, a dream, that's right. They're still in there and it's okay to speak them.* Nelson, who had lost a leg on his fourth trip to the United States, had a sly look on his face and spoke next.

"I know what I'd do. I'd make love to some Chinese girls." The place cracked up. Even Donald smiled. Dona Olga left the room abruptly. From that point on, people began talking freely and happily about their dreams. Wilmer, a young coffee farmer from Honduras, said he would go back to growing coffee.

"How could you do that with no legs, you idiot?" someone shouts. Things got quiet as Wilmer looked down at two stumps cut off above where his knees were. *Oh no, too much too soon.* But Wilmer looked up defiantly.

"I'll make some paths through the fields for my wheelchair. I can pick from the chair!" Everybody laughed and applauded. When it got to the two women in the room, everybody was silent. The bigger and bolder of the two, a one-legged woman from Nicaragua, said, "I will start a hair salon. I don't need legs for that!"

"I will be your first customer," said one of the men. The place erupted into giggles and grade-school ditties about young love. It was Maria Magdalena's turn next. She was a small, shy woman from El Salvador. She spoke quietly.

"I have always wanted a little store in my house. I could keep watch over my three kids. They are with their grandmother now." The revelation of family connections brought up the sobering truth that many of the people here were parents who had left their young families with older relatives, thinking they would return soon or send for the kids later. As a dad, my heart reached across the room to Maria.

Everyone shared his or her dreams. Even Donald said that he wished he could get an education. He had left school after the third grade to help his family. When we left much later, the shelter seemed a more content place, as if a small, deep piece of each person's wound had been healed. Marta smiled and hugged people goodnight. I asked Donald to tell Dona Olga that I wanted to talk with her in the morning. I had an idea.

That evening I called Michael, the director of the Polus Center. We talked about what it might take to get some technical training for some of these folks, and what the cost of repatriation and setting up small businesses might look like. It was obvious that almost everyone desperately wanted to go home, if they could find a way to support themselves and not be a burden on their families. At the same time, over six hundred thousand coffee farmers in Central America alone were in the same economic situation. There were no jobs on the farms and few in the cities. Where would twenty-three Death Train amputees fit in, forgetting about the new ones each week? We worked out a rough plan. Donald could be trained to be a caseworker for intake at the refuge. He could interview all of the Death Train victims and organize individual files for each one. We could provide needed training for each person and then find work or set up a small business back home if it looked like a good match. Polus Center would develop individual service plans to assist each person with the often difficult dynamics of reintegration into his or her former, now radically different life. Dona Olga would be happy that her clients were being provided for and helped back to a productive, meaningful life. I agreed that Dean's Beans would pay for the first two repatriations, and we would then have a track record with which to approach other groups for future funding.

In the morning I met with Dona Olga. She seemed happy with the plan. I told her it was small scale and manageable, so that we could see results or problems pretty quickly. Donald was very excited about his possible new position. He could stay with Dona Olga, get some computer and literacy education, and help people. She suggested that we start with Nelson, whom I guessed she wanted to get rid of as soon as possible after that very un-Christian remark about the Chinese girls and his general self-assured attitude. He was the only resident of the refuge who didn't seem in awe of Dona Olga. Polus Center already had a relationship with Beatrice, a Salvadoran social worker, who could work on the repatriations and be on the ground to help the transitions at home. She was meeting with the Salvadoran consulate in Tapachula that day to discuss our proposal for repatriation of the Salvadoran residents of the refuge. We agreed to begin with Nelson.

Later we visited with the Salvadoran Consul. He was a tall, older man who was delighted with the idea of repatriation of the Death Train victims. He promised to pay "special attention" to this project. After all, he said with a wink, the president of El Salvador was a college classmate of his. That evening, Beatrice called the hotel elated.

"Where have you been? I've got great news! The Minister of Foreign Relations wants to hire Nelson!"

"To do what?" This was too sudden. "He has no education and no particular skills besides dishwashing and chasing Chinese women."

"They want him to return to San Salvador and be the case manager for repatriation at the ministry. He has the best qualifications for that and he speaks English so he can communicate with the officials in the United States, too!" She was off the wall with excitement.

"And he wants to go back and do this?

"He is crazy with excitement and can't wait to tell you. Let's go!"

As I entered the refuge the atmosphere was celebratory. Everyone was talking rapidly and with great animation, except for a new guy with one arm and leg, who lay rolled toward a wall—was he the young man I had seen in the hospital? Nelson was across the room. He put two thumbs up and beamed at me.

"You are the world's luckiest motherf---er!" I shouted in English.

"Motherf---er! Motherf---er!" came the laughing chorus from around the room. Oops! I didn't know that this was one of the few truly global phrases. Nelson hopped over and hugged me.

"This is so great, man!"

"Congratulations. Guess we'll have to get you some shoes, eh? You might need a suit, too." Nelson's eyes widened.

"You mean that? Will you help me?"

"Sure," I said warmly. "That'll be my 'welcome home' present to you." Nelson suddenly looked worried.

"You're not gonna forget, will you? I'm really gonna need that stuff."

"No problem, my friend. In fact, when you get back I'll come down to El Salvador and we'll go shopping together."

"You're a great guy, man!" A big bear hug and a few furtive tears from both of us.

We held another pizza party that afternoon to celebrate Nelson's good fortune. Most of the residents were genuinely happy, but the newer men held back, not able to see anything bright in their own futures yet. While the radio cranked out tinny tunes, several of the men strapped their legs on and danced with Marta. We all clapped in unison and cheered them on. The festive air was broken when Dona Olga and a film crew arrived.

A director, a cameraman, and a guy with a boom mike charged into the front room. They immediately began filming the refuge, thrusting their camera (with its intense, focused light) into the faces of the men and women. Some of the men hurried into the back rooms. The camera and light searched the room like the spotlight in a prison yard. Nelson, who was the most handsome and presentable guy, was caught like a deer in the headlights. They pummeled him with questions about his accident, life in the shelter, and so on. His self-confidence and happy smile disappeared as he lowered his face and mumbled responses. Satisfied with the sound bites, the crew moved on toward the others, pushing aside wheelchairs and knocking over crutches in their determined bid to grab brief snippets of sad lives for the evening broadcast. They left as suddenly as they had entered, the tinny radio playing a festive tune in sharp contrast to the shell-shocked quiet of the residents. In response to my what-the-hell-was-that? look, Dona Olga shrugged.

"We need all the publicity we can get. That will be shown on the news tonight."

That night we went out drinking and dancing with the Salvadoran Consul. Beatrice was turning out to be a miracle worker as well as a social worker. She and the consul talked about Nelson's repatriation and quickly turned their energies toward Maria, who had captured both of their hearts. Beatrice wanted to submit a plan and a budget to Polus Center for renting a home for Maria and establishing a community general store there—and reuniting Maria with her children. We called Michael and he readily agreed. Maria would be the second Death Train victim to be repatriated.

Before leaving for the mountains of Chiapas the next day, Marta and I went back to the shelter. Dona Olga said she was not happy about Maria's repatriation. Maria had been betrayed by so many people: her former husband who had abandoned her and the kids, the guys who let go of her hand when they were helping her board the Death Train. She thought Maria was better off at the refuge. Donald was also expressing reticence about his new career possibility and gave us a long sermon about God's intentions for him. I had a feeling that Dona Olga was feeling threatened, that her "flock" was being taken away. I castigated myself for these cynical thoughts. After all, saints are selfless beings who don't have egos, do they? Dona Olga was probably just concerned about the welfare of her favorite charges.

The bus from Tapachula to San Cristobal de las Casas, high in the mountains to the north, took nineteen hours. Thankfully, it was one of the fleet of air-conditioned modern buses that race through the nights of Mexico, blaring nonstop kung fu movies with Spanish subtitles for their semiconscious passengers. As we rose higher and higher, the bus stopped frequently at police roadblocks. The cops were looking for *indocumentados* or troublemakers coming to Chiapas to provide aid and comfort to the Enemies of the State—the Zapatistas. I was a businessman going to visit coffee farmers. No problem. But Marta, an Ecuadoran with a U.S. green card, was a suspicious character. The fact that she was young and very pretty only emboldened these guys, who tried to make her get off the bus at each roadblock for a private search and questioning. Fortunately, our firm insistence that we were working together, her papers from Polus Center, and a few of those knowing, raised eyebrows worked to keep the men at bay.

The last time I had been in San Cristobal it had been an armed camp. The rebellious Zapatistas and their peasant farmer supporters had held the city center. Battalions of federal troops had cordoned off the city. The air had been tense. The strong foreign tourist, supporter, and media presence had kept a lid on the extreme violence that waited for obscurity to provide its cover. But that was a decade ago. Now, the city was a clean, renovated colonial tourist destination. Internet cafés competed with swank, expensive restaurants for the visiting dollars and euros. In the central square, tanks were replaced by tank tops, bayonets by baguettes.

I had gone back and forth with our friends in Chiapas about the proper etiquette when visiting one of the autonomous zones, the areas liberated from the federal government and under Zapatista control. Have Cooperative Coffees e-mail ahead and let them know you are coming. That will smooth things. Connect with Eva or some of the other solidarity people in San Cristobal. They know the system and will help you get through. Visit Enlace Civil or Junta de Buen Govierno, the Zapatista support and governance offices in San Cristobal. Explain your reason for visiting the farmers. Bring documentation of who you are. Bring coffee in a Dean's Beans bag to prove it. Be prepared for long delays. Get permission to visit Oventic, the regional headquarters nearest our farmers. They didn't respond to your e-mails? Well, don't go without approval, or things could get pretty difficult for you. Hire a private car for the visit. There isn't good bus service and you might get stranded up there. It seemed overly bureaucratic and burdensome. I just wanted to visit the coffee farmers.

With all that was on my mind from the Death Train visit and the hassles getting up to San Cristobal, I completely forgot all of that protocol stuff. Marta and I wandered down to the local van area, where hundreds of minivans and cars waited to take locals all over Chiapas. We walked several blocks looking for signs, but none of the destinations were posted. We were suddenly approached by a young man asking if we would like to go to Oventic. There were a thousand locals and foreigners milling about, so how did he know we wanted to go to Oventic? Did the hotel clerk put the word out? Did we look "the type"? We climbed in a small van and roared out of town and higher up into the mountains. The vistas from the exposed, winding mountain roads were stunning. We stopped in several small villages to participate in the commerce of the rural countryside: letting people on and off, taking on chickens, and dropping off cases of bottled water. Finally, the van pulled over next to a small hut next to a metal cattle gate. A few women sat in the hut, and I could see that the gate closed off a dirt road leading to a cluster of adobe buildings and a school. We had arrived at Oventic.

A sign on the gate said to wait there for a security clearance. I leaned against the gate and waited. Five minutes later a man with an old .22 rifle (the kind for shooting small birds and soda cans) came over and asked what we wanted. I told him I wanted to visit the farmers of Mut Vitz a few miles

up the road. We were invited to sit in the hut. He took our passports to be
processed. We sat for almost an hour. There was a small store across the
dirt road that sold woven peasant shirts with EZLN (Zapatista National
Liberation Army) sewn on the breast pocket. Revolution tourism. I bought
one to support the cause. Finally, the old man returned and said we could
go to the regional headquarters down the road for our interview. We walked
down the road as far as the school. We looked around for the regional
headquarters and walked back.

"*Lo siento mucho*, I'm very sorry," I said humbly, "but we can't find it."

The man walked us to a one-room building with a brightly painted door.
The painting was a giant ear of corn. Each kernel was a masked Zapatista.
What an appropriate symbol, as corn was first discovered by these very same
Tzotzil indigenous peoples. It was a beautiful symbol of revolutionary art.
Marta got very nervous and I felt a powerful swoon as some inner connection
was made between these people, the earth, social change, and my own life's
work. We knocked on the door and waited . . . and waited. *Man*, I thought,
the revolution moves at a snail's pace around here. I looked around and there
was a *caracol* (snail) painted on another building. Hmmm.

Finally the door cracked open. A woman's dark eyes looked at us through
a full-faced balaclava. She asked our names. She closed the door and came
back after ten minutes. We entered and were directed to sit on a bare wooden
bench before a bare wooden table. There was nothing else in the room. After
several more minutes, the local Junta de Buen Govierno committee came in
from a small back room. Two masked men and the woman, now with a baby
suckling her breast. My fool's mind wondered why the infant didn't have a
baby balaclava on. Marta was shaking when one of the men began to speak
in a quiet monotone. They told us the history of the Zapatista struggle in
that area, how they never received schools, health care, or any attention from
the state. The people suffered terribly, especially after hurricanes and mud
slides. The coffee price was desperately low, and the people here were so
distant from even regional markets that they were constantly victimized by
coyote middlemen and corrupt officials. For them, the Zapatistas represented
true liberation and a chance to have a say in their own lives. We would see
this for ourselves when we went up to Mut Vitz. I explained about Dean's
Beans and Cooperative Coffees, which had a steady presence in Chiapas

through several of its members, such as Higher Grounds, Just Coffee, and Cloudforest Coffee. I talked about our support for Mut Vitz, Maya Vinic, Yachil, and several other small cooperatives here over the years, and how Mut Vitz had been our first grower partner at Cooperative Coffees. They asked me a few perfunctory questions. Nobody asked if we had checked in at San Cristobal. None of the interviewers had ever heard of Cooperative Coffees or Dean's Beans, but they were gratified about our long connection with Chiapas and believed us. Then I talked about our work with the Death Train. Dark eyes glistened through the balaclavas as we told the tale of despair and now hope. There was a long silence after we finished. They met in the back for a few minutes and returned.

"You are welcome in the Autonomous Region of San Juan la Libertad. You are our friends and allies. Go out to Mut Vitz with our thanks and our blessings."

We were told to return to Oventic after our visit to collect our passports. If we waited outside of the gate, we would get a ride up to Mut Vitz when a truck or van came along. Hitchhike in peace.

Several cars, trucks, and vans passed as we waited outside the gates. None of them stopped to get permission to enter the Autonomous Zone. Nobody tried to stop them. I realized that we were in more of a psychological than a physical territory. We had not experienced laws at Oventic but more what you call "guidelines." Surely the well-equipped Mexican army could roll over the old guy with the .22 and the few other lightly armed farmers we had seen here and there. But the Autonomous Zone was really about liberating the people's minds from fear and dependency. It was about holding strong to your relationship with your community and your land; about the ability to take control of your own destiny in the face of a system that alternately failed and oppressed you. This was the deep message of the surreal corn on the door in Oventic.

We hitched in the back of a pickup to the Mut Vitz office and warehouse in El Bosque. Along the way we passed several army outposts. Machine-gun emplacements bristled out of the hillsides like the quills of a pissed-off porcupine. Heavily armed troops glared as we passed. For a liberated zone, there sure was a massive federal military presence.

The office was a small cement building, clean and freshly painted. The warehouse was new, built in part with the $1,200 profit share from Dean's Beans that we had sent down the year before. We were met by Victor Gonzales Ruiz, a board member of the cooperative. We pulled back one of the massive red loading doors and toured the empty warehouse (all the coffee had been processed and sold by that time). Victor told us the story of Mut Vitz (Bird Mountain).

The group started in 1997, when Tzotzil coffee farmers from several municipalities got together to share experiences: problems with local *coyotes*, difficulties accessing the local and international markets, and violence by the military and from the thugs paid by the ruling PRI party.

"We decided that we should work collectively, form our own association and see if we could sell our coffee in the Fair Trade market. We weren't getting any help from the government, so we had to work hard to get information and techniques to improve the quality of our coffee. We also had to learn about organics to get certified. We had used chemicals in the past. The government gave them to us for free until we were hooked, then they started charging more and more. Then some of our members got sick from the chemicals. We knew that was not the right path for us or for our land."

In 1998 Mut Vitz obtained an export license, allowing the co-op to get out from under abusive private exporters. This was an important milestone on the road to self-sufficiency. The co-op began with five hundred members and grew to over a thousand in three years. All of the members supported the Zapatista resistance to the federal government, and Mut Vitz formally declared itself an Autonomous Organization, eschewing assistance of any kind from the state and federal governments. Its members could not be bought or bribed, but they were also on their own. The cooperative suffered continual commercial and physical harassment over the years (even the murders of several members) but kept on its autonomous path. Mut Vitz held firm during the worst years of the coffee crisis, paying its members almost twice what the *coyotes* were. They thought things would get easier when the international prices rose.

Yet the upward surge of the market price was a mixed blessing. Victor shook his head in bewilderment.

"The higher price brought back the *coyotes*."

The *coyotes* have always been around the remote farm regions of the world. They live at the margins of commerce, like their feral namesakes, waiting for their chance to feed. I once stopped and talked to one who sat at the bottom of a hill in Nicaragua, waiting for the farmers to come by carrying their heavy sacks of beans to town. He lounged in his red Toyota pickup, a briefcase full of cash at his side. He did not see himself as a bad person. He was a buyer of coffee, he said, just like me. To some farmers, the ready availability of cash (and not having to carry the beans any farther) outweighs the thought of waiting for months for a greater payment. Maybe the farmer has a sick kid and needs money for medicine now. Maybe there is some other immediate need that temporarily outweighs the commitment to the politics of liberation. As I talked to the *coyote* that day, I realized they were not entirely evil. It was hard to see it, but sometimes they provided a service.

"This caught us by surprise," Victor admitted. "Our cooperative was there all of those years, providing money, market access, and support to our members. The market prices got better, so we thought we were out of the worst of the crisis. Then these *coyotes* came along with more upfront money than we could give and some of the families took it. When you have no food on the table, that money look really good. We couldn't compete. Then we didn't have enough coffee to fill all our contracts to you guys and some of the others." Victor was clearly embarrassed by this.

"What about prefinancing from Cooperative Coffees? If you had the prefinancing you could offer your members more upfront money," I asked.

Victor breathed deeply. "That's really complex. Many of us don't want to rely on any special treatment from you buyers. That's like more dependency, even though you are on our side. It's new for us and it makes some members nervous. We are an Autonomous Organization." He pulled at a shriveled leaf on one of his plants, examined it, and tossed it to the ground. "The *Junta* has some issues with prefinancing, too. Mostly about one co-op getting something that the others don't. So if all the co-ops were able to get prefinancing that would make it easier." He looked at me hopefully.

"Yeah, I know. But you know that there is not a lot of prefinancing money out there."

He raised his voice a little. "It is a rule of Fair Trade. The buyer is required to give prefinancing if the growers ask for it."

"That's what the rules say, it's true. But most of the buyers don't even offer it, and for those of us that do, there simply isn't enough money to prefinance everybody. It really sucks, but that is the reality." I didn't want to make him more upset by telling him how many companies include prefinancing in their advertising about Fair Trade, even though they don't actually do it. Victor was right. It was very complex.

As we walked through the coffee landscape up toward the main road, the sound of birds gave way to the singing of children. We came across an elementary school, its outer walls ablaze with colorful slogans and Freida Kahlo–esque paintings. Beautiful earth goddesses exclaimed that education was the path to liberation. Victor explained that before the Autonomous Region was created, there were no schools here, nor any health clinics. The Zapatista movement focused on what truly mattered to the community, he said firmly.

Victor left us at the road. We had trouble flagging down a ride. Finally a burly trucker pulled over and offered us a lift back to Oventic. But after a half hour we realized he had turned off the main road and was going in the wrong direction. He wouldn't stop or even slow the truck down. He just ignored us and drove on. I was getting very worried, as the level of violence against members of Mut Vitz and other communities in resistance was increasing. Coffee trees were being uprooted, corn destroyed, people beaten, and more. Even tourists, usually sacred cows in rural zones of low-intensity conflict, were being grabbed and robbed. Finally the driver stopped in a remote indigenous village. He simply ignored us and we walked away, not knowing where the hell we were. We sat at the side of the road to consider our options. None. The people up here didn't speak Spanish, and there were no cars on this minor back road. After a few deep breaths, we began walking back up the road. Within minutes a van stopped and hailed us. We got in. It was the same van that had taken us to Oventic that morning. Marta and I just looked at each other. The driver smiled and took us back to Oventic, no charge. We got our passports back from the old guard and went down to the *Junta* headquarters to pay our respects and report on our visit. We waited a long time for the masked woman to open the door. The eyes were not the same. Apparently the Zapatistas were "on call," and different local committee members were there now. I thanked the woman through the barely opened doorway. I started to tell her about our time at Mut Vitz. She shrugged and closed the door before I could finish.

———

Two months later, Michael and I were headed to El Salvador to celebrate the repatriations of both Nelson and Maria. Beatrice met us at the airport in a battered rental car without windshield wipers (how did she know it would rain the day we arrived?). She was trying to save money for the project. Beatrice had arranged everything—the housing, the work, Maria's inventory, and the reunion with her children.

Maria had been back for almost a month. Our budget for Maria had included six months' rent on her one-story house, furniture, and cash for living expenses and inventory. In the front room, Maria had established her store, selling bread, Doritos, toothpaste, and other sundries to her neighbors. She met us at the door in her wheelchair, saying it was too hard to get around her new home on the two prosthetic legs that had replaced her own, cut off at the knees when she fell from the Death Train. She was twenty-six and engulfed in the energy of her two boys, Manuelito and Javier, ages five and four, who couldn't get enough of their mother, now that she had returned after six months in the Tapachula shelter.

Maria told us that the business was growing slowly. She predicted she would be able to make the rent and take care of her family after six months (pretty good for a small business anywhere!). She wanted to expand her offerings to include cosmetics, which were not readily available in her neighborhood. We gave her a cash grant to buy the inventory. While we were visiting, several customers stopped by. Maria filled their orders from her wheelchair. The boys raced the bread, fruit, and soft drinks over to the barred window and returned to Mom with the money.

Maria's mother and brothers had come from the countryside to help Maria get set up but had recently returned to their village. Maria said that she was ready for that, as her two teenaged brothers ate lots of food from the store and never paid for anything. I told her that was common with visiting relatives the world over. I played with the wild-haired, hyperactive boys for a while. They relished the male roughhousing. We made plans to meet Maria and the boys for lunch at a downtown Mr. Pollo (a sort of McDonald's for chicken and rice) and headed off to visit Nelson.

We drove up to the apartment where Nelson lived. He hung over the balcony and bellowed a welcome.

"Wait a minute! I gotta put on my leg!"

He lived in a cramped apartment, but he said it felt like a palace after the refuge. He told us about his new, wonderful job. He was a special assistant in the Ministry of Foreign Relations. His job was to help find other illegal Salvadoran migrants whose families were trying to locate them or who wanted to come home.

"I know what it's like to be an *indocumentado* and have no place to go. This job is perfect for me. I thought my life was over, losing a leg," he said plainly. "But when I saw all those guys in the shelter without any arms or legs, I knew what a lucky guy I was." He looked at me tentatively. "Do you remember your promise?"

"Sure, brother. Let's go shopping!"

We hit a pretty nice clothing store. The sign on the door said "No Guns Allowed." Nelson held up a number of suits with the help of some eager, solicitous saleswomen. He was a very handsome man, and his happiness was like a magnet. I picked out a light blue tie and a white shirt to go with a dark blue suit chosen by the women. Nelson disappeared into a dressing room. He came out and stood in front of the full-length mirror. He looked like a million bucks. As he stared in the mirror, his big dark eyes became full and wet. I walked behind him and put my hand on his shoulder.

"This is the first time in my life I feel important."

We dropped Nelson off at work and visited with his coworkers. They all expressed their gratitude for our having brought Nelson to them. They said he added a level of experience and compassion to the department that did not exist before. He was "a gift." The department head, Geraldina Beneke, said that this was the only successful repatriation program in Central America, thanks to Nelson. When we were alone, Nelson confided, "I know what a good thing this is. It has changed my life and I'm not gonna screw it up."

Maria pulled up to the Mr. Pollo in a local taxi whose driver had outfitted the car to accommodate people with disabilities. The gentle driver took the wheelchair off the top of the taxi and helped Maria inside. The boys were dressed smartly, their hair combed and struggling for liberation under gobs of gel or cooking oil. They had never been in a place like this. The smell of the fried chicken was inviting and overwhelming, but the boys were focused on a big cage of plastic balls that other children were leaping into with the abandon of mythical virgins into a volcano. Maria was nervous about letting the boys out of her sight. I realized that as much as she loved them, she hadn't gotten a break from childcare for over a month. I decided on two things. First, I would play with those boys until they dropped. Second, I would buy Maria a television set. Beatrice's first reaction was that a TV was evil for children (good social worker), and I would ordinarily agree. But Maria was nearly exhausted from corralling these two wild ponies all day long, and politically correct or not, this woman needed an electronic babysitter. I grew up watching too much TV as my single mom worked long hours, and I'm here writing this book, aren't I? The strangest part of the experience was paying for everything in U.S. dollars. The year before, El Salvador had begun using the dollar as its national currency. In theory, it would increase and facilitate trade between the two countries and stabilize the currency. Unfortunately, the government decided to devalue its currency by 30 percent against the dollar the night before the transition. So when the workers of El Salvador woke up they found their buying power, their paychecks, and their savings diminished by 30 percent. When the business owners awoke on that same morning they were treated to a 30 percent decrease in labor costs and a 30 percent spike in profits. Dinner at Mr. Pollo became a luxury overnight.

The Death Train continued to take its toll after we returned north. Marta quit the Polus Center after the hard trip. We read reports on the Internet of more victims jamming the shelter and other refuges along the tracks. Finally, God had had enough. Exactly one month after Katrina had pounded New Orleans, Hurricane Stan roared across Central America. It smashed through Tapachula, its twenty inches of rain flooding out the city and cutting off communication for weeks. The shelter was inundated by the rising Coatan, cleansing the little haven of its pus and squalor. Many of the donated crutches and wheelchairs floated out into the city streets. Dona Olga headed for higher ground as her new shelter, paid for by Canadian donors and built by one-legged carpenters, was nearly finished. The tracks of the Death Train were torn up and twisted by the water and the wind. For the moment, the Death Train was stopped.

While Beatrice oversaw Nelson and Maria's progress, Michael and I worked on a plan to make the plight of the Death Train victims known to the world. For a while it looked like we would have an unlikely ally—the United States Congress. Washington was on fire with the debate on illegal immigration, and we had the only successful and humane program for addressing at least one source. We contacted several members of Congress to arrange for a delegation to visit Tapachula. The governments of Nicaragua and El Salvador were fully in support of our approach. Even Larry King interviewed a *Los Angeles Times* reporter who was hawking her book on the Death Train (although there was no mention of proceeds going back to the unfortunate subjects of her masterpiece). But Congress couldn't be bothered, and neither Larry nor the concerned reporter ever returned our phone calls and e-mails. Twenty-four disabled *indocumentados* just didn't rate in this debate.

We decided to find out who owned the train and the tracks, thinking that they might fund some of the work or at least take steps to ameliorate the problem (like ordering their conductors not to speed up or slam on the brakes when the migrants tried to board). There was little information on the Chiapas Mayab Company, but the tracks were owned by a company based in Connecticut—the romantically named Genesee & Wyoming.

Michael tried to contact their President and CEO, Mortimer Fuller III (whose granddaddy had founded the company back in 1899), thinking that the company might be interested in understanding the problem better and participating in finding a win-win for all concerned. Fat chance. He never got past the executive secretary. He was lucky his telephone ear didn't get frostbitten from her arctic treatment. After several unsuccessful attempts to speak to Mr. Fuller and each time receiving the Fuller Brush-off, Michael gave up. I said I would try a more corporate approach, using language that I was certain they would understand. I called the same executive secretary. I told her that I was a CEO of a coffee company who had visited the Death Train because I had heard many coffee farmers had died or been injured on it. I told her that I thought they should be aware that they could be held liable for the behavior of the conductors or the condition of the track, if any of those soft-hearted disabilities or liberal immigration activists found out about this. She was still guarded, but she thawed enough to give me the name of their Vice President of Safety and Compliance, Gerry. He returned my phone call in a week and we discussed the issues from a business perspective. I told him that they had an opportunity to be a good corporate citizen and fend off activists and lawsuits at the same time. What would the press and their shareholders say if a bunch of amputees in wheelchairs picketed their head office in the privileged confines of Greenwich, Connecticut? Wouldn't it be better if they took a proactive stance and helped solve the problem? Gerry said he would look into it and the company would decide what to do. I never heard from him again, but we read online that the Genesee & Wyoming had decided to abandon the Tapachula tracks as being a total loss after the hurricane. We can't take credit for an act of God or of corporate self-interest, but I know that we played a small part in derailing the Death Train.

After taking out a full-page ad about the Death Train in a café magazine, we were flooded with offers of help. Several Dean's Beans customers went down to Tapachula and worked in Dona Olga's new facility, helping feed and care for her remaining clients. Local priests and human rights organizations report that there have been no new Death Train victims in Tapachula since the company abandoned the track, but other Death Trains loaded with indocumentados *continue to thunder north from different locations in southern Mexico. As long as the "free trade" systems of coffee and other commerce continue to deny people a sound, locally based economy, the Death Trains will not lack for human cargo.*

The farmers of Mut Vitz and other declared Autonomous Organizations continue their struggle for dignity and the resources to live a decent life. They continue to be harassed by the government and increasingly by paramilitary organizations. They also continue to be supported by their international friends in both commerce and social development. Recently, it was discovered that Mut Vitz owed several hundred thousand dollars in unpaid taxes to the government, which took the opportunity to come down hard on the Autonomous Organization. The cooperative is in danger of collapse, and many members have left to join neighboring co-ops. Fair Trade is no guarantee of survival in hostile environments.

We are also working with Honor the Earth, an indigenous rights organization, to send reservation youth from the United States to work with their indigenous counterparts in Chiapas to install solar power on local health clinics.

7

Coffee, Land Mines, and Hope

NICARAGUA, 2001

Jose Gonzales was a typical twelve-year-old—bright, curious, and just a little too mischievous for his own good. Jose peeked into the back room of his small wooden house in San Juan del Rio Coco, Nicaragua, which his coffee-farming parents had rented to a stranger for a little extra income during those hard times. The stranger carried a military backpack, like so many of the unemployed people wandering the mountainsides, and he had left the backpack in his room when he went out. There was something green and round poking out of the backpack. It was the size of a Coke can and Jose couldn't resist checking it out. Nobody else was in the house, so Jose crept into the back room. He pulled the object from the backpack and examined it. He couldn't read the English on it, nor decipher the numbers. Jose tossed it in the air a few times and caught it, then hit the metal casing where four small metal prongs extended outward. Jose was thrown back against the wall as the American M16A2 antipersonnel mine exploded. A few days later Jose regained consciousness. He could barely see, as one eye was gone. He looked down and screamed—both his arms were missing.

The coffeelands of Nicaragua were sown with more than a hundred and thirty thousand land mines during the decade after the revolution ended in 1979. Many were placed along the Honduran border by the newly elected government, to intercept the U.S.-funded and U.S.-organized counterrevolutionaries, or "Contras." The Contras were a hodgepodge of the former dictator's brutal National Guard and security teams, disgruntled farmers, conservative businessmen, and just plain thugs. President Reagan called them "Freedom Fighters" in a pre–Karl Rove marketing campaign. When he couldn't get congressional support for funding them anymore, our president turned to the Iranians, who had stormed the U.S. embassy in Tehran and captured all the personnel, and began the Iran-Contra "guns for hostages" scandal. The Contras, in turn, planted many of the mines throughout the country, where they were used primarily as weapons of terror, but the mines had no politics. They indiscriminately dismembered or killed whoever stepped on them or tripped the wires attached to their triggers. The mines hung in trees or were buried in the roads and paths of the Nicaraguan countryside. Most insidiously, the Contras planted them in the coffee fields to maim or kill soldiers who went to help with the coffee harvest, the largest source of income for the population and the country. Unlike organized minefield operations, the mines in Nicaragua were placed here and there, in what seemed at the moment to be a strategic area, or where a resting soldier or Contra felt like getting rid of them. They were covered over by growing vegetation. The flooding, earthquakes, and hurricanes that ravage Central America annually moved the land mines around the countryside, presenting new dangers every season to the farmers in the fields and the children on the roads to school. The vegetation and erratic movement have made the job of finding the mines for removal nearly impossible.

The mines in Nicaragua came from the United States, Russia, China, Czechoslovakia, Belgium, and another dozen countries, off-loaded in foreign aid programs or purchased on the open market. The mine that blew off Jose's arms was probably made by Thiokol Corporation in Utah, which had a federal contract to manufacture the M16A2. Other land mines that littered the countryside could have been made by Raytheon in

Massachusetts, Accudyne in Wisconsin, Alliant in Minnesota, or Lockheed in California. All of these companies had lucrative contracts, but none of them fully manufactured the mines. Instead, they would subcontract out for the parts. Perhaps the timers were made by a small company in the Midwest, the casings by another, and the ball bearings that would become deadly shrapnel by a third. There were subcontracts at the time to companies in Florida, Illinois, Massachusetts, Connecticut, California, Alabama, New Jersey, Nebraska, and Pennsylvania. Clearly, the explosive pork barrel was spread among Red and Blue states alike. Even Native Americans got in on the action. While I was working on Fort Belknap Reservation in Montana to stop cyanide-leach gold mining in the 1980s, Fort Belknap Industries was cranking out parts for the M87 "Volcano" land mine under subcontract to Alliant. In most instances, the subcontracting companies would send the components to government facilities managed by private companies for final assembly, such as the Louisiana Army Ammunition Plant in Shreveport, where Jose's M16A2 was likely assembled by Thiokol, or the Iowa Army Ammunition Plant or the Lone Star Army Ammunition Plant. In this way, company execs and workers would be divorced from the final tragic results of their labors (one vice president told me that they didn't make mines, they only made trigger mechanisms—somebody else made the whole mine). Jose and his parents might not have appreciated the technical distinctions. Nor the parents of eleven-year-old Julio, who stepped on a mine while chasing a rabbit, nor the parishioners of Franciscan Brother Tomas, who died when his old red truck hit a Russian TM62M antitank mine.

Fortunately for Jose and many Nicaraguans like him, a small nonprofit clinic had been started in the old colonial city of León in 1999 to provide prosthetics and therapy to land mine victims and other rural poor who could not possibly afford the technology. The project is called Walking Unidos. It was the first international outreach program of the Polus Center for Social and Economic Development, a Massachusetts-based organization that provides services and advocacy for people with disabilities. The Walking Unidos clinic was housed in a modest, one-story structure in a commercial district of León, across from a small supermarket and a movie theater (where I saw my first *Harry Potter* movie in Spanish—"*No soy un magi, solo soy Harry!*").

Inside the building there was a workshop, an examination room, a small office, and a courtyard with parallel handrails for exercising. The workshop contained dozens of donated power tools, including drills, saws, and a router, for shaping and sizing the prosthetic legs and arms that were cast of plastic in the commercial oven nearby. During its first full year in operation in 2000, the clinic provided over one hundred new artificial limbs, eighty-eight prosthetic repairs, and seventeen sets of new braces to Nicaraguans in need. Several of the staff members were amputees who received their limbs and training in prosthetic services at the Walking Unidos clinic. Esteban, the forty-eight-year-old chief prosthetist, grabbed a freshly formed leg and worked its top with a rasp, taking down a sharp edge from the mold. A seventeen-year-old boy sat patiently, waiting for Esteban to bring his new leg over for a test run. An older man walked back and forth in the courtyard, holding on to the handrails. This was a groundbreaking program—a community-based clinic instead of the large, foreign-run operations usually associated with these expensive and high-tech programs. But it sorely needed financial support. Polus had set up the clinic with grants and fund-raisers in Massachusetts, but ongoing operational expenses for developing-world clinics are very hard to come by. I knew firsthand, from working in Guatemala, where the survival of women's health programs was dependent on the continued interest of fickle donors (this year health care, next year chicken projects!). In fact, many development programs around the world begin with great fanfare, only to be closed when the original donors move on to other start-ups or more high-profile projects. Schools are built without money to pay for teachers or books. Solar ovens are installed without spare parts or technical support for the inevitable problems, and so on. Multimillion-dollar USAID programs are abruptly ended, leaving people without jobs and the much depended-upon services.

I had been approached by Michael Lundquist of the Polus Center to supply coffee for the Polus annual dinner and fund-raiser for Walking Unidos. He knew that we purchased coffee from Nicaragua and did development work there. As Michael told me about the project, I realized that we could do a lot more than donate coffee or money. Michael and I talked about ways to generate a steady stream of income to support the clinic. I suggested opening a café. After all, Nicaragua was a great coffee-growing country and many of the victims of the land mines were coffee farmers and their families.

Thus, whole coffee-growing communities were being impacted. León was a university town and many foreigners wandered through as well, so there should be a good customer base for the café. Business Plan 101—have customers. Maybe we could even roast coffee on the premises, just like we did here in the United States. I called around in the coffee industry up here, asking buyers of Nicaraguan coffee if they knew of many café-roasteries in Nicaragua. No one had heard of any. I e-mailed the farmers of Prodecoop, the cooperative I was working with in the mountainous (and mine-impacted) region of Esteli, asking if they were aware of any. Not a single one. It looked like we had the jump on Starbucks at last!

Within a month, Michael and I were in Nicaragua, sipping Victoria beer in the old Hotel Colonial in León with Santiago, the director of Walking Unidos in Nicaragua. Santiago is a big bear of a man, with a thick mustache and a ready grin. He had been a soldier in the revolution and for a time a bodyguard for Daniel Ortega, the president of Nicaragua. But the war was long over, allowing Santiago's immense heart to take center stage. When Santiago heard about the clinic, he came to volunteer and would do anything to help this important project. He quickly worked his way up to director, as Michael realized the talent and commitment of this big man.

In the middle of the splendid, decaying courtyard of the once grand hotel, we planned the creation of the first café-roasterie in the history of Nicaragua. The café would be owned and operated by Walking Unidos. All profits would flow to the clinic, to pay for operating expenses, prosthetic materials, router bits, and anything else that was needed. We drove around León looking at possible sites. Business Plan 101—location, location, location! We decided on a corner shop across the street from the hotel and near the university. It needed a little work. Its colonial tile roof was in need of repair, a paint job was called for, there were no lighting fixtures, and something had crawled out the back and died. Otherwise, it looked pretty good.

I went into the little supermarket to get a few things and see what coffee was going for on the shelves. I wanted to know what the café could charge so that we could make some reasonable income predictions—after all, this was supposed to be a business! As I squatted in the aisle, a young blonde woman walked past. I glanced up to see that she was wearing a faded Dean's Beans T-shirt. It was a sign from the coffee gods.

I left León for Esteli with a very full heart and a head bursting with ideas about the new café. Santiago was going to see about a lease, organize work crews to repair the place, and look for new lighting fixtures (we had gone to a few stores together, but Santiago seemed to favor the heavy black twisted-metal style, sort of "Early Inquisition," which Michael and I felt might send the wrong message to customers). I wanted to spend a few days at Prodecoop visiting the farmers. We needed to talk about the coming harvest, the situation of Fair Trade, and some possible development work together. I also wanted to see how Cooperative Luis Alberto Vasquez in San Lucas, one of my favorite co-op villages, had recovered from the devastation of Hurricane Mitch a year earlier. We had helped put together Hurricaid, a fund-raising concert at the University of Massachusetts that put eleven thousand dollars directly into the farmers' hands after the hurricane. Since I had direct connections with these farmers, we could bypass the government and large aid groups that were taking a slice of the pie from relief donations and holding up supplies in Managua warehouses. The money went to Prodecoop, which bought food and assembled relief packages, brought in roofing and building materials, and rebuilt roads to support the beleaguered coffee communities. Many of these small grower groups had lost their entire coffee crop, their sole source of income for the year, as the high winds had stripped away the flowers, the beans, and the leaves of the plants. One-third of the actual coffee trees were uprooted by Mitch, and new trees would take three to five years to produce. In the absence of government and large aid organizations "helping," the farmers worked quickly and effectively to rebuild their lives with the funds we raised. Then Prodecoop sent us a down-to-the-last-dollar description of where the money went. It was an awesome piece of accounting that we shared with the good folks of Massachusetts who gave so freely at Hurricaid. I only wish that Prodecoop had been in charge of the reconstruction of New Orleans after Hurricane Katrina instead of the feds.

I arrived in Esteli at nightfall and roved the peaceful streets and parks until I was ready to sleep. In the morning, we drove from Prodecoop's office up into the mountains to reach San Lucas. At the base of the last left turn up the mountain sat a forlorn man in a red pickup. He was the same *coyote* who sat there every harvest, offering ready cash to the farmers who carried their beans down the mountain. But there were few customers this year. The final road, which wound around the ledges to reach the village, had been washed down the mountain in several places. The village had thus been completely cut off from Prodecoop and the rest of the world for two weeks. The farmers worked by hand to rebuild the road, which now resembled its former, barely passable self. Manuel, one of the directors, handled his truck like a pro over that terrain, as Merling, the steady, irrepressible manager of Prodecoop, rattled off the statistics of reconstruction. The Hurricaid money had paid for the reconstruction of eight kilometers of roads and one wet processing plant here. The villagers had received 20,700 pounds of corn and 1,600 pounds of beans. Three hundred corrugated zinc sheets for roofing were purchased and ten homes reconstructed. More food relief, road repair, and housing were provided to three other cooperatives, as well. As we approached the cooperative, the sun flashed off the new zinc roofs around the hillsides. Old mud and wattle houses had been updated by brick and mortar. But the sun also baked the earth where large patches and long rows of coffee plants had been yanked out like so many old teeth. Sadness and hope churned inside my guts at the sight of this little mountaintop paradise that had been turned upside down.

The village was very quiet. This was in sharp contrast to my previous visit during the harvest before the hurricane. When we entered the village at that time, the hills on both sides were alive with human and bird sounds. The entire village was engaged in the communal harvest, and laughter and singing were carried down the hills on the soft breeze. The village was made up of resettled families who had been displaced during the civil war. According to a plaque at the entrance to San Lucas, the land had previously belonged to a large landowner who was very well connected to the former dictator, Somoza. Coincidentally, the land had been bought by the dictator's crony with money embezzled from the international reconstruction funds from another natural disaster, the massive earthquake in 1972.

"The landowner lives in Switzerland and doesn't need it anymore," noted Merling with a smile.

We met with the members of the cooperative. They thanked me and all of the people who contributed to Hurricaid for helping them get through this difficult time. I told them that we were with them in good times and bad; that was our commitment to the members of Prodecoop. The farmers had little time to entertain me, as they were hammering, sawing, carrying, and resting all day. It was important to be there as an act of solidarity, but it was also time to leave. On the way down the mountain I explained the idea for the café in León to Merling as we bounced from rock to rock. I wanted to use the green beans from San Lucas for roasting at the café. I asked Merling if she could put the coffee on my account as a continuing contribution to the café from Dean's Beans that would help San Lucas recover.

"*Seguro*, sure. You are a good man," she said, as my head cracked against the roof of the pickup truck.

Merling took me to see the new *beneficio* (processing plant) on the road to Managua. Since it began in 1994, Prodecoop had to have its beans dried, milled, and bagged at a privately owned facility for hire. This limited the value the farmers would ever see from their hard labor. So the farmers of Prodecoop agreed to save their Fair Trade premiums toward the building of their own *beneficio*. The coffee pricing crisis that began in 1998 hit them hard, but it had a silver lining. Many local *beneficios* went out of business, including the one that Prodecoop had used. The farmers were able to purchase the rundown building and grounds and set up their own processing capacity. When I first saw it on this trip the cement drying patios were cracked and weeds grew everywhere. The machinery looked rusted and unusable. But Merling and the rest of the Prodecoop looked at the place with eyes of an unrequited lover and with the same steely determination that had overthrown a dictator. Within a year, Prodecoop was processing all of its members' coffee, thereby controlling the quality to its own satisfaction and keeping a big chunk of the upstream value of the coffee. The money went right back into the farmers' hands.

By the time we returned to León, Santiago had already secured a lease for the site. The Nicaraguans at the clinic named the café Café Ben Linder, after the young Seattle engineer and amateur clown who had been murdered by the Contras in 1987, while working on a small hydroelectric dam in rural northern Nicaragua. It is believed that he was the first U.S. citizen to be killed in the U.S.-funded counterrevolution. On a rainy afternoon Michael, Santiago, and I stood outside the future café, sprinkling ground Prodecoop coffee on the building as a blessing. There was an incredible air of excitement at the clinic that day. It was clear that the Walking Unidos community had claimed the project as their own before we had even roasted the first bean.

Over the next few months, we gathered equipment for the café back in Massachusetts. I found a small, five-pound used roaster for sale in the *WantAdvertiser* for five thousand bucks. It was, amazingly, a Diedrich—the same company that had manufactured our bigger roasters, so I knew how to set up and run the little machine. The owner gave me a pretty good deal when I explained that the machine was headed to Nicaragua for this project. He even threw in a lot of triple-walled exhaust piping, which may have been the only safe exhaust piping I would ever see in Nicaragua. Our funky café was going to be up to code. We packed all the equipment, roaster, piping, grinders, bags, cups, and everything a little café would need into a shipping container that Polus was filling with medical equipment and supplies for León. As the container headed south, a motley crew of one-legged carpenters with tools borrowed from the clinic, and many volunteers replaced red roofing tiles and installed Santiago's heavy metal fixtures (he snuck a few in there after all).

A fully equipped café-roasterie greeted me on my next trip to León in February 2001. A beautiful mural showing the life of Ben Linder was on the wall, painted by Northampton artist Greg Stone. A bank of computers was set up against another wall, donated by Wired International so that Walking Unidos could offer free computer literacy courses to the children of León. A small gift shop of local arts and crafts was nestled in another corner. Manuel had arrived from Prodecoop that morning with a 152-pound bag of green beans for roasting. The green beans were really fresh, clean, and free of the broken beans and other defects usually found in coffee sold internally.

"This project deserves our best quality," said Manuel. I asked him for the bill. He shrugged and said that was Merling's department. Later, I asked Merling for the invoice. She hemmed and hawed and said she couldn't find it. I looked at her with suspicion.

"What's the deal, Merling?"

"Look, this project is a beautiful thing and helps the *amputados*," she said simply. "We don't want to make any money off it, so we are donating the beans."

Manuel stayed and helped us install the little roaster in the back kitchen courtyard (it was open to the sky, so we didn't have to cut through any walls or ceilings!). We received some needed telephone assistance from Steve Diedrich in Idaho.

"It won't start."

"Did you take the shipping cap off the exhaust stack?"

"Uh . . . no."

We set up the brewing and grinding equipment and did a mini-Roastmaster's Course for the staff. Everyone cheered as Santiago dropped the first roast. This first batch of self-sufficiency emptied into the cooling bin and the smell of success and hope wafted into the street. It was the beautiful smell of Sabor de Segovia, the name Prodecoop had given its beans. We sampled the strictly high-grown quality coffee from San Lucas. As always, it delivered abundant body and a mild acidity that stayed on the tongue. In ten minutes the front room was filled with curious and thirsty citizens of León.

The next evening was the official grand opening of Café Ben Linder. It was also the last game of the Nicaraguan World Series of *beisbol* (baseball, obviously!). The León Lions were facing the Managua Boers (named after one side in the Boer War, a common way to name Nicaraguan *beisbol* teams in the old days). Santiago had scored us great seats behind home plate (tickets—fifty cents; beer—a quarter; the experience—priceless). *Beisbol* had come to Nicaragua as the only positive by-product of the invasion and occupation of the country by U.S. Marines during the first decades of the twentieth century. It has become an all-consuming passion over the last century. Nicaragua has long played internationally against Cuba, the United States, Japan, and everyone else and usually fields a respectable team (they totally clocked Team USA in 2007!). But the international team must have taken all of the top players, because the national teams were kind of lackluster. This may have been the result of two significant tactical blunders made by the Sandinista government in the late 1980s: They banned beer from the ballparks (silly socialists!) and banned foreign players from the national teams. So, not only were the fans fall-down drunk on illegal sugar cane moonshine or worse, but without the agile Cubans or hefty Dominican Republic hitters on their teams the players couldn't reach the fences even if they had one of those hurricanes behind their backs. Fortunately for us, the new right-center government—true believers in globalization—had changed the rules again. We were escorted to our seats by the National Police, who gave me a police cap as a respectful thank-you present. This was not because of Café Ben Linder, but because I had funded a coffee-cup-shaped sign in right field of the stadium that read "Café Ben Linder—El Hogar de Dean's Beans" (The Home of Dean's Beans). As the impromptu amateur band wound down its pregame show, I was handed the stadium microphone to deliver an important, beer-soaked message: "Dean's Beans will give one hundred U.S. dollars to any player—even the *gorditos*, the little fat ones from Managua—who hits the sign with a home run!" The crowd went ballistic. But no matter how much beer we drank and how much the crowd derided the *gorditos* and everybody else, no matter how many wild pitches flew into the crowd nor how many errors each team committed, nobody hit a home run that night. Some chucklehead tried to ignite the team's passion by throwing an iguana onto the field with a firecracker tied to its tail (a bizarre León *beisbol* tradition), but it was to no avail. León's hulking homegrown first baseman, Sandor Guido, did whack a few out of the stadium, but they were all foul. Fortunately (except for the iguana), León squeaked past Managua to take the game 4-3. The home team had won the Nicaraguan World Series. Afterward, a delegation from the León Lions came hats in hand with a request.

"*Con permiso*, please, could you move the sign to left field next season? Nobody ever hits home runs to right field. The players are complaining. We want a chance at the money."

The crowd in the streets was wild that night. Cars drove up and down in front of Café Ben Linder honking and swerving, the passengers singing, waving, and occasionally puking out the windows. Even the churches (all thirteen of them) peeled out joyously on their old bells. León was one happy city. The noise was so loud that it echoed off Acosasco Hill at the edge of town, temporarily erasing the screams of tortured political prisoners that some people in León say can still be heard from Somoza's notorious El Fortin prison. The eternal bonfires at the massive municipal garbage dump on the hill, scavenged daily by the poorest of the poor, seemed to glow cheerfully. People poured into Café Ben Linder all night long. We didn't sell much coffee that night, but it was one hell of an opening celebration.

Over the next few years, the café grew. In the first year, it paid for one prosthetic each month. By 2007 it had provided the Walking Unidos clinic with cash for prosthetics and related services for many of the rural poor who entered its doors. The café has also provided meaningful work for many people with disabilities, such as Roque and Mario, who fought on different sides during the counterrevolution and had both lost legs. They work together in the café and the Walking Unidos clinic. Roque and Mario have forgiven their differences and try to help others affected by the war. The roastmaster is Denis, who lost an arm during the war when a homemade bomb he was carrying went off unexpectedly. Denis is the only one-armed roastmaster I know. But a business requires more than good people, good intentions, and equipment. It has been hard to find skilled restaurant managers in León, and the Latin American style of making everything by hand when it is ordered instead of having things prepped and ready has led to a loss of customers, especially among the foreign students and visitors to León. As with any new business, there has been a constant need to reassess the way the café operates and bring in the resources needed to meet the expectations of your customers. This has been an ongoing struggle for the little café-roasterie. At the same time, Café Ben Linder has reached beyond its walls and allowed others to begin to take control of their lives. At the World Trade Organization meeting and protest in Cancún two years later I met a man from Nicaragua selling roasted coffee from his small community of Porvenir. I asked him if they roasted the coffee themselves.

"Oh no, *señor*," he replied. "It is roasted at the Café Ben Linder in Leon."

We also learned a lot about providing economic opportunities for people with disabilities. In 2002 I traveled to Ethiopia with Michael and Esteban. I was working with the Oromia coffee farmers, while Michael and Esteban were investigating whether the Café Ben Linder model could be transported to Ethiopia. Although he worked in the poorest country in the Western hemisphere, Esteban was deeply disappointed with the state of prosthetics in that even poorer country. In one hospital he found the prosthetist carving a foot for a patient out of a block of wood. We agreed that there was much to be done to assist the caregivers of Ethiopia before we could set up an operation like the one in Nicaragua. At the same time, there was an increased need for these services right over the border from Nicaragua in Honduras. This became obvious as more and more of the people seeking help from Walking Unidos had come from that neighboring country. Many of them had suffered from the same land mine problem as the Nicaraguans, as so many of the mines were planted in the border regions by the Nicaraguan combatants. In response, Polus Center and Walking Unidos set up a sister organization called Vida Nueva and a second clinic in Choloteca, Honduras. During one visit to Honduras, Polus representatives came across seven men at a bus stop; all of them were land mine victims—and all of them were coffee farmers. The stories were much the same as across the border. Roberto's son had gone out on his eighteenth birthday to clear a small piece of land he was taking over to plant more coffee. Fifteen minutes later Roberto heard the blast, a frequent sound echoing across the hills in the borderlands. But Roberto knew that this was closer. He ran to the field and found his son dead. Margarit was clearing grass around the base of a coffee tree to improve the air circulation and keep the plant healthy. His machete hit an old mine, blowing off his right arm.

It became clear to Michael and me that there was a relationship between coffee and land mines in Honduras and Nicaragua. Did this problem exist elsewhere? We took maps of the most heavily mined regions of the world and layered them over maps of the coffeelands. Even this crude attempt at Geographic Information Systems immediately revealed an ugly picture. Land mines scarred the lush coffee landscapes all around the world. They ranged from Ethiopia, where the mines were primarily in parts of the country where there was no coffee, such as Tigray by the Eritrean border, to Colombia, where mines and less formal explosive devices were inextricably intertwined with coffee, creating three new victims each day. There was Angola, which once earned over 90 percent of its export dollars from coffee. That number had dropped to less than 2 percent, as the roads were so heavily mined that even if the coffee could be picked it would be nearly impossible to get it to the ports safely. Angola had seven million mines planted in a country of four million people. Southeast Asian countries, such as Vietnam, Cambodia, and Laos, all rely on coffee exports. Yet many important coffee areas in those countries are terribly heavy with unexploded mines from long-ago conflicts. The Central Highlands region of Vietnam is among the largest coffee regions in the country. However, it was also the site of major U.S. bases during the Vietnam War (or the American War, as they know it), and the fields of Pleiku, Da Nang, and Khe San still carry on the war through unexploded land mines and other munitions. Even though we were the first to connect the dots on this, it was clearly a massive, worldwide problem. And it certainly was bigger than Dean's Beans or Polus Center, no matter how much coffee we drank and how hard we worked. We decided that since this was a problem endemic to the coffeelands, it should be addressed by the coffee industry. We chewed it over during a series of lunches and decided to create a trust that coffee companies could both contribute to and participate in. After all, many coffee companies (but surprisingly not all) know where their coffee comes from, so they have a role to play in identifying affected coffee-growing communities. That kind of on-the-ground data collecting would get us right to the places where help was needed. The companies could then fund work in the very communities where they bought their coffee if they so chose.

But the land mine problem is multifaceted. The mines have to be cleared, which is an extremely expensive, massively labor-intensive, and skilled undertaking, usually done by governments and specialized groups. That was beyond our resources and experience. Communities needed to be educated and made aware of the presence of mines and how to identify and avoid them. This is called "mine risk education" and was also done by governments and many NGOs. The other significant piece of work to be done was called "victim economic reintegration." Simply put, getting the victims or their supporting family members back to work. In fact, Michael told me that meaningful work was one of the first things a land mine victim would say when asked what kind of support he needed. The other most prominent concern was the loss of a spouse ("I am afraid my wife will leave me," or more commonly, "My husband left when I lost my leg"). As we dug through the academic literature, reports by nonprofits in the field, and National Mine Reports from affected countries, it became increasingly clear that significant resources and attention were not available for economic development here. Even where line items existed for this work in budgets, they tended to be very small and the actual details rather vague. There were few successful back-to-work programs for land mine victims out there.

We decided that this was where we could make the biggest contribution. After all, we had been in the business of job creation and creative development work since the beginning, and Polus had the expertise in working with people with disabilities. There were plenty of innovative people in the coffee industry who could add ideas to the mix. For example, many of the cooperatives we and others work with have started to set up their own cupping labs to check the quality of their harvests. You don't need legs to cup coffee, so there could be great work here for impacted farmers. There are many other opportunities within coffee for land mine victims, if the training and support are made available—and that's the job of the Coffeelands Landmine Victims Trust.

Polus applied for a grant from the State Department Office of Weapons Removal and Abatement (the Good Guys), who were charged with cleaning up the mess created around the world, in part, by the other branches of the State Department (the sometimes Good Guys, sometimes Bad Guys). Jim and Stacy from the Good Guys were completely supportive and saw this as a model for the kind of public-private partnerships that everyone in Washington was talking about but not that many privates were stepping up to join. The grant allowed us to map more seriously the relationship between coffee-growing areas and land mines and to begin educating the coffee industry about the problem and seeking its support. We put together a DVD with testimony from coffee farmers who had lost limbs and loved ones to land mines, mixed in maps and our commentary, and hit the road. Our first stop was Green Mountain Coffee Roasters in Vermont. Even though I had been a bad boy to Green Mountain, constantly challenging their trade practices in the past, I knew that they would be a sympathetic audience. In fact, Rick, one of the old-timers at Green Mountain, had been one of the first Coffee Kids supporters when Bill and I started the group and was now the chair of its board. Rick was a very committed guy, and we had become very close, despite the smoke and thunder of competition between our two companies. Michael and I went up to Vermont and came back with a commitment of support from the company. We next hit the West Coast, hoping to corral some of that Starbucks money that flowed from all those ten-dollar Grande Immenso Lattes or whatever they are. We didn't plan far enough ahead, as there was not enough time to organize a Seattle roasters meeting, even though we had gotten a lot of interest in response to my e-mails. Starbucks would have to do.

The Starbucks corporate office (the Mothership) is in an old industrial building near the Seattle waterfront. The decor is sort of industrial chic, with exposed pipes and columns painted white and pastels. We waited in the reception area for Sue to come get us for our meeting. The steel elevator opened and out came six young businessmen, obviously there to try to convince the mermaid to buy their wares. They were all dressed in immaculate suits, but curiously, they had no ties on. The two Japanese men in the group seemed uncomfortable in the semiformal wear, as if their zippers were open instead of their necklines. A Starbucks employee walking by told me that the dress code was "enforced casual." The men had taken their ties off in the parking lot before entering the building. We met with Sue and Megan, both higher-ups with portfolios that included aspects of social responsibility. I had known Sue ever since I launched a massive assault on her company as we shared a panel at the SCAA in Berkeley years back. It was the year that both Dean's Beans and Starbucks decided to sign on to Fair Trade. After her feathers deruffled from the shock and awe, Sue realized that my inartful comments were nothing personal, and in spite of my sometimes lovingly affronting style, we have become good friends. Of course, moving Sue and Megan to tears is my forte, but that was not the same as getting a commitment from one of the largest companies on the planet. Fortunately, thanks to Sue, Starbucks quickly came through with financial support for the program.

We flew down to San Francisco to meet with progressive importers Royal Coffee and some of its customers. Royal puts out a newsletter to its several thousand customers, so the company would be a great avenue for disseminating information about the project. Also, since it bought from coffee communities around the world, it would be a big help in getting the word out to farmers. As always, the crew at Royal was receptive to my offbeat ideas, even though they tend to get ensnared in stuff outside the normal course of business, such as helping me import organic Fair Trade sugar from Peru ("Dean, we're coffee importers, remember?"). All of the roasters at the meeting were interested in getting involved. In fact, coffee communities and their governments universally supported the project. The Colombian Coffee Federation, those Juan Valdez guys, were completely open to the work. The organization of the coffee industry in Colombia makes information sharing about social issues like this very straightforward. Michael and Jim went to Colombia to meet with government service providers and land mine victims. They met farmers' kids who got hurt collecting firewood, hunting armadillos, and doing many of the ordinary things kids on the farm do. The kids were more worried about how they would care for their moms as they got older than about themselves. I went to the Sierra Nevada region, where indigenous farmers do not often seek help after getting hurt by land mines, as the culture tells them that the earth is punishing them somehow. I didn't get much information as those societies are pretty closed to strangers, even though I was one of the first buyers of their coffee for export. After a second visit to the Manizales region by Michael and Santiago from Walking Unidos, we started to draft a formal relationship with the government and the Coffee Federation to do victim economic reintegration work in Colombia.

We had heard that it was not easy to work in the coffee-growing regions of Vietnam, despite the large number of land mine victims and the huge number of mines still there. But the uniqueness of this program seems to melt away barriers. Thanks to Michael Sheridan from Catholic Relief Services, I was introduced to Mr. Giang, who is in charge of foreign nonprofits doing work in Vietnam. Before our phone call, I called every Vietnamese restaurant in the book, in hopes of learning some polite expressions to impress Mr. Giang. The owner of a restaurant in Philadelphia helped me out.

"*Sin giao. An goh kwey kong?*" I said with some trepidation. ("Hello. How are you?") Mr. Giang was pleased.

"Where did you learn such good Vietnamese? Have you been to our country?" he asked.

"*Gam uhng.* (Thank you.) Well, to be honest . . ." I told Mr. Giang the truth, as I didn't want our relationship to start with a lie (I gave that up after my first marriage). He laughed and was even happier that I had made the effort for him.

We talked for a long time about the land mine situation in Vietnam and my ideas on working with the Vietnamese coffee industry as well as ours to address the problem. I then took a chance and shared something deep.

"I also want you to know that I have a personal motive here," I began softly. "My brother Randy was a marine in Da Nang during the war. I have spoken to him about this project and he is happy that I am doing it. This is a small way for me to make amends for my family's involvement, to give something back to your country." There was silence on the other end for a moment.

"Thank you very much," replied Mr. Giang gently. "Your thoughts are greatly appreciated. Our country will welcome you."

Café Ben Linder has seen its ups and downs, as any business does. Many coffee people have volunteered to go down and teach refresher courses in roasting and help with menu planning and café management. We are going to install an espresso machine and train a person with disabilities to run it. He or she will be entered to compete in the International Barista Competition at the SCAA in Minneapolis in 2008.

The Coffeelands Landmine Victims Trust is becoming better known in the industry. More companies are stepping up to support the work with contributions of time and money. We have identified many affected communities and coffee workers and are designing creative ways to reintegrate them into the workforce. But our work has just begun.

PART FOUR

ASIA

8

Good Friends, Cold Beer
... and a Water Buffalo

SUMATRA, 2003

When Umesh, the owner of Zumi's Espresso in Ipswich, Massachusetts, brews up a pot of our Sumatran French Roast, he is continuing a New England tradition dating back to 1803. In June of that year, the ship *Margaret* tied up at the wharf in Salem, unloading the first shipment of Sumatran coffee in the young United States. The cargo was an afterthought, a hold-filler for the more important cargo of pepper from Sumatra. Brawny sailors from Ipswich, Essex, and a dozen small New England towns swayed the burlap bags of beans out of the hold and onto the dock. At that time, the only Starbucks was a prominent whaling family on nearby Nantucket (and they probably drank tea).

The *Margaret* had fared better than many ships from Salem that plied the spice trade to the East Indies. During those early years of the trade, several ships (most notably the *Putnam* and the sadly named *Friendship*) lost crew and cargo to the jagged-bladed *kris* knives of Malay pirates off the Sumatran coast. The American ships were seen as easy prey for the locals, as they were lightly armed, unlike the Dutch, British, Spanish, and Portuguese, who sought territory, slaves, and spices in convoys of heavy merchant warships.

War, peace, and coffee remain front and center in Sumatra. While Umesh poured the dark roast in Ipswich, I sat in the Vermont office of Senator Patrick Leahy drinking some lesser brew. I was there with Iswandi and Salim, two ethnic Gayo Sumatran coffee farmers, and Tomas Fricke, the founder of Forestrade, a progressive company that helps organize coffee and spice cooperatives around the world. Iswandi was the chairman of Pertusan Petani Kopi Gayo Organik, known as PPKGO, a successful farmer's cooperative. Salim was the head of quality control for Forestrade's Indonesian operation. We were there to talk to the senator's staff about the worsening human rights situation in Aceh and Sumatra Uttara, the two northernmost provinces of Sumatra. There, the long-running battle for autonomy from central Indonesian control had spilled into the coffeelands of Iswandi and Salim, bringing death and destruction to a region known for its tolerance and peacefulness. Senator Leahy was the author of the Leahy Law on Human Rights, which requires cessation of international aid to countries where human rights violations are found. It was hoped that the senator would work to stop massive U.S. arms shipments to Indonesia that were being used on the citizens of Sumatra.

After the meeting, we went to a local saloon for lunch and a cold beer. Although both men are Muslims and that religion generally forbids the use of alcohol, Salim and Iswandi sipped at their beers as an act of solidarity with the Vermont farmers who grew the ingredients. I had been dealing with their cooperative, PPKGO, since its inception in 1997. At that time, Tomas was working with Sumatran farmers growing spices but wanted to branch out into coffee at the request of the community. He brought me samples of their coffee and asked if I would try it and give him feedback. The bright green beans were fresh and aromatic. They were rock hard, guaranteeing that they would hold their taste profile deep into a dark roast. When we roasted and brewed them, the beanery filled with a smooth, full scent. We immediately agreed to be among the first buyers. I have been drinking their Sumatran coffee every morning since that day.

Salim told us how the low-intensity war had frightened away many people, especially young men who would otherwise work the farms. They were afraid of being conscripted by one side or the other or feared the random violence that accompanies such conflict. Although the war generally raged on to the north of the farming regions, it occasionally washed over their lands, as members of GAM (Free Aceh Movement) slipped away from pursuing government forces into the thick rain forest of the Gayo region or took refuge in the nearby Gunung Leuser national park. Further, the low coffee prices of the world market translated into lesser amounts in the farmers' pockets, so there was little money to pay for labor or needed organic fertilizers. Iswandi wondered how the farmers would be able to keep the fields healthy without labor and fertilizers, and we drank and talked late into the afternoon. I noticed Salim, who was a trained agronomist, scribbling on a notepad as we talked. I asked him what he was writing.

"I am thinking about the water buffalo," he said, not lifting his hand from the diagrams and notations on the pad. He only looked up quizzically when Iswandi guffawed at my comment that I missed my family on long trips, as well.

"No, it is not that," he said soberly. "Look at this." Salim held out the pad as we slipped off our bar stools and gathered around him. "The water buffalo urinates about ten liters each day, and this is what I calculate his fecal load to be." He stabbed at the page, his brows deeply furrowed. His hands were permanently browned and scarred from a lifetime of working the soil.

"Nice lunchtime conversation, Salim, but what does it mean?" I asked.

"This is the right amount of nitrogen, potassium, and other natural compounds to fertilize one hectare of land each year. And one hectare, about two acres, is the average holding of our farmers. A water buffalo could provide enough fertilizer to a farmer to care for his land. Also, the water buffalo is a ground feeder. He would eat the weeds around the coffee plants but probably not eat the coffee plant itself. This may be the answer to our problem. The water buffalo is what you call an 'eco-management' system!" He put down the pad with a satisfied smile. "Yes, this is a good possibility."

"But Salim," I questioned, "there have been water buffalo in Sumatra for centuries. Hasn't anybody figured this out already?"

"We use water buffalo in the rice fields and to plow in the lowlands, but they are not generally found in the mountains."

"So how much would it take to buy a water buffalo, transport it to the mountains, and take care of it?" My "development mind" was starting to kick into high gear.

Salim grabbed his pad and began scribbling numbers. "I think it would cost about four hundred U.S. dollars."

"I'll make you a deal, Salim. I will fund the first water buffalo eco-management project for five hundred dollars, but on three conditions. The first is that you name the Buffalo Paman (Uncle) Dean. The second is that you monitor the progress of Paman Dean in a very scientific manner for six months, to see if your scribbles were accurate and to make sure that Paman Dean does what he is supposed to do." I took a final swig of my beer.

"And what is the third condition?" asked Iswandi.

"After six months I will come to Sumatra. If Paman Dean is a success, we will have a big celebration."

"And if he is not?" Salim was writing this down.

"We will eat Paman Dean."

Maps are incredibly deceiving when it comes to time and space. I was already working in New Zealand on my first visit to Indonesia in 1991. As I looked at the map, Indonesia was only a few inches away, closer than the mainland United States or even Hawaii. Yet it took twelve hours to fly from Auckland to Jakarta direct. Curse the famous Dutch mapmaker Gerardus Mercator for that one. Mercator projections, the standard for wall maps, distort size and distance in the southern hemisphere, making the United States and Europe larger than South America and Africa (which they are not), and screwing up my perception of the distances between southern points. So even though I appreciated Mercator's revolutionizing maps past the old Ptolemic woldview, and the fact that he saved hundreds of sixteenth-century mariners from falling off the earth or ending up on wrongly charted reefs, he did make a mess of my first Indonesia trip.

Sumatra is almost the furthest point on the globe away from Boston (actually the honor goes to Shark Bay on the coast of South Australia, but no coffee grows there). For centuries, the Muslim Kingdom of Aceh, at the northern tip of the massive island, was the gateway to the fabled Spice Islands. The ever-greedy European powers of the day wanted to get direct access to the Spice Islands, cutting out the middleman king of Aceh, but the kingdom was simply too powerful. So the Europeans paid duties and tribute each time they passed the tip of Sumatra to move into the Strait of Malacca and on to the Spice Islands. In 1511, after a tremendous battle involving warships of many nations, war elephants, and poison arrows, the Portuguese under Alfonso de Albuquerque (of New Mexico fame) pummeled their way into control of Malacca, the port city-state that controlled the strait. But the ancient spirits of the region were not so easily subdued. Albuquerque and his treasure ship, *Flor de Mar*, loaded with the greatest plunder the world had ever seen (including one hundred Asian virgins for the obviously over-testosteroned King Manuel of Portugal), sank in a typhoon off the Sumatran coast. Albuquerque survived the disaster only by spearing many of his officers as they tried to grab on to his lone lifeboat. Although Malacca vanished as an independent entity from that point forward, Aceh remained an independent kingdom until the late nineteenth century, when superior Dutch armaments finally overcame the tenacious resistance of its warriors (including the curiously named "Acehnese murderers"—suicide bombers who were told they would go straight to heaven). The proud Acehnese have been fighting for independence ever since. When the Dutch ultimately relinquished power in 1942 after a decades-long bloody insurrection, the Acehnese found themselves under the control of the Japanese invaders. Finally, after the war, the new lords of Sumatra were the Javanese, who made up the political hierarchy of the new nation of Indonesia. The new princes were the multinational oil, gas, and minerals companies that had discovered substances more valuable than the pepper and spices coveted by earlier invaders. In the latest iteration of this long struggle, the Acehnese GAM had fought the Indonesian army to a standstill in the mountains of Aceh and North Sumatra, while seeking a political accommodation for greater autonomy from Jakarta.

The end of Paman Dean's probation period coincided with the eve of the U.S. invasion of Iraq in late March of 2003 to rid the world of Saddam Hussein's weapons of mass destruction. Representatives of two other companies buying PPKGO coffee (Equal Exchange and Green Mountain) were going to join me on this trip, as neither company had visited these farmers before. Both companies backed out, fearing some sort of retribution from the locals (98 percent Muslim) due to the impending invasion. I knew better. The most populous Muslim nation on earth was also the most religiously tolerant, and Christian, Muslim, Hindu, and Buddhist communities lived in relative harmony. I learned this firsthand on my maiden visit to Indonesia in January of 1991. After clearing customs I sat in a taxi in the notorious gridlocked traffic of Jakarta. A newspaper boy slammed a paper against the window with the huge one-word headline "PERANG!" I wondered out loud what that meant. The cabbie turned to me over the seat and said in a friendly, matter-of-fact, *Year of Living Dangerously* voice, "That means 'war,' boss."

That was the start of Desert Storm, the first large-scale U.S. invasion of the Fertile Crescent. The entire time we traveled Indonesia during that trip we encountered young men claiming to be Saddam Hussein or George Bush, or otherwise making jokes about the invasion. Others asked politely why we were involved in the subterranean oil tiff between Kuwait and Iraq. There wasn't a moment of serious anti-Americanism. If anything, people were universally friendly and pro-American. The big lesson, as always, was "these Muslims aren't the same as those Muslims."

This time, in the post-9/11 world, it was hardly different. The 2003 U.S. invasion of Iraq brought riots outside the U.S. embassy in Jakarta, but my Indonesian friends told me they had more to do with returning students being charged high fees to apply for visas and being refused without an explanation or a refund by some very unfriendly embassy staff.

The Gayo in particular have enfolded the values and practices of Islam into their animist worldview with amazing grace. The ancient Gayo tradition of open debate, including men and women, has meant an Islam accommodated to their open and welcoming society. Further, although centuries of trade and population movements have brought myriad cultural influences to the coasts, the high mountains and remote valleys have allowed indigenous cultures to remain strong, accepting change at a more measured pace. Change also comes slowly to the Gayo, not because they resist it, but because they think about it, debate it, and massage it before incorporating new ideas or practices. This helps explain why the manager of Forestrade in Indonesia, who works closely with the farmers and is heavily involved in the decision making at PPKGO, is an ethnic Chinese woman. Lucia is a short, round-faced, energetic woman, prone to wearing fuzzy pink sweaters and toreador pants. She has been known to break up a long business meeting by calling for an aerobics session or yogic stretching. Trust me, these are not common practices among the coffee farmers of the world. The farmers of PPKGO see and appreciate her managerial and business skills and have made her the liaison between the complex worlds of buyers and sellers. Lucia was born to trade. Her father and uncles were businessmen and her grandfather was a spice trader on the coast at Padang. Her distant relatives could have sold that first cargo of coffee to America.

PPKGO is also an interesting mix of ethnicities. Although predominantly Gayo Muslims, membership includes Javanese, Acehnese, Padang, and Batak farmers. The farmers' religious affiliations include Muslim, Christian, Hindu, and animist. Since its formation in the late 1990s, PPKGO has been an important force for promoting peaceful conflict resolution and economic stability in the tense border region with Aceh. The group has even provided shelter and sustenance for people fleeing the conflict.

The visit also coincided with the latest in a series of ceasefires between GAM and the Indonesian army. Even though we would see many burned homes and hear horror stories about the conflict, we would be able to travel Sumatra in safety. Just as important, the farmers were really excited about our visit.

I took a meandering course to get to Medan, the city in Aceh that was "closest" to the Gayo farming region (it took fifteen hours from Medan by car to get there). I went via Jakarta to take in some special sights. The late-night welcome to Jakarta was a ride down the broad avenue from the airport to town. As if to remind you of the intensity of poverty in the country, the median grass strip for miles outside the airport was crammed with cardboard and corrugated shacks, where thousands of homeless and desperately poor Indonesians lived. The hundreds of small kerosene lanterns that lit the shacks added a surreal festivity to the scene. After a short night at the Wismah Bumi Asi hotel (the minaret across the street started loudspeaker prayers at 4 AM), we headed down to Jakarta's ancient and historic harbor, Sunda Kelapa.

I stood on the wooden docks, staring up at the tall masts of the fabled Bugi schooners as they offloaded their coffee cargos from the outer islands of the archipelago. The ancestors of these gnarly, hard sailors may have attacked the *Putnam* and the *Friendship*, as the Bugis are a race of *orang laut* (sea people) who have been pirates and merchants in these waters since anyone can remember. When British and Dutch colonists wanted to make their children behave in these parts, they would threaten them by saying, "If you don't go to sleep, the Bugi-man will get you!"

I watched the Bugi-men carry 150-pound sacks of coffee on their backs up and down a gangplank that was, in fact, a narrow board hacked from a tree trunk. The Bugi-men offered to let me come on board, provided I carried a sack like everyone else. I looked down into the tetanus-laced waters of Jakarta harbor and demurred, whereupon they offered to carry me and a sack of beans up on one of their backs. I sprinted up the plank on my own to the laughter of the crew. The hundred-foot vessel was made entirely by hand, without power tools, on the beach of one of the islands in the Makassar Strait (just the other side of Borneo!). I can't even put in a screw without an electric screw gun anymore. The planks were held onto the ribs of the schooner by trennels (tree nails), carved wooden pegs. The masts were gigantic tree trunks, still exhibiting the twists and turns of growing on a windy coast. Much of the rigging was hand-wrapped hemp, which is surprisingly strong, although hunks of iron plate and probably pirated steel wire appeared here and there. The crew let me look into one of the coffee bags on deck (I politely declined their offer to go into the hold below). It amazed me that these burlap sacks and their contents would survive the trucking, shipping, craning, and overall abuse they would be subject to on their wonderfully long journey from village Indonesia to the cafés of America and Europe. When I show farmers photos of their coffee in the burlap bags in our roasterie, they are as amazed as I am.

Medan is a massive industrial city on the northwest coast of Sumatra. Most of the coffee groups, including PPKGO, send their beans here for export. The ships at the port of Medan are no Makassar schooners. Rather, they are the huge container ships that pack as many as four hundred containers on deck, each coffee container carrying forty thousand pounds of green beans. The container ships steam out of the port on their thirty-day voyage to California. On their way, they pass dozens of *jermal*, offshore wooden fish traps and processing stations on stilts, largely served by debt-pledged or abducted children aged twelve to sixteen. Children's welfare groups in Indonesia and internationally have long fought to end this abusive situation, but the Indonesian government has spared few resources to help these low-priority young citizens.

Salim, Iswandi, Lucia, and Tomas met me in Medan, along with several Indonesian soldiers who would accompany us during the visit to the farmers. Apparently, part of the ceasefire required soldiers to stick with all foreign visitors. In theory, the practice was meant to keep the visitors safe, but there was a lot of talk as to how this enabled the government to keep its eyes on foreigners going into GAM-friendly territory. The soldiers were all from the neighboring island of Sulawesi, to ensure their loyalty to the national government instead of to family and ethnic group. This is a pretty common practice in multiethnic societies and can lead to terrible human rights violations, as the soldiers feel little kinship with the local population. These soldiers were pretty laid-back, however, and I came to realize that they really got off on being with foreigners, as we asked them to eat and drink with us at every meal. Thus, as the trip progressed, the number of soldiers swelled from the original two to around a dozen, and the bar bills grew accordingly. By the time we visited the last village we were followed by three trucks full of soldiers, all very friendly and happy to slap "Make Coffee Not War" bumper stickers on their military vehicles. I asked Lucia about this.

"The soldiers are as tired of war as we are. They agree with your bumper sticker." At the same time, our passenger car sported an automatic weapon tucked next to the stick shift, with the barrel pointed toward our backseat. I prayed for smooth roads.

The long drive from Medan toward the coffee-farming regions passed through the entire history and ecology of Sumatra. The coastal lowlands beyond Medan's industrial zones were full of rice paddies and tobacco farms, both introduced over the centuries to cater to the shifting populations of Malays, Chinese, and Europeans. In the hills we passed abandoned or poorly tended nutmeg gardens, victims of the nutmeg blight of the 1960s that destroyed a premier export. Now even the endemic clove cigarettes of Sumatra are rolled on other islands. Further on, the oak and hardwood montane forests were broken up by palm or rubber plantations. The palm provides oil for cooking and now is being looked at as a source of biofuel, as the world cooking oil market has become saturated. The rubber trees were being tapped to make the condoms of the world, as that impervious substance had made a comeback in the face of the relentless HIV/AIDS crisis.

Each small town seemed to have the same pattern of development. A mosque, a few cafés and restaurants, and an agricultural supply store. Outside of one of the general stores stood a pallet stacked with paper sacks emblazoned with the large block letters SEMEN.

Tomas noticed my slight smile and whispered, "Don't go there, Dean. It means 'cement' in Indonesian."

We spent the night at a palatial resort on the shore of Lake Tawar. Our small entourage of farmers and soldiers constituted the entire guest list, although it took a while for the manager to find our reservation. We were waited on solicitously by a staff twice our number.

"Times are very hard," said the manager through a sad smile. "But we do not let the staff go. The violence will end someday. We must be prepared for when things will get better."

Lake Tawar sat in a bowl of steep hills. I could see ripe coffee plants all throughout the hillsides. Sharp-eyed (and taloned) fisher hawks dove into the lake to grab fish feeding on surface insects in the early morning glow. Just beyond the hotel, fishermen cast nets from small canoes to haul in the huge mountain lake's bounty. The fish were brought to the hotel and immediately put on the grill for breakfast. They weren't even gutted, so I carefully pulled the meat off the bony skeletons. The insects were still in there somewhere, and I didn't want to see them at breakfast. This cultural sensitivity wasn't shared by the soldiers, who held the fish by the head, put the whole fish in their mouths, and sucked everything off the skeleton. *Must be a Sulawesi thing*, I thought as I looked away quickly. We were soon joined by a half dozen members of the PPKGO board of directors, who wanted to accompany us to the welcoming ceremony ahead (and maybe, like the soldiers, enjoy the free eats at the hotel). We headed even higher, entering the Bukit Barisan (Parade of Mountains), the thousand-mile-long range that grows like a twelve-thousand-foot-high spine down the center of this enormous island. Bukan Barisan is the home to many rare and endangered species, including the Sumatran tiger, elephant, and rarely seen rhino. Monkey life was active and evident in the trees all around, but we didn't see any of the dwindling population of Sumatran *orang utan* (forest people).

We pulled up to the iron gates of the processing plant at the compound of C. V. Trimaju in Takengon. Here, farmers from throughout the surrounding hills brought their red cherries to be soaked and fermented, depulped, and dried in the sun on Trimaju's huge cement (that's *semen* in Indonesian!) patios. As we got out of the cars, the sound of drums, flutes, and gongs reverberated around the walls and out into the hillsides. We entered the gates and were met by hundreds of farmers and their families, smiling, clapping, and singing welcoming songs in Gayo. It seemed as though the two sides of the welcoming path were arguing happily with each other in song. This was *didong*, the traditional Gayo version of a poetry slam. Teams of men and boys trade songs and insults, or in our case, praise and welcome. Each team vies to outdo the other but follows the format of a swaying song and response, accentuated by rapid, complex hand clapping. *Didong* has always been a means of transmitting culture, myth, and morality among the Gayo, who don't have a written language (which drove missionaries crazy, as there was no local language into which they could translate the Western Bible). Churches and governments over the years have tried to subvert *didong* into a vehicle for the propaganda of the moment, but the Gayo have always resisted this invasion. Many of the *didong* singers were dressed in traditional clothing, including a Gayo version of a cowboy hat, fabulously embroidered with the gold and red patterns of Kerawang Gayo.

A group of women met us as we entered the compound. One by one they chanted prayers over us as we were sprinkled with water (purification—yes, please) and rice (fertility—no, thanks) and given floral leis and palmlike leaves to carry. We walked through the crowd as big brass *mong-mong* gongs were played with padded wooden mallets and *bansi* flutes and three-stringed *arbab* zithers carved from jackfruit trees danced around us. Women played the *rapaii pasai*, a tambourine covered in goat's skin. We were led to a small covered stage and sat on couches surrounded by tables of beautiful exotic fruits. A tent stood before the stage, and in it sat forty to fifty Muslim women, swaddled in Gayo blue dresses and white head cowls or scarves. In Gayo culture the women do not cover their faces, so we were met with half a hundred smiling, almond-shaped faces. A handful of gold teeth glimmered in the crowd.

Ringing the tent and the stage were a hundred more farmers and their families. Most of the men and boys were dressed in a mix of T-shirts, gym shorts, jeans, cotton short-sleeve shirts, and knit polos. There was little to distinguish them from rural folk anywhere from Africa to Arkansas. The air smelled of sharp clove cigarettes and sweet fermenting coffee cherries.

On stage we sat with the elders of the community, including Mr. Misradi, the founder of the facility, and his son, Adi. After opening prayers, we took turns giving speeches of praise and thanksgiving for our relationship. During one speech, I asked Adi quietly who the women in the tent were.

"Those are the widows of the farmers killed during this conflict," he said sadly.

"But there are so many!" I was shocked by the number, but also by their friendly demeanor.

"We honor and support them, so they are taken care of even without their husbands or fathers. That is our responsibility in this community."

After the speeches, each widow came forward and was given an envelope with cash and a beautiful piece of sarong cloth as a gift. I gave out special T-shirts I had made for the trip that sported a map of Sumatra and the words "PPKGO/Dean's Beans/Forestrade 2003 Kopi Friendship Visit." When the ceremony ended, the women spontaneously began playing the tambourine and singing. I got up and began dancing with the widows in the front row. It was good for a laugh

After the beautiful ceremony and dancing, we retired to Adi's large house for a huge buffet. There, among the many exotic *belimbing* (starfruit), *ubi* (sweet potato), *jambu* (guava), the unrecognizable fruits and vegetables, and the fish, shrimp and meats, I came face-to-face with the dreaded durian, known as "The World's Smelliest Fruit." Guests are forbidden to bring the durian into hotel rooms in Indonesia. I had seen one of those international "forbidden" signs, red circle on top of a durian picture, in the Medan hotel lobby. Its repugnant odor is reputed to cling to bedspreads, draperies, and maids like the body odor of a triathlete. I had only heard stories about the durian but thought, *hey, how bad can it be?*

Iswandi, Salim, and several farmers gathered around, and Lucia headed to the other side of the room with a pinched look on her face, as I prepared to dissect the forbidding fruit before me. It is an innocent-looking, brain-shaped yellowish green fruit the size of a soccer ball. Its thick, horny hide was difficult to cut but gave way under my full body weight. Inside were thin membranes covering sections of custardlike goo, each containing a large brown pit. *Harmless enough.* I raised the durian toward my nose and was hit with a nasal sledgehammer. High-school boys' locker room with a dash of periodontal disease? A donkey ride into the Grand Canyon on a hot August afternoon? A public toilet in Tehran? It was all that and more, as my mind grasped to identify and escape from the rude stench. I swooned and let out an involuntary "arrrrggghhh!" as the farmers howled with pleasure. I fell forward with my tongue out like Galahad's lance and pierced the offending goo. It was sweet and quite good.

I went to the *mandi* to wash the durian off my face and learned another lesson in Indonesian etiquette. Never mind the durian. After handling and eating immensely hot peppers, it is a really good idea to wash your hands *before* using the toilet.

On the way back to the meal, I was waylaid by Adi's twin fourteen-year-old daughters. They had taken off their ceremonial robes and were sporting jeans and T-shirts like any other kids. I had told them earlier that I had two daughters, and the twins wanted to show me their room. With Adi's permission, we went upstairs to what could have been a teenager's room anywhere in the United States. A large poster of Queen adorned the wall, along with cutouts of magazine fashion ads and movie stars. Their school notebooks sat on the desk plastered with Japanese cartoon kittens and photos of Leonardo, Brad, and Ashton. I felt right at home.

After a long day of ceremony, food, and discussion, the men retired to the *meresah*, a traditional thatch and wood dormitory attached to Adi's family house. The soldiers drove off to sleep elsewhere or to do night patrols through the area or to get drunk. In the humid darkness of the spartan *meresah* we talked about hope and fear, about caring for your family in a time of violence and uncertainty. They shared the difficulty of getting their coffee down to Medan through government and rebel roadblocks and shakedowns, worrying about theft and overfermentation from the delays. They talked about curfews that made returning from the forests or from coffee deliveries a calculated risk of injury, disappearance, or death. Out of the darkness came a tentative question.

"Do many Americans hate Muslims?"

"No," I responded clearly. "Most Americans have never met a Muslim, but I don't think they blame all Muslims for the problems caused by the jihadists. I think if more Americans came here, they would really like the Gayo people."

"Then they should come here and be welcomed," replied the voice.

"There wouldn't be enough room in the *meresah*!" shouted a tired voice. "Now be quiet and go to sleep!"

We all slept on thin pads on the hard plank flooring. The Gayo men slept on their sides, putting rolled mats they called "Dutch wives" between their legs to keep their knees comfortably apart. The mosquitoes were surprisingly fierce that night. I wondered if they were drawn to the durian smell that wouldn't come off my fingers and face.

In the morning we cruised the small villages of the Takengon region on the way to Wonosari, the home of Paman Dean. We stopped in at several farmers' houses and town squares. We saw three of the water supply systems that we had helped fund over the years. These were simple gravity piping systems taking water from mountain streams down into the villages for distribution. These systems were familiar to me. I had put together Coffee Kids' first and only Asian project on just the other side of this mountain range in 1990. I had interviewed four different community-based groups before deciding on one to do the project. The group was called Bina Insani. It was one of the hundreds of grassroots, on-the-ground community development groups that dot the Indonesian landscape. Bina Insani helped the farmers figure out how much material to buy, coordinated the shipping and setting up of the pipes and cement, and worked with the farmers to set up a fair labor system for installing the pipes. It was a great and successful project. The farmers and their families had dug the pits to lay the pipe through the mountains and bring potable water to the fifteen hundred people of Simalungun for the first time ever. Here, since PPKGO was such a strong, locally based organization already, the farmers had organized themselves to do the work without any intermediary group. The water ran cold and clear out of the pipes.

We also visited a few mosques that had been repaired and expanded through Fair Trade and other monies the farmers had received. The mosques often had *madrassas*, schools of Muslim learning, in the compound. *Madrassas* got terrible press after 9/11 as breeding grounds for terrorists, and there are many such schools teaching hatred and intolerance in Pakistan, Afghanistan, and elsewhere. The Bali and Jakarta bombings in 2002 were tied to the terrorist group Jemaal Islamiya and their small, radical *madrassa* in Java. We were in Sumatra four months after the Bali bombing and *madrassa* bashing was big in the Western press at the time. But generalizations are dangerous. *Madrassa* has the same meaning in Arabic as *shul* does in Yiddish: "a house of religious education." These Gayo mosques and their associated schools were full of young boys and girls learning the moderate form of the faith, and they were as curious and friendly as schoolyard kids anywhere. I was probably the first Jewish person to visit this area, but that was merely a curiousity; there was no negative association. If Barack Obama had lived in Takengon instead of in Jakarta, he would have been comfortable in one of these schools.

We walked through the incredibly lush Sumatran coffeelands. Everywhere, thick shade covered the healthy plants. It was hard to navigate between the coffee, as the interlaced, full branches and wide, serrated leaves nearly hid the paths from view. The paths were also obscured by thick webs of *laba-laba* (large spiders that live in the trees). In the organic world, spiders are an "indicator species." Their presence tells you that there are no toxic chemicals in the soil or sprayed on the leaves.

The coffeelands were abundant with intercropped fruits and vegetables. Salim told me that there were over two dozen different species enlaced in the ecology of coffee here. Spices such as ginger, cardamom, pepper, cloves, and vanilla wiggled up and around bushes of oranges and limes, guava, papaya, starfruit, banana trees, and a riot of colorful unrecognizable and unpronounceable edibles (*nangka*, *rambutan*, *nipis*, and *zurzat*—now repeat that three times, fast). There were twice as many intercropped species here as there were in Latin America. Salim showed me why, as he grabbed a handful of moist earth. The rich volcanic soils in Sumatra are almost a foot deep—twice the depth of the soils of the Americas.

We were served fresh coffee at every stop. The long, bumpy rides between farms forced me to stop often and pee. At first I was able to cover by saying I wanted to stop and admire a certain vista or patch of rain forest. But my hosts soon caught on and loudly proclaimed, "It is time for a Dean stop," whenever they saw me squirming in the backseat. At the farm of Mahamad near the village of Tanah Abu the coffee was roasted over a wood fire until it was black, charred, and smoking fiercely. One of the Sulawesi soldiers lay aside his automatic weapon and took delight in grinding the beans in a giant wooden mortar, saying that he had always ground coffee for his family. This simple act greatly softened the military presence. Aminah, the farmer's wife, brought out some old ceramic cups for us to use. They handed me a cracked one with a large Starbucks logo on it. Tomas stifled a laugh as I tried to explain that the look of shock on my face was for the mug, not the coffee in it. The farmers waited in anticipation as I made an elaborate ritual of smelling the coffee, swirling it in the cup, slurping it, and swishing it around in my mouth. After the eternal silence of three seconds I pronounced the coffee excellent.

"This coffee has a full body, very low acid, and no bitterness. There is a lingering smoothness on the palate, a nice mouthfeel." The farmers were smiling and happy. I shook my head sternly. "But you've got to do something about that cup."

In Bintang Bener, just a grenade's throw across the border from Aceh province, we saw ample evidence of the conflict. A school and a house were burned down. Farmers told us almost casually about losing their cows to gunfire or a leg to a land mine. One man showed us his scarred throat, where he had been garroted with piano wire by government troops seeking information about GAM movements through the area. This was Iswandi's home village. His wife and four children lived on and ran their eight-acre coffee farm, large by Gayo standards. Iswandi juggled the family business and the chairmanship of PPKGO, providing technical assistance and logistical support to the far-flung farmers of the cooperative. Iswandi admitted that it was nerve-wracking to live in a zone of hot conflict, but his commitment to his community and his family kept him strong. He told me that in order to carry on under such circumstances, he had to hold a vision for the day when peace would come.

Finally we reached the village of Wonosari, where Paman Dean the buffalo roams. By this point, the farmers and soldiers in the entourage had built up enormous excitement at seeing the famous water buffalo eco-management project that we had been talking about the whole trip. We met Paman Dean's guardian, Mr. Sawadi, at his small house deep within the coffee forest. He was a burly man with a sweet disposition and a blade of grass sticking out of his mouth—the karmic twin of Paman Dean. He greeted me like a relative, with a joyful "*Selamat datang!*" (Welcome!) and a big hug. The fifteen of us squeezed into Mr. Sawadi's living room—an eight-foot by ten-foot space. It felt like a Manhattan subway car during rush hour, except no one here was picking my pocket or asking for contributions for dubious charities. Mrs. Sawadi brought in the coffee. I asked if it had been fertilized by Paman Dean.

"Of course!" bellowed Mr. Sawadi. "And that's why it tastes so good!"

Iswandi reminded the group that I was here to inspect Paman Dean's progress to determine if the project was a success.

"Or if we get to eat Paman Dean!" interrupted one of the farmers with obvious, well, relish. There was a lot of laughter and talking. I couldn't tell which side the majority was on.

We walked out into the forest. The small wooden hut of Paman Dean waited about a football field away. The young water buffalo was tethered inside, chewing some grass and looking fairly content. He was brown and gray, with big liquid brown eyes. For a water buffalo, he was pretty cute. I walked into his shed, passing under a wooden, handwritten sign that read: PAMAN DEAN, ECO-MANAGEMENT PROJECT, THANK YOU DEAN'S BEANS.

The benefits of corporate sponsorship, I mused as I stroked his head gently. I talked with Paman Dean awhile, asking all of the obvious questions: was he treated well, did he like it here, was he lonely? The farmers cracked up, not because I was talking to the animal (which they also did), but because I clearly expected an answer and they knew I didn't speak Gayo. Fortunately, Mr. Sawadi knew the answers and filled me in.

We walked through the coffee forest to see how Paman Dean's handiwork was being managed. Mr. Sawadi showed me how he and his helpers had collected Paman Dean's Frisbee-sized offerings and dug them in around coffee plants in a specific area. They took out their clipboards to demonstrate the record keeping (weight, frequency, date) and showed me the yields from those plants versus others sans contributions. Six months was a little early to tell, said Salim, the agronomist, but there did seem to be an increase in yield. In any event, the Paman-powered plants were lusher and apparently healthier. There were larger leaves and they appeared a deeper green. Further, these plants had fewer weeds competing for plant nutrients, as Paman Dean had, in fact, nibbled the weeds away. The crowd followed more closely than paparazzi in Paris, waiting for any hint of the final outcome—project or prime rib?

We returned to the packed living room for another cuppa. The farmers sat still, craning their necks to hear the final pronouncement. I told Salim that I was satisfied that Paman Dean was doing his job. His idea was a good one, and I thought that the project was a success. A broad smile graced Salim's weathered face. He turned to the room and said proudly, "*Proyek Paman Dean berjalan suksess! Suksess!*"

There were equal amounts of happy and disappointed faces in the crowd. A small cluster at the back went outside for some discussion and returned shortly. The leader of the group asked if he could speak. He was from another village, as were some of his companions. They wanted to know if they could receive water buffalo, too. They added that if they could have females and males they could breed their own Paman Deans and would not need further assistance from the project. Plus, the females would provide milk for home consumption and sale, and maybe they could learn to make cheese as well. I was deeply touched that our small investment could bring such meaningful possibilities and hope to the community. The farmers went home happy.

After the successful visit with Paman Dean, I wanted to wander the coffee forests of Wonosari a bit. I do this often when I travel. It takes me back to my, uh, roots. I think about the blessings in my life that have flowed from this venture. I have been able to travel, meet interesting peoples, and experience different cultures. I get to help people work toward their goals. And to top it all off, it actually pays the bills. During my perambulations I came upon a massive coffee tree, about thirty feet tall, dwarfing the human-sized coffee plants around it. I could barely get my hands around the trunk. It was acting as a shade tree for the plants around it, but it dripped with ripe berries. I went back to the house and asked my hosts about the tree. Mr. Sawadi walked me out to the tree and told me that it was a robusta plant, and that it was about fifty years old. Considering that the useful life of a coffee tree is five, ten, or twenty years, depending on how much pruning and grafting it will take, this was astounding. I looked around and saw other trees almost as large. We were standing in a high-altitude, ancient robusta grove.

Unlike arabicas, robustas generally thrive in lower altitudes, happily sprouting away at sea level to about three thousand feet. The variety was first found in the West African lowland forests and cultivated commercially beginning in the mid-1800s. Robustas do well in hot, moist conditions but can't stand the sharp, cold nights at the higher altitudes. The beans are generally smaller than those of arabicas, but what they lack in size they make up in punch—robustas carry a caffeine wallop 30 to 100 percent greater than arabicas. They are also more bitter by nature, regardless of what country they grow in. Indonesia was the world's largest robusta producer until it was surpassed by Vietnam around the new millennium. The Vietnam robusta resulted from a massive World Bank program to bring Vietnam into the world economy. The backlash, unfortunately, was that the world market became flooded with cheap Vietnamese robusta beans, greatly precipitating the coffee-pricing crisis of recent years. No good deed goes unpunished.

Since the 1950s robustas had crept into the blends of the big American commercial roasters, Maxwell House and its brethren, as a way to cut costs. It also cut taste, leading to a slow decline in coffee consumption during the 1950s and 1960s. More recently, robustas have made a comeback as an addition to espresso blends. The highly caffeinated robustas throw off an attractive *crema* that makes the espresso look more, well, European, like an espresso should. Since most roasters use very dark roasts for espresso, the bitterness of the robusta can be hidden in the bitterness of the roast. But the robusta trees of Wonosari were not the cheesy, quick, and dirty ones I had seen elsewhere in Asia. These were strong, ecologically established, and strangely compelling.

Could we try the coffee? Sure. We went back to Mr. Sawadi's house and his wife roasted a few handfuls in a wok over a charcoal fire. The taste was stunning. No serious bitter notes, but the same earthy, full body as the Sumatran arabica. I asked Mr. Sawadi if he sold these beans.

"We do, but we get only a few *rupiahs* for them because they are robusta."

Talk about prejudice! To me, a good coffee deserves a good price. Since the tree was in a certified organic field and the co-op was certified Fair Trade, I offered to buy one hundred bags (15,200 pounds) at the going Fair Trade organic price for arabicas. Mr. Sawadi and the co-op members were stunned. This was the first organic Fair Trade robusta sold in all of Indonesia— actually in all of Asia (probably in the whole world!). Our purchase alone would effectively triple the income of the villagers from the entire harvest. Iswandi later told me that this one sale kept the village together that year, as people were beginning to flee the violence of the civil war and had no real income off the robustas to help keep them there.

Yet as I fawned over this garden of earthly delights, a darker side of the Sumatran robusta trade was unfolding at the other end of Bukan Barisan. There, deep in the national park, endangered tigers, rhinos, and elephants of Sumatra found sanctuary. Illegal robusta plots were being carved out of this wilderness. Thousands of acres of ancient trees and complex habitat were being cleared at an alarming rate that could lead to the collapse of the resident endangered species in our lifetimes. Unscrupulous growers and traders were mixing the illegal crop with the legitimate robusta beans of the surrounding Lampung province and selling the tainted harvest to unwitting American and European coffee giants, including Kraft, Nestlé, Lavazza, and possibly Starbucks (which denied the allegation). After hearing about this scandal, we decided to make a blend of Sumatran arabica and robusta, roast it dark and strong, and call it "Ahab's Revenge." The cursed captain of the *Pequod* may have died on his mad quest to save the world from evil, but at least in our coffee he would have the last laugh over his morally uncertain first mate.

As we prepared to leave the Gayo region we heard that the United States had invaded Iraq. A television in one restaurant showed the night sky of Baghdad lit up by tracer shells and enormous explosions. There was never a hard look or a cross word from anyone I encountered for the rest of the trip, although many people asked me why this was happening. But there may have been a more subtle response.

We stopped at a Muslim restaurant in one small town on our way back to Medan. We ate curried chicken and vegetables with our fingers. I needed something to drink to wash down the *panas* (spicy hot) meal. I had been scrupulous about not drinking untreated water, drinking beer instead. But there was no alcohol in this strictly observant establishment, so I took the chance on a cold glass of sweet *lassi*, a blended yogurt and ice concoction. What was I thinking?

We were in the car again for only five minutes when the televised explosions in Baghdad replayed in my stomach. For the next seven hours I had to stop the car often and anywhere we could. This happened to be on the only busy truck road back to Medan, and there was little privacy anywhere to be found. At one point we passed a massive political rally in support of one of the major candidates in the upcoming national elections. Yellow banners waved for miles along the roadside as thousands of people walked, talked, picnicked, and sold goods. It took all my Yankee ingenuity to find a square meter of privacy to deal with the constant amoebic attacks, but the yellow banners came in handy.

As we approached Medan airport, Dani, my driver, turned up the radio. The announcer was saying that the truce between GAM and the government was over, as ten thousand Indonesian paratroopers and army forces had just invaded Aceh. Dani struggled with some of the words.

"How you say *perang* in English?"

"That means "war," boss."

The conflict raged again until the great tsunami of December 26, 2004, smashed Aceh into pieces. Hostilities were suspended as both sides searched among the hundreds of thousands of dead and displaced for loved ones. The shock waves reached up into the Bukit Barisan in the form of earthquakes, shattering buildings, water supply systems, roads, and fields. Fortunately, only two members of PPKGO lost their lives, but a deeper tragedy was to unfold. As there were few high schools and no colleges in the mountains of the Gayo region, many farmers sent their kids to Banda Aceh, the capital, for schooling. In the weeks that followed the tsunami, Salim searched desperately for two of his daughters, eventually finding them safe from physical harm. Thirteen other farmers were not so fortunate, and the hills of Takengon echoed the wailing of Gayo funeral rites for the lost children.

Like so many other coffee companies, we raised money for the relief efforts. We sent twelve thousand dollars directly to PPKGO, which set up a very effective operation that didn't have the government interference, red tape, or confusion of some of the foreign efforts. The farmers of PPKGO loaded up their trucks with rice, vegetables, bottled water, clothing, and everything else they knew the people in the affected communities would need. They went to zones that were declared off-limits to foreign aid agencies as being under GAM control, bringing essential supplies to people otherwise left alone in the wake of the tsunami. While the peace-loving farmers of PPKGO brought relief and compassion to their neighbors, the government and GAM negotiated a meaningful solution to the centuries of Acehnese struggle. The peace accords granted more autonomy to the region while keeping Indonesia whole and provided for a greater regional say in the management and environmental regulation of natural resources, including a larger share in the economic benefits.

As if the gods rewarded their efforts, the Gayo harvest that followed the tsunami was the largest on record. Salim said that the subterranean movements had unlocked deep mineral and nutrient deposits, but many farmers had a different understanding. Four other member companies of Cooperative Coffees donated water buffalo (females!) to the eco-management project. Within a year the farmers' wish came true. They had many "Paman Dean babies" and the herd doubled. A better rate of return than my 401(k) plan! Lucia told me that the farmers attributed this to the spiritual power of my masculinity. Salim and I gave the credit to Paman Dean.

9

The Three-Hundred-Man March

PAPUA NEW GUINEA, 2004

The flight attendant gracefully navigated the narrow aisle to serve plastic packs of tropical juices to the twelve passengers on Air Nuigini Flight 701, from Port Moresby to Goroka. The ancient prop plane lumbered, hiccupped, and yo-yoed over a mountainous and thickly forested landscape. I was plastered against the window, envisioning the tribes, the rare animals, and the riotous fauna of Papua New Guinea below, as I had read in those *National Geographic* magazines growing up in New York City. (I didn't even have to hide those "cultural" photos from my mom!) In fact, two thousand feet below us a team of researchers from Conservation International and several universities were discovering new species of tree kangaroos, butterflies, and a host of previously unknown plants. Folks were terracing garden plots here seven thousand years ago, when my European ancestors were hunting mammoths and drawing stick figures in caves. Yet the vast island north of Australia still held lands and peoples unknown to us.

"Man, this is wild!" hooted David from the opposite seat. An Emmy-winning documentary maker, David had been pretty much all over the world — but never here. In fact, I had never met anybody who had been to Papua New Guinea. I had called the embassy in Washington DC to try and learn a few welcoming phrases in *tok pisin*, the invented mélange of German, Dutch, English, and smatterings of the eight hundred local languages that is used throughout the island nation. The embassy officer shared a few basics, adding with a sniff, "I generally think of *tok pisin* as rather bad English."

David and I had made a deal: I would pay the expenses and he would film the trip without a fee. Even at this early stage in the trip, David thought he had gotten a pretty good bargain.

We were met at the Goroka airport by Iggy and Kekas, our hosts. Iggy was a muscular thirty-year-old with a round head accentuated by the shaved noggin. He wore an old T-shirt and cargo shorts and had the widest bare feet I had ever seen. His feet reminded me of the old R. Crum "Keep on Truckin'" character. Iggy was trying hard to organize the tribal coffee farmers in this part of the Eastern Highlands and Simbu provinces. No easy task—these peoples have a reputation for fierce independence and quick tempers. But Iggy had an easy disposition and a ready laugh, just the kind of guy for the job. He also chewed a lot of *buai* (betel nut), the mildly narcotic nut used throughout Asia. Like most chewers, Iggy's teeth were outlined in a dark red stain, and he left a trail of red saliva stains on the sidewalks of Goroka as we headed to the Bird of Paradise Hotel for the night. There was no particular reason to stay in Goroka; it was just that the battered roads between here and the highland towns we were headed for were deadly at night. As Iggy casually explained, "There are lots of *raskols* out there after dark. They stop your car and take everything. Even your life."

Kekas was trying to organize the farmers in Henganofi, in the Eastern Highlands. She had lived in New York for five years with her husband, an accountant at the United Nations. She hadn't gone out much during that time because she was afraid that New York was too violent. Her arms were covered with small tattoos.

"The old people did their faces," she remarked, rubbing a finger over a name on her left arm. "But the kids don't want the pain, so they put theirs and their friends' names on their arms with pins and charcoal." She offered to do it for David and me, but we both demurred. Our wives were already a little suspicious of our intentions on this exotic trip to the far side of the world, and we didn't need to stoke the fires—just yet.

Kekas's husband had died in a car accident three years earlier on the same bad roads we would be driving, leaving Kekas to raise their three kids alone. Kekas was immensely intelligent and present and was totally dedicated to raising the living standards of the coffee farmers of Henganofi through better organizing and crop improvement. Her sixteen-year-old daughter Theresa and fourteen-year-old son Avdoh stood nearby. They spoke the Queens English—not the one from Buckingham Palace, but the one from the borough of New York where they had spent time while their father worked. Avdoh quickly showed that he had a very analytical mind and that wise-cracking attitude that I knew and loved from my youth in Queens (although outside of the City, few people really appreciate it).

Our hosts rather abruptly dropped us off at the Bird of Paradise Hotel, one of the two hotels in Goroka that offered twenty-four-hour security (it was owned by the provincial governor), and promised to be back for dinner. I opened the door to my room and was met by a naked, skinny Indian fellow sitting on my bed.

"Sorry, I was taking a shower." He wrapped a towel around his middle and left. David and I settled into our rooms and hit the bar. A surly Aussie woman demanded another room key, as she couldn't find hers. A rather large Nouméan told me that he was waiting for his rental car at the airport and heard that it had gotten carjacked.

"The police chased the *raskols* and shot the driver. When I got the car it was full of bullet holes, broken glass, and blood." He leaned close to me and whispered, "Frankly, I don't like these people. They are very violent."

We took our beers and wandered over to the open-air restaurant. There was a stream rushing by and the songs of birds and insects gave a peaceful, meditative air to the place. Only one other table was occupied. In a far corner four huge, black, really mean-looking guys sat hunched over bottles of beer. Our pleasant waitress, Abar, smiling through reddened teeth, told us they were waiting for a "compensation meeting."

"People here have *tok-tok* meetings to resolve problems. They sit down, *tok,* and decide how much an insult or an injury was worth. It is very civilized." The guys in the corner did not look like mediators, but this wasn't the Happy Valley of Amherst, Massachusetts, either. Abar asked us what we were doing in Goroka. I told her about our upcoming visits with the coffee farmers and her eyes brightened.

"I sell coffee, too!" Apparently, everybody in Goroka did. "I buy a few kilos in my village every week and sell them to the buyers here in town. I don't get a lot of money but I want to sell more someday."

It was dark when two cars approached the high chain-link fence surrounding the hotel grounds. We strained to see if it was Iggy and Kekas. There were loud voices. The mediators rushed out to the fence. From the distance, we could only hear the shouting and see people silhouetted in the headlights. There was a scuffle and two shots. Police sirens screamed. The Nouméan walked by us and chuckled.

"Guess we'll eat here tonight."

After twenty minutes things died down, all the police cars and mediators left, and a Land Rover entered the gate and pulled up. Iggy poked his head out smiling. I asked what had happened.

"Land dispute. They were gonna meet here and negotiate. That's why those guys were in the restaurant. This other clan came and the guards wouldn't let them in. They fought. That's our tribal warfare." He laughed. "Welcome to PNG!"

"They've had seven thousand years to work it out and they're still fighting over boundaries?" I asked.

"You see, the population has doubled since independence in 1975, so there is a lot of pressure on land. You will see that tomorrow. Also, before independence, the government gave a lot of land to white settlers from Australia and other countries, and they sold it or changed owners by some shifty paperwork. It is all very confusing and people are having trouble getting their clan lands straightened out."

In the morning, we loaded up the Land Rover with food, water, and other consumer goods for the trip to Henganofi. Iggy drove southwest out of Goroka toward the misty, bluish mountains in the distance. We maneuvered around massive landslides. The road looked like some giant animal had taken huge bites out of it. No warning signs or barricades would prevent an inattentive driver from plunging headlong into the holes or off the mountainside. There hadn't been a single road so far that wasn't in complete disrepair. As I bounced off the ceiling and rammed my knee into the dashboard, I asked Iggy why there were no roads from the Eastern Highlands to the capital, Port Moresby.

"If the government built a road, the farmers would drive to the capital and burn it down," he said mildly. "Sometimes these roads get a little repair around election time, but that's only every couple of years. Anyway, these are the good roads. It's much worse over in Simbu."

We didn't pass through a single small village all the way to Henganofi. Much of the foothills were deforested and broken up into rectangular farm patches. Lone huts made of woven mat walls and thatch roofs poked out of the soil here and there. Several large brush fires smoldered on the slopes. David stopped to get a little "B roll," background footage. I just wanted to get out of the car and stretch. Iggy sidled over and pointed up the hillsides.

"You can see a hut over there and one way over there. People in this area live in very small family clusters. These people are different from the people in Simbu, who live in bigger tribal groups. You see, everywhere in PNG is different from everywhere else. We are a new nation of over eight hundred small nations." He laughed and shook his head. "Everybody got different languages, everybody got different *kastom*. It's a crazy place." Iggy had spent two years learning accounting and office management in Brisbane, Australia, so he had something to compare his country with. He had worked with another guy trying to organize farmers, but that guy had apparently spent much of the farmers' money on his gambling and drinking problems.

"This country is like the frontier everywhere. It is difficult to communicate between people, difficult to keep proper books, and difficult to trace money. It is easy to steal from the farmers who can't read or add and have to rely on the middleman for all the information." He aimed his face to the sun for warmth. "We really have to change that."

Way up it looked like the fires had caught a few huts; their charred remains sat on the hillside like blackened, fallen-down sand castles. I asked Iggy if people accidentally burned houses often when they were clearing land. He looked over and smiled.

"No, people are pretty careful about that. Those huts were burned on purpose in a family dispute last month. One family hired some gunmen from Goroka to settle the score. They attacked the other family, wounded six people, and burned the huts."

I thought back to the old picture book called *Peoples of the World* that I had found in a local library when I was trying to get information on the tribal groups from the Eastern Highlands. One picture showed a guy dead on a huge rock in the middle of a river, ten spears sticking out of his back and legs. I didn't show my wife, Annette.

"I thought tribal warfare was done with spears and arrows around here."

"No, not around here. That is way up the Sepik River or in some of the other distant places. Most people use guns these days. We are starting to see a lot of automatic weapons, like M-16s and AK-47s."

"Jeez, that's pretty heavy stuff for a neighborhood argument—and very expensive. Where do the people up in these mountains get money like that?"

Iggy sighed.

"You see, lots of people are growing marijuana now to sell to the coast, and sometimes they take guns instead of cash. They don't have too much use for money, but the guns are handy."

As we crested a ridge, Iggy turned sharply to the right, onto a very flat, red dirt road. We followed it along ridgetops for several dusty miles.

"The farmers dug this road by hand. They had no machinery, but they couldn't wait for the government. It took a couple of years, and the rain messes it up every year, but it's the best road around."

Iggy wasn't exaggerating. We snaked along the road smoothly—a nice change from the kidney-pounders we came up here on. People began to appear alongside the road, walking in the direction we were driving. First they appeared in groups of twos and threes, mostly women and children, then groups of five and ten. They all shouted greetings to Iggy and Kekas. Most of them asked for rides, but we rolled along waving as we passed.

"They are all going to Henganofi for our meeting," observed Kekas.

I didn't remember seeing any villages during the entire ride that morning. I asked Kekas where all these people had come from.

"Oh, they live all over the place. They walked about eight hours to get here."

"That's amazing!" I exclaimed. "At home, most people don't walk more than a quarter mile to do anything." Kekas laughed.

"Yes, I know from New York, but here everybody walks. There's no choice and nobody thinks anything of walking for a day or two for a visit. Besides, the farmers are really excited to meet you. They have never had a buyer visit them before. Just your showing up here is a sign of respect that they have never experienced."

The walkers increased on both sides of the road as Iggy noted we were almost there. We drove over another small hill and David and I screamed at the same time. Well over a thousand people lined the road ahead of us. There were countless clans gathered together, wearing a range of outfits from the sacred to the profane. Bare-breasted women covered in ash and bark stomped the ground, their belled ankles chiming rhythmically. Boys in dirty shorts, their bodies blackened with charcoal, carrying pointed short spears, sang a squeaky welcome. We stopped the car and Iggy said it was time to walk. A roar went up from the entire crowd as we got out, and drums, flutes, and yells filled the hot, dry air. A muscular man with a long devil's tail and an oversized, scary black mask writhed slowly our way, only to turn and move away without a word. Kekas and Iggy were greeted by a committee of men and women who looked like small-town businesspeople in their street clothes. The group spoke rapid *tok pisin*; I could pick up a word here and there, but mostly it sounded like, well, bad English, or a poorly tuned radio.

"*Apinun tru!*" (Good afternoon!)

"*Where blong dispela?*" (Where's this guy from?)

"*Dispela comin long waya long here.*" (They came a long way.)

Several clans in turn came forward and welcomed us (I think) with their particular dance, song, or ritual action. One group carried a thirty-foot replica (I think) of a freshwater eel.

"They are the Eel people. They believe that they came from river eels and they worship their Eel God. But they are also good Christians, of course," Iggy instructed us. David was in seventh heaven, running up and down the road, filming everything in sight. I was amazed at how unobtrusive he was. He came, he went, he engaged and played, and he filmed. People either ignored him or enjoyed him, but he never got in anybody's face or disrupted the flow of events.

A brass and percussion band, 796, came forward. Each of the twenty men and boys was charcoaled completely black and had a chalked "796" on his back or chest. I asked Iggy what the significance of "796" was. Maybe it was a secret code for the clan, or the key to survival on *Lost*, or a spiritual metaphor. Iggy shrugged and popped another betel nut.

"It's just '796.'"

The band cranked out a repetitive, rhythmic cacophony, like a Midwestern junior college band. They were flanked by a group of eight-year-old boys, who stepped forward with the most serious demeanor. They started to grind their pelvises forward in violent beat to the music, while pumping their fists backward and forward. Nobody in the crowd cheered or reacted at all to these minilove machines expressing their not-yet-manhood, but I had to honor them. I leaped forward and started to do the Pelvic Thrust with them, at least until my lower back went out. Some of the men and women in the crowd laughed and cheered, but the little love men pulsed on uninterrupted until the music stopped. They never changed their serious pusses, even as they turned and marched away.

Many of the people in the crowd, especially the teenagers, wore T-shirts emblazoned with the logos of globalization—Nike, Asics, and sport teams from everywhere. That's not unusual, as factories that make the shirts sell off odd lots and travelers trade shirts for whatever. But one young man wore a black shirt with the stern face of Osama Bin Laden staring out. I asked Iggy if the Al Qaeda leader was respected here.

"Who is he?" he asked.

"The guy behind the World Trade Center bombing," I replied, a little surprised. Iggy shrugged his shoulders. "Al Qaeda? International terrorists?"

"Never heard of him, and I don't think that kid has either."

The shirt was probably made in Indonesia or Malaysia, worn there, and then "consolidated" with other used clothing for resale throughout the developing world. This is the fate of much used clothing in the United States as well. After all, if the poor in America don't want your shirts, what should the Salvation Army or Planet Aid do with them? They sell them by the pound to consolidators, who categorize them by value (new jeans in this pile, worn-out T-shirts in that pile), bundle them into shipping containers, and sell them to their counterparts throughout the coffeelands and beyond. Once the container hits PNG, for example, the local businessmen go through the piles and buy what they want to resell. Outside of Goroka we drove by Bigpela Klos Stoa, the J. Peterman's or Target of PNG (specializing in fashion for the large warrior?). It was basically a couple of giant shipping containers side by side, bursting with used clothing. We also passed huge outdoor markets with acres of cast-away clothes on bamboo racks. Nobody outside of the capital buys new clothes. Iggy remarked that he had never owned anything new before I had given him a Dean's Beans T-shirt at the airport (which he wore every day of the visit).

From behind us two vine- and moss-covered chairs appeared, with long poles beneath to allow the guests of honor to be hoisted high on broad shoulders and paraded up the hill. David and I mounted our chairs and were marched away. I felt pretty self-conscious at first, sure that there were people in the crowd thinking, *Oh shit, another white guy on the throne.* But Iggy told me that there had never been a *whiteman* honored here before, and I couldn't detect any negativity in the raucous and friendly crowd. I guess they really did appreciate the visit.

At the top of the hill was a flat area where the folks had built a roofed bamboo platform for our visit. There were no other structures as far as the eye could see. Henganofi, it appeared, was a feeling, not a town. We were brought up the four bamboo steps onto the platform and seated next to a number of local dignitaries. To my right was the pastor of Henganofi, an Evangelical Christian who immediately shook my hand and queried, "Are you Jewish? I am Jewish, too!"

The dignitaries took turns welcoming us to Henganofi, exhorting the residents to grow more coffee and start working together. If they grew good coffee, they would earn more money and be able to take care of their families better.

"*Yu lukautim cofi, na cofi by lukautim yu!*" It became the motto for our trip.

Several groups performed before the platform. One group danced in and planted coffee branches. They mimed watering and pruning them, while a narrator sang the coffee cycle. One man from the audience was so taken by this that he ran up, lifted his grass skirt, and waved his personal warrior's spear at the trees. Iggy was delighted.

"Oh! He's celebrating the fertility of the soil! We love the earth in PNG!" David remarked that we should get that guy to appear at an Earth Day festival back home.

Then two faux *raskols* came forward and mimicked stealing the coffee cherries from the new trees. This was a big problem, Iggy related. But the farmers came back and beat the tar out of the *raskols*, to the delight of the crowd.

It was my turn to speak. Iggy introduced me as the man who came all the way from America to help the farmers organize and get more money for their coffee. I was ready to try out my *tok pisin*.

"*Apinun tru, ol meri na man blong Papua-Niu-Gini!*" A roar from the crowd. A good start, but I knew enough to quit while I was ahead. I told them in English that if they organized into cooperatives and worked together, they would be able to sell directly to exporters and roasters and go past the middlemen who had always cheated them. They would get much more money.

"How much?" yelled a man from the crowd.

"Yeah! How much?" chimed in others.

I tried a quick mental calculation of dollars into *kina* and pounds into kilos. I told them I wasn't completely sure, but I thought they'd get between six and nine *kina* for a kilo of beans (that's about eighty cents per pound). Kekas had told me the farmers sold a kilo to the middlemen for one *kina* now (fifteen cents per pound). The crowd paid closer attention after that, applauding most of my statements. Figuring I had spoken enough for now, as we were going to have more *tok-tok* over dinner, I decided to close with my well-rehearsed line.

"*Tank yu tru, tank yu straight. Mi tok-tok pinis now!*" I expected a final round of cheers, but the crowd stayed seated and looked even more attentive. Iggy leaned over to me and whispered, "You just said, 'Thank you, I am going to talk about my penis now.'"

"But I thought *pinis* meant 'finished'!" I was totally embarrassed.

"It does, if you say it right. It's more like *pin-nis*."

"Thanks, I'll remember that."

"Well, you got a choice now, you can end the speech or talk about your penis. Nobody here has ever seen a *whiteman pinis*. I think they're pretty curious."

"Nope, that's it for now. Maybe after dinner."

Iggy got up and told the crowd that my talk was over. Big applause and cheers, a couple of disappointed looks. He smiled at me and added graciously to the crowd, "When you start a fire it takes a while. Sometimes, it needs a little wind to make it kick in." The crowd murmured agreement. It must have been a local expression. Iggy ended with a flourish. "But Mr. Dean here is not a little wind. He is a big wind! He is a very big wind!" The crowd went wild. The band 796 clanged, tooted, and thrust the meeting to a close.

We sat on the ground, on our butts or on logs, in a makeshift canvas tent put up behind the bamboo platform. Iggy and Kekas convened the meeting after a short prayer from the pastor.

"JesusChristinheavenpleasehelpusgetmoremoneyforourcoffee."

"Amen," replied the congregation.

Iggy spoke at length about the need to organize with other farmers in the province and beyond. I asked lots of questions about how the farmers planted, harvested, and processed their coffee. Group cooperation for economy of scale was an alien concept. Every family did for themselves. They harvested in small family groups, trudged the beans down to the nearest river to depulp them by hand, smashing a handful at a time with river stones to remove the beans from the surrounding red fruit. Afterwards, they carrried the beans back to their huts to dry. The family had to stay with their beans by the river and at the hut for fear of *raskols* who would steal their only cash crop. Since the farmers had no cars or trucks, they carried the beans on their backs miles to the road and sat, waiting for a buyer to come along. Sometimes they waited a day and a night and a day again. They took what the buyer offered, no negotiation. I asked how long they waited to depulp the beans after harvest, the time it took to depulp a bag of beans, and how long they dried them in the sun. The farmers talked and talked, arguing about the times, which seemed different for each family. It got a bit rough-and-tumble. One farmer went on a bit about how hard it was to get his beans down the mountain.

"Enough! You talk too much!" shouted another man.

"This is a democracy, he can say what he wants!" replied another, as several of the farmers jumped up to shout at and gesture at each other. Iggy turned and smiled.

"We are very aggressive."

"That's okay," I replied. "Thomas Jefferson said 'liberty is a boisterous sea, meeker men prefer the calm of tyranny.'"

"Tell him I agree with him."

The men calmed down as a huge, charred bush pig with a pole up its rear and out its chest was carried in. Large corrugated sheets full of yams, taro, fruit, and vegetables I couldn't identify were laid before the assembly. Dinner time.

Iggy said that as the guest of honor, I should cut the pig for everybody and put it on their plates or in their hands. He handed me a foot-long, homemade carving knife. I looked at the pig. The pig looked at me. I silently prayed that this would not endanger my kosher certification at the beanery back home. Iggy whispered, "Make sure you give the best pieces to the headmen here, otherwise they will be insulted. And you know how violent we are."

So is the haunch the best? The ribs? The flank steak? Actually, what *is* a flank steak? Do different cultures prize different cuts? Where was Anthony Bourdain when I needed him? The crowd watched me intently. I put the tip of the knife on the fat ribs and looked up. "Nnnnnnh," came a grumble from the crowd. Iggy shook his head subtly.

"Try again," counseled Iggy. "But you better get it right this time."

I pointed to the shoulder. Same unhappy reaction. Finally I put the knife against the rear haunch. "Mmmmmm!!" Smiles and vigorous head nods. Dinner was served.

I forked over prime cuts to most of the crowd, but Kekas and her children declined the repast for "religious reasons."

"Are you Muslim?" I asked in surprise. There were some along the coast, but not up here.

"No, we are Seventh-Day Adventists," she replied. In the worldwide race for souls, the motto was "No Tribe Left Behind." Papua New Guinea had for a century been prime pickings for Baptists, Mormons, Lutherans, and a new wave of Evangelicals led by the Summer Institute of Linguistics (SIL). If the Jesuits were the Marine Corps of the Catholic Church, SIL was the Evangelical SWAT team. Their mission was to translate their Bible into indigenous languages, convert the local populations, and rack up more souls for their heaven. SIL was still very active in PNG.

"I used to love hot dogs in New York," Avdoh pined.

After a very greasy meal, we talked about possible ways of working together at each part of the cycle, as many people do in other countries. We talked about ways to control fermentation rates and other aspects of bean quality to get a uniform taste from their coffee. I mentioned the hand depulping machines used in other remote regions. Perhaps these inexpensive machines could be installed in each village and used cooperatively. The river stone thing was very exotic, but the farmers didn't feel like it was a necessary part of their culture. They did it because they had no choice. They knew that if it took six hours to depulp a bag of coffee, the first beans had a longer fermentation time than the last beans, so the quality of the bag would be uneven. Multiply that over three bags in three days and the beans wouldn't even look like they came from the same area, let alone the same harvest. The farmers were eager and appreciative listeners. They had been growing coffee in these mountains for only about fifty years and had little technical assistance from the government or the coffee industry. As a result, these very capable farmers didn't have the knowledge of what the market wanted and what they could do to make their product more attractive to buyers. They just grew it and sold it. I showed them photos of farmers from around the world engaged in cooperative work. They were really taken by the photo of farmers in Yirgacheffe, Ethiopia, standing before a beehive hut similar to their own housing. I told them that those farmers had a half wall in their huts and brought their animals in at night to warm the place up. They were astonished.

"*Waaah!*" exclaimed a man with a pig tusk in his nose and a piece of cloth around his waist. "*Dispela em so primitif!*"

It took a full day of driving to reach Kundiawa, a small, bustling frontier town in the foothills of Simbu province. On the way we passed entirely deforested mountainsides tucked into explosively lush rain forest. Each of the deforested areas had stone and log markers delineating small patches. Iggy noted sadly that this was population pressure. People cut all the trees and put in garden plots for their growing families.

"If we don't get control of our population and get some money into people's hands, this whole country will be deforested!" he said, tightening his hands on the steering wheel.

We also passed through Asaro Valley, the home of the Asaro Mudmen. The Mudmen were the warriors of the Asaro Valley. When they went out for revenge raids or other forms of local justice, they coated their bodies with the white mud of the Asaro Valley and put on huge mud helmet masks.

When they approached their victims, they slowed their movements to a ritualized crawl. I could see where they could be terrifying. But I thought they would be Asaro Mudpies if they came up against any of those AK-47s. Iggy noted that the Mudmen would be at the Coffee Culture Festival that he had organized in the village of Kup two days from then. As we were getting further and further away from Goroka and anything resembling a road, I was certain that the Kup festivities would be smaller than that huge celebration in Henganofi.

We stayed in one of the few hotels in Kundiawa, a ring of cottages with a galvanized tin sheet for a security gate. A dance had been organized at a local bar next to the hotel to raise money for the festival in Kup and to announce the formation of the Digne Coffee Growers Association in Simbu, Iggy's attempt at a cooperative venture here. The dance was pretty well attended, with lots of in-town couples and singles out on the dance floor. The local band was good, belting out *tok pisin* and English reggae, disco, and whatever. The bar kept serving up cold beer from behind a massive iron cage for safety, but it was a peaceful night. The Digne committee wouldn't let us walk back to the hotel alone, even though it was fifty feet away. Even peeing out the back door was kept under close surveillance.

"Too dangerous at night," was their stern admonishment.

After a morning of traditional Aussie fare (a can of baked beans on toast, with a side of canned spaghetti, washed down with tea or instant coffee), we packed for the trip to Kup. Iggy told us we would have to wait a while, as an incident outside the dance needed a little compensation meeting. Apparently, some drunk threw a rock at the committeemen, missed, and hit the side of a rented car. The driver wanted compensation from the Digne group. I asked why they would be responsible, and Iggy gave me a lesson in PNG jurisprudence.

"They were the guys who he was aiming at. And they put on the dance that the car was parked at." He told us to just sit tight, it wouldn't take long. After three hours, though, David and I got antsy and decided to walk over to the police station, which was a block away. Besides, we hadn't had the chance to walk around the two blocks of Kundiawa yet. The streets of Kundiawa were paved and there were sidewalks. There were only ten or so businesses in town. All of them seemed to be heavily defended general stores or shipping companies. The town was full of people, although we were the only nonresidents, it seemed. The sidewalks were absolutely splattered with red streaks of betel, as if Jackson Pollock had given art lessons to Dracula here. Walking down the street was like being in a salivary version of paintball, as we dodged red loogies left and right. Beteljuice, Beteljuice, Beteljuice!

There were a hundred people milling about the entryway to the police station. Some of the Digne guys were there, and they ran up to see what we were doing out of the hotel grounds. Michael, one of the headmen from Kup and the founder of Digne, got Iggy, who explained to us that the compensation meeting was going well and would be over soon. Now that we were here, we should stay put. David and I leaned up against a relatively red-free wall and waited. I looked behind the "reception desk" (a half wall cut out from a cement bunker) and noticed a printed sign:

SORCERY

TOO MANY PEOPLE ARE TORTURED AND MURDERED BECAUSE THEY ARE ACCUSED OF SORCERY. DON'T TAKE LAW INTO YOUR OWN HANDS. REPORT SORCERY TO POLICE.

The photo under the headline showed a man full of spears on a boulder in a river. Suddenly, a man rushed into the crowd, shouted something, and began to pound on the head of another man. The crowd parted and let this happen, with much laughter and hooting. The police came out from behind the reception barricade and began pleading with the man to stop, lightly patting him on the back as he beat the stuffing out of his victim. Finally, the assailant gave up and walked away. The victim was helped to his feet, his face like red mashed potatoes and one bloody eye nearly hanging from its socket. As he was led away, it was impossible to differentiate between the blood and the betel stain on the ground. Iggy came out and said everybody was happy, we could go on to Kup. I asked him about the beating that just took place. He shrugged his shoulders.

"They are very religious men here. They go back to the Bible. An eye for an eye." Literally.

Iggy was right about the roads in Simbu. Five big men piled into the back of the Land Rover as we left Kundiawa.

"We need them in case we get stuck in the mud or fall off a bridge," Iggy explained comfortingly. We nearly went off the best bridge. Fortunately it had a metal side rail, so we only smashed in the rear passenger window, grinding glass shards into one of our human jacks' forearms. Unlike the road to Henganofi, this road passed through muddy wallows and thick rain forest. We went over many small bridges that were merely downed trees aimed in what I thought were the wrong direction—we didn't cross the trees as much as we shinnied along them, the wheels slipping between the trees constantly. Iggy talked about ecotourism as a development possibility. He thought about whitewater rafting on some of these rivers we were crossing.

"That sounds like a good idea. Has anyone ever rafted this river?"

"Yes, two Aussie guys got killed on it last year. It's full of dangerous rocks and whirlpools a little further down," he noted.

"I think the idea needs a little work, Iggy."

"Maybe," he added thoughtfully.

A group of people had to move over to let us pass down one of the muddy, narrow roads. They were carrying three fat pigs tied on spits.

"They are going to a wedding ceremony. It will be a big one," Iggy observed.

"How can you tell?" I asked. Iggy thought it was obvious.

"It's a three-pig wedding."

We rarely passed any other people, but when we did, they waved at Michael, who said they were going to the Kup Coffee Cultural Show. Cultural shows are the most popular form of mass entertainment in PNG, and they present a great opportunity for different tribes to come together and strut their stuff. This was going to be the very first Coffee Cultural Show ever held in Simbu. As we climbed over ridges we caught glimpses of the towering rock face of Mount Elibari. On the other side of the mountain, large, foreign-owned gold and copper mines tore open the earth, leaving behind terrible untreated toxic legacies while sucking the mineral wealth out of the country.

Eight thousand people were waiting when we pulled into the forty-acre field that was Kup. There were hundreds of men and women wearing towering bird of paradise headdresses, large ocean *kina* shell necklaces, and grass skirts (known as *arse-gras* because it covers your rear end). There was a contingent of fifty Asaro Mudmen, some of them bopping in their lethargic, ethereal way to a transistor radio atop one Mudman's shoulder (his other one carried a spear). Everywhere people were a riot of plumage, earth, and animal. Possum skins, hawk feathers, snake skins, and totally unknowable objects adorned the young and the old, as each group mirrored its ecology. A delegation of broad-shouldered warriors with six-pack abs, feathered headdresses, and boar tusks piercing their noses came up to greet us formally. They shook their spears at us and sang a song of welcome. David and I were approached by two comely young women, bare-breasted and smeared with pig fat, their faces painted with ash and plant dyes. They would be our "honor guards" and stay by our side throughout the festivities. Joe, one of the headmen from Kup, wanted to make me feel right at home.

"We want to honor you!" he said with great enthusiasm. "We will make you a member of our dancing society." I really love that stuff, so I readily accepted.

"Yes! Now we will smear you with pig fat and paint your body. You can have a special bird of paradise headdress! You can be naked and have a headdress!" Joe started to give orders to get my pig fat ready. David was cheering me on. He was enjoying this.

"Yeah, *brata*, go for it! My camera is ready!"

"Uh, thanks, Joe. This is really an honor. But could I pass on the naked thing? How about a boar tusk necklace?"

The crowd laughed.

"Okay, just a necklace." He was disappointed but cheerful. My honor guard, lovely Rita, from the nearby village of Bi, put a necklace of boar tusk and flowers around my neck. The crowd laughed and let out a crescendo-ing "Wooooo!!" Iggy told me that people didn't applaud here; their *kastom* was to shout "Wooooo!" as a group. It was amazing and beautiful how the community response would begin in unison, swell quickly, and crest. It was like a wave of sound rising up and crashing over us. Michael smiled and told me that the necklace I had gotten was the one used in a wedding ceremony, and that's why the crowd was so excited when I put it on. Rita smiled shyly. David took his off and stuffed it in his pocket, but not before an ancient woman with bare breasts and four teeth hugged his arm and joined us. He visibly squirmed.

"See you at the show, *brata*!" I shouted above the crowd, as I left him to plan his honeymoon.

Tribal groups were performing songs and dances everywhere. A dozen different languages joyously split the air. One group of warriors sang:

> *We are the men of this land.*
> *We must go out and harvest the coffee.*
> *That is how we feed our families!*

A women's group in reed skirts and bodies completely dyed red responded:

> *We are the Mothers of Coffee!*

A "stadium" had been erected for the Kup Coffee Cultural Show. A large area of the field had been cordoned off by an eight-foot wall made of carefully woven banana and pandanas leaves. Iggy told me it had taken three full days to build. A large bamboo speaker's platform had been built inside the stadium. There would be speeches and entertainment all day and all day tomorrow. Michael and the Digne committee had decided to charge one *kina* for the show, which was affordable and would bring in some revenue to pay the people who built the stadium and platform and worked thc show. We worked our way into the stadium and toward the platform, pulled here and there to watch the dozens of tribal groups perform. One large group of men was engaged in the PNG version of pro wrestling. Two groups squared off against each other in semimock combat. They charged each other with clubs and pretended (mostly) to bang away at the enemy. Sometimes the buffoonery was obvious, but one of the guys really got clocked and was carried off the field. The groups chased each other over long distances, forcing the screaming, laughing crowd to part wherever they passed. Local bands sang to guitars that had never been tuned, as percussionists beat on huge bamboo trunks with old flip-flops, making a wonderful "boink-boink" rhythm. Pigs were steam-roasted atop hot rocks in *hargis* (underground pits covered with banana leaves). Women sold peanuts, oranges, and stogies of tobacco and marijuana rolled in newspaper ("All the News That Fits the Spliff"). People who had never seen a *whiteman* came up to ogle at us (especially the six-foot-two David with the movie camera). There was food and celebration all over Kup. And everywhere, people were festooned with branches of coffee beans.

Kekas found us in the crowd. She had come up separately from Henganofi with some farmers. She was beaming.

"After you left, the farmers talked and talked. They talked all night long about what you said, how to organize and work together. This is new to us. In our country everyone works alone. But working together, that's the way to go! The farmers are very excited!" Kekas left us again to brew coffee next to the speaker's platform. I had brought several bags of Tribal Aromas coffee with the names Digne and Henganofi on them to brew up at the festivals. None of these farmers had ever had fresh coffee. They rarely even drank instant. Kekas was doing the first Dean's Beans coffee sampling in Papua New Guinea. The farmers crowded around her to try the brew. Kekas used the sampling to educate the farmers about the need for quality control and all sorts of technical matters. She was on fire.

As we mounted the bamboo platform, I asked Iggy where all of these people came from and how the heck they got there.

"Everybody walked. Some of them walked for a week to get here. They will stay for two days and walk back."

"How did they find out about it?" I asked, realizing that there was no television here and the newspapers were used for smoking and wiping.

"That was thanks to Brata Kennedy," Iggy beamed.

Brata (Brother) Kennedy was the most popular radio host/disc jockey in PNG. He was about thirty and very handsome and had a sweet, smooth voice. Brata Kennedy was on the air every night on one of the few radio stations. Of a national population of five million, Brata Kennedy could count a nightly audience of four million. He came to the Kup Coffee Cultural Show because he felt something good was happening for the people of the highlands. Brata Kennedy loved his people and used his popularity to educate, entertain, and encourage them. He had agreed to be the host for the show. He did a great job of keeping the show going while politician after politician, sensing a rare opportunity to address such a large crowd, came up and gave stump speeches that included support for the Digne initiative (along with an occasional intimation that they had something to do with it). Many of them urged the crowd to plant more coffee and to work together. Some of them used what I came to understand was a unique PNG tribal means of persuasion—outright shaming. James Pia Pia, a district officer, shouted, "If you do not plant coffee, shame on you! There is something wrong with you!"

Luke, a committee member, advised, "You need a coffee garden to keep a good name in your community. Otherwise people will think that you are a no-good *raskol*!"

Still another speaker added, "If you want a good mattress to sleep on, get out there and plant more coffee!"

Some speakers blamed the government for their lack of development. John said, "The government is stupid. It does not take care of the farmers. Those Melanesians give each other jobs on the government payroll and build big buildings, but the farmer has to live in *tumbuna* time, the time of our grandfathers!"

Others spoke more specifically to important issues. A woman from a national women's rights organization spoke of the need to treat women and children with respect and to end the violence that passes for dispute resolution.

"When you fight, you destroy the coffee. Women and children are the helpless victims of the fighting. Their rights must be recognized. Only when there is peace will there be development."

But none of the politicians or speakers held a candle to Honorable Member of Parliament Alfonsus P. Willie.

Hon. M.P. Willie was an enormous man with betel-red teeth and deep-set yellow eyes. I knew it was terribly un-PC to think this, but he looked to me like a mountain gorilla that had just humped Jane Goodall. He had arrived at the show in a police Land Rover with the inscription on the side:

THIS VEHICLE PROVIDED BY FUNDS OBTAINED BY
HON. A. WILLIE, M. P.

The stage sagged as Hon. M. P. Willie took the bullhorn. He railed on about his contributions to the community. He talked about the new road to Kup that he would get funded to get their coffee to market. He talked about repairing bridges. He talked and talked . . .

"Shut up, you!" someone shouted. The crowd laughed. "Wooooo!"

"We want to hear the *whiteman*, not you!" another yelled. Democracy in action. Jefferson would have been proud.

Hon. M.P. Willie took it gracefully. He quickly ended his remarks and was thanked by Brata Kennedy. The bamboo sighed audibly as he left the stage. BrataKennedy announced that we would next hear the music of the popular band Dop Doit (Firefly). The crowd went nuts. Suddenly, thousands of people rushed the banana leaf fence. What took two days to put up came down in less than a minute.

Iggy looked around and sighed. Then he shrugged and said, "Well, people really want to hear the music and see Brata Kennedy. Maybe they can't afford one *kina*. It's okay." He popped a betel nut and relaxed back on the chair. The legs of the old office-style chair popped through the bamboo floor of the platform and Iggy was on his ass with his legs in the air.

"Wooooo!" sang the crowd.

Jerry, the leader of Dop Doit, wore a scraggly beard, a cowboy hat, and a long trenchcoat. Jerry Jeff Walker meets Detective Columbo. He and his band let fly with a wild combination of reggae, zouk, makossa, and everything else that the BBC and every Asian pirated CD had brought this way over the decade. They were great musicians. The crowd danced, little boys humped the air, and the Mudmen moved real slow. It was one helluva performance.

As the band cranked along, David got up and began to dance onstage. He flailed his long arms and legs gracefully and had the crowd screaming. He turned and smiled.

"Your turn, *brata*!" So much for my professional demeanor. I did what I could but didn't come near the Coffee Dance that David had offered the crowd. Brata Kennedy had an amazed look on his face when he came up after the number ended and the band began to pack.

"I didn't know *whiteman* could dance," he said admiringly. He and Iggy introduced me again and I had another chance to do my *tok-tok*. I looked out over the most incredible sea of peoples.

"*Apinun tru, ol meri na man blong Papua New Guinea . . .*" I asked how many people grew coffee. Well over half the hands went up. I told them that something powerful and exciting was happening in PNG. Their excellent coffee, which was mostly unknown in the world, could be the key to development. Not gold or copper mining. Not timber. Those were already there, and the results were destroyed environments, low wages, and alcoholism as people were forced off their lands. Coffee could provide for their families—if they learned to improve the quality and consistency and were able to trade directly with the outside world.

"Yu lukautim cofi, na cofi by lukautim yu!" If they built a strong organization of farmers, it could bring other benefits to the communities. It could be the vehicle for health care, microloans, education, and many more things. I knew this to be true. I had seen it in many countries. It could happen here too. "Your job is to grow great coffee, make a strong organization, and keep your culture strong. My job is to introduce your culture and your coffee to America. If we work together, everyone in America will taste your coffee and say '*Dispela cofi em swit moa yet!*' (This coffee is delicious!)"

"Wooooo!"

My *tok-tok* was finished. I let Iggy translate that one.

At night I had a visit from one of the speakers who had exhorted the crowd to work together to get more money. He had raged about the need to get rid of the rapacious middlemen.

"These farmers must get past these middlemen, and I will help them." He gave me a typed letter. "I am proposing to be the person who buys all of the coffee from the farmers and sells it to you." What about Iggy, Michael, and Digne, I asked incredulously.

"Oh," he said conspiratorially, "they don't know the farmers like I do. I can get them all to sell to me. I am an important man around here."

The next morning, half the people were gone. I asked Iggy what had happened.

"Last night there was a fight between two drunken guys. They each called on their *bratas* and cousins and soon there was a big brawl. Lots of people got scared and just packed up and walked away in the night."

The festival carried on, with tribal groups dancing and putting on morality plays about young kids dating and how to take care of coffee. It was a more mellow atmosphere, but it was a peaceful day.

Late in the afternoon, Michael said it was time to go up to the villages. He wanted me to see the coffee being grown and harvested.

"Only one *whiteman* has ever been to Uwage and Bi. He was a nice man. He was a missionary."

"Where is he now?" I asked

"Buried."

We could drive only a few rough miles into the rain forest. The bridges got smaller and the rivers got bigger. We left the Land Rover at a small group of huts in a village called Mur and walked on. Michael explained that we were going to cross many tribal boundaries, and that we had to pay respect to each tribe as we entered its lands. We walked for miles. Every so often we would be met by a group of women or men who would howl out a welcome (or a warning). Within minutes we would be met by tribal peoples with spears and masks.

"This is Enduka territory" or "This is Kumai territory," Michael would say. We would stop and talk for a few minutes, introducing ourselves and describing our reason for crossing their land. They would sing a song of welcome and let us pass. Bandi, Dage, Nauro, Komkane, and on and on. We came upon a family carrying heavy bags of coffee beans down the mountain. Michael asked them how far they had to go. They told us that it took them eight hours to walk to a road. They were the lucky ones. The tribes on the other side of the mountain had to walk two days, sleeping on their coffee bags by the side of the road at night to protect them from *raskols*. They would stay by the side of the road until a truck came by and somebody offered to buy their beans. They took whatever was offered, then walked to the nearest *stoa*. There, they bought rice and cooking oil and carried it back up the mountain. This was the extent of their participation in the global economy.

They were not unique. All over PNG, farmers from remote villages were carrying their beans over mountains and rivers, through mud and landslides, to wait by the road for buyers. In fact, the majority of coffee in PNG finds its way to market in this manner. The middlemen know where the farmers will appear, usually next to the *stoa* built there specifically because that's where the farmers appear. The coffee goes through any of a score of small hullers and baggers and ends up on the docks of Lae port. Here, as Michael told me, "it is all swept together and bagged for the exporters, who ship it off to Germany and Holland. That is why the world doesn't know our coffee."

Yet few farmers were as remote and challenged as the coffee growers of Marawaka, four hundred miles to the southeast. There, the farmers sat with their bags of coffee staring at the sky. They were waiting for a break in the thick cloud cover that had socked in the region for almost two weeks. When the sky opened, an old Twin Otter aircraft from the Missionary Aviation Fellowship (MAF) could land at the remote airstrip. After dropping off supplies for local missionaries, the plane would take on the farmers' coffee and fly it to Henentu, almost an hour away as the Otter flies, where the closest paved road was. The airstrip had been built by the Summer Institute of Linguistics (missionaries already knew how to work together). Here, the beans could be trucked to the nearest processor, bagged, and taken to the north-coast port of Lae for export. MAF proudly reports on its Web site that they brought out eight hundred tons of coffee for the farmers that year, the only way those farmers can get their coffee to market. What they don't reveal is that they charge the poor bastards fifty U.S. cents per kilo to fly the coffee. Basically, MAF gets the farmers to pay for the fuel and labor, and the farmers end up netting a *kina* or so, if they are lucky. But this week the farmers weren't so lucky. As they sat on the runway waiting for the planes, the beans continued to ferment. They would shortly be rotten and useless. That's what happened the year before after the great Asian tsunami had hit. Although the floodwaters didn't reach the mountains, the weather patterns that followed brought heavy cloud cover, thunder, lightning, and rain. The nearest roads were rendered impassable and still remained that way. The MAF planes were grounded. Many of these remote villages lost their entire cash crop for the year. The villagers merely shrugged their shoulders and went home, leaving the beans to rot on the runways. As the farmers were self-sufficient in food production, this wasn't too bad, but two years without any cash would be a serious problem. So the farmers of Marawaka made a desperate decision. If the planes wouldn't come to the airstrip, they would walk out of the mountains.

It was the largest attempted human movement of coffee in the history of PNG. Three hundred men, plus an equal number of women and children, carried on their backs bags of coffee weighing up to ninety pounds for up to six days and nights. They carried the bags over hard, rocky terrain, steep slopes, and tricky ridges, over rivers and mudflats, easing the headstraps that distributed the weight of the beans between their backs, necks, and foreheads. Most of them gave up, selling their coffee at whatever small crossroads they encountered, wherever someone offered a price—any price. Many just abandoned their rotting beans and walked back home.

After a few more tribal border crossings we were met by a band of twenty men.

"Eeeeyooooh! Eeeeyooooh!" they intoned in unison, and ran toward us. They hoisted me on their shoulders and ran with me for about a half mile through mud, streams, and over rocks. We finally came to a halt at a big gathering of bird of paradise feather headdresses, boar tusks, and dancing. We had arrived at Uwage. Leo, the powerfully built headman, welcomed us. After more brief speeches we continued walking until we came to a clearing with a lone hut at either end and an old wooden table set in the middle. The village was surrounded by neat gardens of yams, bananas, cassavas, and melons. Leo offered the hospitality of Uwage to David and me.

"You can choose any woman here between the ages of thirteen and seventeen. Before thirteen they are not yet women. After seventeen they will be married." I thanked him but said that David and I each had a wife, and they would kill us if we took another.

"Only one?" Leo looked surprised. "I have two, my other wife lives in Bi. I have two pieces of land. Two pieces of land, two wives." I couldn't dispute the logic.

"I have only one piece of land," I lamented. Leo patted my shoulder solicitously, wondering how a man as poor as I could possibly have anything to share with his village.

About fifty people showed up and took seats along the clearing. Each of the men, women, and children was incredibly muscular and fit. They were totally self-sufficient in food up in these mountains, so even though the coffee prices were low, their daily lives were not impacted. These were the healthiest people I had ever seen in any coffee country. No, in the world! An old man came up to greet me joyously.

"Even though this path is harsh you came to our village. I am so happy. If I were a dog I would wag my tail and lick your face! Welcome!"

I thanked him and was led to my seat at the table facing the crowd. I noticed that on the side of one hut several woven plastic rice bags had been strung together to make a three-and-a-half-sided enclosure, open to the clearing. Iggy saw me looking at the curious structure.

"They have made you and David a toilet." I was pretty grateful and confided to Iggy that I kind of needed to use it badly. I hadn't minded peeing in front of thousands, as I could turn away from the many curious eyes. But this was Number Two—the big time.

"Don't worry, it has all been arranged for you." He turned toward the other hut at the far end of the clearing.

"Hey! Mr. Dean needs some toilet paper!" he shouted clearly. A minute later Leo's Uwage wife, a tall, thin woman named Lilien, came out of the hut carrying an old roll of toilet paper (probably left by the missionary, may he wipe in peace). She carried it before her like a treasured relic and placed it on the table before me. She smiled.

"Uh, thanks. I'll just be a minute," I muttered.

"Hey, *brata*, we'll be watching!" laughed David.

I walked into the enclosure, painfully aware that all eyes were on me and that several small children were walking in with me to stand and stare. I tried my best to squat over the new hole in the earth with dignity and not defecate all over the pants I held bunched up before me. Using the paper under these circumstances was a disaster as well. I didn't know how to say "go away!" in *tok pisin*. I thought it was something like "*come yu behain*," but it felt weird to be a stranger in a strange land with my pants down, shouting something I didn't understand to little kids. Instead, I used the universal "back off" sound of a barking dog. The kids thought this was so funny that they ran and brought their friends over. They barked back at me, probably thinking it was some bizarre American toilet ritual. My only comfort during this ordeal was that ultimately David would be next. I gathered my dignity and returned to the table.

It was dark by the time we polished off the pig and the tons of incredible vegetables and fruits placed on the table. I commented that studies in Africa link diets steady in certain yams to incidence of twins. Michael and Leo laughed and asked how many families there had twins. Half the hands shot up. As kerosene lamps were strung around the clearing, we talked for hours about how to organize cooperatives, how they were managed, and what they might mean for the price of coffee they would receive. One by one, the people in the clearing told their stories.

"They called us cannibals," an elder related. "For fifty years coffee gave us no money and did not change our lives. Now I think this will change."

"All my life I give them coffee. They give nothing, they get heaps."

"We don't need any more wars, we need money and development."

I talked for a long time about the growth of community organizations in coffee, how they start small like a new plant and grow. I told them the stories of other groups that began where they were and now had their own mills, trucks, and even banks! We talked about quality issues, and all the farmers agreed that they wanted to get hand depulpers to use instead of the traditional method of pounding a handful of beans with a rock by the river. One old woman added, "I can't even get to the river. If my boys are not here, I have to chew the cherries off the beans." Several of the older people admitted this practice. *Well*, I thought, *that's one way to begin the fermentation process.*

The farmers gave a resounding "Wooooo!" to most of my statements. I was on a roll and figured that it was a good time to talk about the role of women. Kekas had told me that even though women worked hard in the field and cared for the family, they were not part of decision making in most villages. I noted how the United Nations had studied many countries and found that the richest countries were the ones where both men and women had opportunity in the working and managing of the economy. I tried an agricultural metaphor.

"If the women in the village don't participate fully, it is like planting half of your garden." In the dim light of the lanterns I could see the white smiles of the women. But no "Wooooo!" came from the stone-silent crowd.

"I think the idea needs a little work," Iggy observed dryly.

Many people stayed after the formal meeting broke up. We built a large fire and sat around it sharing big pots of Dean's Beans and talking. I was so buzzed by the coffee and the conversation that I stayed up all night. At one point I needed to pee, so Leo and I walked over to a trailside. As we stood side by side, I looked up and commented on the constellation Orion who hunted the Great Bull overhead. I asked Leo what stories his people told of the stars in the sky.

"We don't have such stories. We don't see pictures in the sky." I couldn't believe it. I had never experienced a culture that didn't have sky stories and constellations. I knew that the coastal Polynesians had an involved sky mythology, but these were Melanesians here. Back at the fire, nobody knew any sky stories. I figured that since the land was so heavily forested, maybe they didn't integrate the night sky into their culture. Leo asked one of the oldest men about it.

"If you see pictures in the sky, the devil put them there to confuse you!"

"He's an Evangelical," Leo informed me.

We spent another three days walking and talking to villagers about organizing co-ops and working together for their common benefit. Iggy felt that our visit was a great success and that he would be able to form and register cooperatives soon. Then we could work on getting the cooperatives on the Fair Trade registry. By the end of the third day I was completely worn out from walking and talking. We were headed back to Mur along the "back trail" and came through yet another tribal boundary, this one of the Sambulga Wagual. We went through the greeting rituals and sat down one last time in the village clearing. Iggy gave his speech of introduction. I told him I could barely stand; couldn't he just give my speech for me? After all, I had said it and he had translated it about fifteen times.

"No problem." Iggy spoke in rapid-fire *tok pisin* for about ten minutes. His comments were occasionally interrupted by grunts, cheers, and an occasional mass spear shaking in my direction.

"Okay, Mr. Dean. That's it. They are very happy that you are here."

"So we can go now?" I asked tentatively.

"Sure, right after you give your speech."

I heard a low chuckle from my right. David was lying back on the grass, his hands cradling his head and a piece of grass casually in his mouth.

"Well, *brata*, looks like it's time for the Dean Show. Better you than me." He snuggled his back on the grass and sighed contentedly.

"*I'll get even with you, smart-ass,*" I muttered as I stood and brushed a few fire ants off my pants.

"*Apinun tru, ol meri na man blong Papua Nui Gini . . .*" I felt a little guilty about not having the energy to give these expectant people something more. I knew that they had heard about our meetings through the coffee vine. But what more could I give? I perked up with a brainstorm.

"Ladies and gentlemen. I have a special treat for you all the way from

America!" That caught the attention of the crowd, including a very curious Iggy and David.

"David is going to do his World Famous Coffee Dance!" The crowd shouted, stomped, and pointed their spears at David. I sat down, unable to contain the Cheshire-cat grin on my face. David got up, whispering as he passed me.

"You asshole."

"You're on!" I replied pleasantly as I lay back in the grass to watch the show.

David didn't miss a beat. As the crowd clapped and sang a local top-forty tune, he wiggled his butt, snaked out those long arms and legs, did a little duck walk, and gave them the best Coffee Dance they had ever seen.

We returned to Kundiawa that afternoon to pack up for the drive back to Goroka and the flight to Port Moresby. Brata Kennedy said that if we came to the capital, we could go on his radio show and get the message out to his four million listeners. I also wanted to take Iggy to meet some folks at an Asian Development Bank office who might be interested in providing microloans and other economic assistance to the farmers once they were formally organized. We would also get the legal papers necessary to register the cooperatives of Henganofi and Digne. Iggy said that he could stay only for a day or so, as he had to get back to his extended family, including his new baby, whom he had named Dean Junior. I asked him why we hadn't visited his family village during our wanderings in the mountains. He sighed.

"Oh, my whole village was burned down in tribal warfare last month. Everyone had moved somewhere else."

"What happened?"

Iggy launched into a long, confusing story of sex, betrayal, revenge, and murder that would have made a Fox News reporter wince.

"But they are having a compensation *tok-tok* now. I have to get back to participate."

"I hope you don't mind me asking, but how much is a village worth around here?"

Iggy thought about it for a moment.

"Well, there were about thirty huts, some animal enclosures, and a lot of gardens. I'd say about four hundred dollars."

—

When I worked in rural Iran back in the day, the villagers would refer to the capital, Tehran, using the Farsi word for "foreign country." Port Moresby could not have been any more different from the mountain towns and villages of Simbu. The commercial and government district was tiny, about five blocks in total. But what Port Moresby lacked in girth it made up for in height. Many of the government offices were perched atop steep hills as if to guard them from the masses below. Our most pressing task in Port Moresby was to find Iggy a pair of shoes. Don Quixote would have given up on this quest. We finally settled on the biggest pair of flip-flops in the world, and Iggy's feet hung over the sides like sumo wrestlers in hot pants.

The U.S. State Department and every travel guide warn visitors not to venture out of their hotels at night in Port Moresby. In fact, most warn not to go to Port Moresby in the first place. I found it charming. The bars were full of the most exquisite polyglot peoples, as Papua New Guinea has been a coastal trading destination for every race of Pacific mariner. People were friendly, the women were stunning, and the beer was really cold. All of my high standards were met.

Our meetings with the Asian Development Bank and several other groups were very successful. Iggy's flip-flops held. Our time on Brata Kennedy's radio show was a smash with farmers all over the country, Iggy reported later. When we saw him off at the airport, he said this trip got him thinking about running for Parliament to throw out the *raskols* and help the farmers. I told him that if he was elected, he would have to wear shoes every day, and maybe share a cop car with Hon. A. Willie, M. P. Iggy shook his head as he kicked off his flip-flops and boarded the plane, saying, "It's not worth it."

Within a year of our visit, Tribal Aromas was formed as an umbrella group of legally recognized cooperatives in the Eastern Highlands and Simbu provinces. The co-ops have been inspected for listing on the Fair Trade registry and have received their organic certification. They are already receiving more than twice the cash for their beans than they were getting prior to my visit. The Asian Development Bank has begun a microloan program with the farmers of Simbu and we have supplied fourteen hand depulpers for the airstrips at Marawaka and beyond. Dean Junior is plump and happy and is reported to have very wide feet.

Epilogue

Our understanding of justice, in trade and society in general, cannot be confined to a formula. Fair Trade, or any movement that is intended to improve the quality of life for people, is more accurately seen as a process. The more we work with the peoples in this book and beyond, the deeper we plunge into the dynamics of their societies, their ecologies, and their economies. Each layer reveals a more profound set of relationships that we must consider as we evolve toward more humane and just relationships. Being open to the experiences of each culture not only makes us more aware but also makes our lives richer. Thus, the tales in this book are only footsteps on a long and continuing trail.

In 2007 we signed two leading-edge trade agreements to step it up a level. After helping the Ethiopian government sculpt an agreement that we thought represented the farmers' interests better than their original draft, we signed a trademark license acknowledging Ethiopia's right to control the use of its geographic names (Yirgacheffe, Harar, and Sidamo), and we are working with the farmers and the government to turn that agreement into a means of raising awareness and money for those special coffees. With a little coaxing from us, Starbucks and others are following suit. We also developed and signed the industry's first long-term Fair Trade agreement, with Oro Verde Cooperative in northern Peru (witnessed by Esperanza from Pangoa). At the farmers' request, we put together a document that spells out what it really means to be committed to each other for the long term, not just to use those words as advertising copy. The agreement includes price, quantity, and quality, but it goes on to include a roasting operation and cafés in Peru that we will own jointly, as well as social and environmental programs that we will work on together. We intend to sign similar agreements with all our cooperative partners and hope that this represents a new way of thinking about relationships in the coffee world, one that others can build upon.

Since the writing of this book, we have begun to bring greater educational opportunity to farmers' kids, both in their own countries and also by finding or funding scholarships here. Rehima is attending university in Addis Ababa.

Tadesse's daughter Fikir will start high school at Winchendon Academy right here in Massachusetts, along with Avdoh and Theresa from Papua New Guinea. It's not exactly "No Coffee Farmer's Child Left Behind," but it is a start!

In Guatemala, we created the concept for a new radio program called "Coffee Talk" that is being aired on several hundred community radio stations pioneered by Cultural Survival, a nonprofit indigenous rights organization. The show affords the farmers an opportunity to share their experiences and techniques and brings on experts and allies to talk about organics, trade, politics, or whatever the farmers want to hear.

In our current age of quantification instead of qualification, it is difficult to assess the "value" of advocacy and activism, so these things don't find a ready home in carbon offset reports or annual U.N. Global Compact filings. But our commitment as Javatrekkers includes working with the farmers, both here and abroad, to bring about needed changes in trade policy and practice, as well as in political and cultural attitudes. We regularly speak at colleges and churches, on radio shows, and occasionally on television. We try to get the message out, whether it's on YouTube or around the late-night fire in some remote village.

There is also a growing movement in the coffeelands, spearheaded by the farmers themselves, to demand change in trade practices, including Fair Trade. Farmers from the Americas have created their own organization, CLAC (Latin American and Caribbean Coordinator for Small Producers), to share information, develop strategies, and advocate on their own behalf. Women like Esperanza, Merling, Kekas, and so many more are taking leading roles in management and activism throughout the coffeelands. There is serious change afoot.

For me, Javatrekking is ultimately about personal and societal exploration. I have never been fully comfortable with what is, when I know in my heart that things can be better, more respectful, more loving, and, frankly, more exciting. It pains me deeply to see cultures crumble and blow away under global pressures (or simply for lack of water), or kids' lives go unfulfilled for want of a pencil or notebook. Javatrekking allows me the vehicle to explore my own relationship to these things and to take responsibility where I can. These may be small contributions in the greater scheme of things, but as an old Indonesian farmer advised me, quoting Arjuna's words to Krishna on the eve of battle, "Add your light to the sum of lights."

Thirteen-year-old Rehima Hussein proudly serves her family's bounty during a coffee ceremony in Ethiopia.

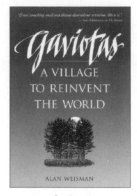